AN AMERICAN SON

With kind regards.

George T. Aratani

11-10-0

Best wishes!

Naomi Hirahara

An American Son: The Story of George Aratani, Founder of Mikasa and Kenwood inaugurates the Japanese American National Museum's biography series American Profiles, which preserves and highlights the untold stories of Japanese Americans who have made significant contributions to the cultural, political, social, and economic life of the Untied States. Through the lives of the famous and the not-so-famous, this series provides a significant contribution to the literature exploring the Japanese American experience as an integral part of American heritage.

The Japanese American National Museum is the first museum in the United States dedicated to promoting understanding and appreciation of America's ethnic and cultural diversity by preserving, interpreting, and sharing the experiences of Japanese Americans. Through the building of a comprehensive collection of Japanese American objects, images and documents, and with a multifaceted program of exhibitions, educational programs, films, and publications, the museum tells the story of Japanese Americans around the country to a national and international audience.

AN AMERICAN SON

The Story of
George Aratani
Founder of Mikasa and Kenwood

By Naomi Hirahara

with an Introduction by Daniel I. Okimoto, Ph.D.

JAPANESE AMERICAN NATIONAL MUSEUM
Los Angeles, California

Library of Congress Cataloging-in-Publication Data

Hirahara, Naomi, 1962-
   An American son : the story of George Aratani : founder of
Mikasa and Kenwood / By Naomi Hirahara with an introduction by
Daniel I. Okimoto.
        p. cm.
Includes bibliographical references and index.
   ISBN 1-881161-15-3 (pbk.)
1. Aratani, George, 1917- 2. Mikasa. 3. Kenwood Corporation.
4. Businessmen—United States—Biography. I. Title.
   HC102.5.A2 H57 2001
   338.7'621381'092—dc21

2001001757

Designer: Koji Takei
Copy Editors: Virginia Stem Owens, Sherri Schottlaender
Printer: Gardner Lithograph

Cover photos
Top: George Aratani and his father Setsuo Aratani in 1928.
Collection of George and Sakaye Aratani, Japanese American National Museum
(NRC.1998.575.3)

Bottom: Setsuo Aratani's farm in Guadalupe, California, ca. 1930s.
Collection of Mary Tamura, Japanese American National Museum (2000.385.1)

Back: Portrait of George Aratani.
Collection of George and Sakaye Aratani, Japanese American National Museum (43.1998.9)

Table of Contents

Foreword

Ms. Irene Hirano, Executive Director of the Japanese American National Museum in Los Angeles, wrote to me recently informing me that the Museum has decided to inaugurate a biography series featuring the lives of Japanese Americans who have made significant contributions to the social, cultural, political, and economic life of America. I was deeply impressed because this endeavor should prove significant in bringing existing Japan–U.S. relations even closer.

Knowing that the first volume of the series focused on the life of Mr. George Aratani both pleased and touched me. Among my many American friends, he remains one of the oldest and closest.

In 1961 I attended Stanford University. In those days, fewer Japanese visited the United States. Sometimes I felt lonely not knowing anyone with whom I could talk freely. By then Mr. Aratani had already established himself in Nagoya as an importer of tableware from Japan. An older acquaintance of mine residing in Nagoya happened to know Mr. Aratani, and he introduced us.

Not a single day passes without me recalling Mr. Aratani's kindness, assistance, and words of encouragement. Later I learned that Mr. Aratani had been a classmate of my cousin, Seiichi Tagawa, former member of the House of Representatives, at Keio University. That made me feel even closer to Mr. Aratani. Mr. Aratani was studying at Keio University in 1938. He had to return to the United States without completing his studies following the serious illness of his father, who had an extensive farming business in California. Then war broke out between Japan and the United States, causing the Issei and Nisei to suffer immeasurable pain.

Mr. Aratani succeeded despite these difficulties. He exemplifies the American frontier spirit as well as the Japanese ideals of diligence and perseverance. The spirit of social coexistence and mutual assistance, which he inherited from his parents, has made him a generous philanthropist.

I am pleased to see the completion of Mr. Aratani's biography by the experienced hand of Ms. Naomi Hirahara, former editor of *The Rafu Shimpo*.

It is my sincere hope that the Japanese American National Museum will be able to contribute immensely to the creation of a new American tradition that incorporates the very best characteristics of both Japanese and American societies.

I still have a vivid memory of the following paragraph in a letter sent by a Nisei grandfather to his grandson, which I saw in one corner of the Museum during my visit.

> *Grandpa is your yesterday, the past; your daddy is today,*
> *the present; you are tomorrow or the future. Whatever you did*
> *yesterday or today will affect you further tomorrow.*
> *But you have a rich cultural ethnic heritage.*

> *Grandpa and Daddy won't be with you in the future.*
> *We only ask that you carry on the family tradition with honor*
> *and respect to the best of your abilities.*

His Excellency Yohei Kono
Foreign Minister, Japan
April 13, 2001

Introduction

The United States is known as a land of opportunity for the poor and oppressed people of the world, a land of milk and honey where dreams of wealth can be realized by enterprising immigrants and their educated, ambitious children. Ever since the good ship *Mayflower* landed almost four centuries ago, scores of immigrants have flocked to America's shores from virtually every continent and country in the world—from Western and Eastern Europe to Africa, the Middle East, Latin America, and Asia. As a consequence, the United States has become the most diverse, multicultural, and pluralistic society that history has ever known.

Wave after wave of immigrants has contributed to America's cultural richness, social distinctiveness, intellectual ferment, entrepreneurial vigor, and economic growth. Where would American art, music, sports, literature, and sociopolitical discourse be without the contributions of African Americans, Latino Americans, and Asian Americans? Where would America's lead in research and technology be without the ongoing assimilation of brilliant scientists and engineers from overseas? Where would America, the economic colossus, be without the energy, creativity, and talents of immigrant entrepreneurs and their children? It used to be that legal restrictions and racial discrimination relegated ambitious immigrants from Asia to very narrow spheres of business activity at the low end of the service sector; Asian immigrants opened restaurants, laundries, grocery stores, and other small-scale retail businesses. The more lucrative sectors, such as manufacturing, processing, assembly, construction, real estate development, and the financial services, were closed to them.

America's restricted playing field meant that Setsuo Aratani, father of George Aratani (the central figure of this biography), channeled his considerable entrepreneurial energies into vertical segments of agribusiness: specifically, preparing, storing, transporting, and selling agricultural products. He also sold miscellaneous tools of the trade—farm equipment, seeds, and fertilizers. Agribusinesses represented one of the few spheres of commercial activity where the loopholes were large enough for enterprising Japanese immigrants like Setsuo Aratani to enter and establish commercial footholds.

But times have changed. Compare the first half of the twentieth century with the second: in the last fifty years, the doors of business opportunity have been pried progressively open. Today, opportunities for entrepreneurial advancement based on hard work and individual merit are more available than ever before. And many Asian American entrepreneurs are making the most of it.

Take Silicon Valley, for example. It is a mecca for technological visionaries, venture investors, strategic consultants, and marketing gurus working in such key fields as computers, semiconductors, telecommunications, applications and systems software, and the Internet. Silicon Valley has become the new-age equivalent of the nineteenth-century California Gold Rush, and it produces, on average, several millionaires every hour of every day. From 1980 to 1998, the two formative decades of Silicon Valley's rise to world prominence, 24 percent of all Silicon Valley start-ups were founded by chief executive officers of Chinese or Indian heritage. Twenty-four percent! Imagine that—the statistic is mind-boggling. It reveals the magnitude of the contributions made by Asian and Asian American entrepreneurs to the revolutionary breakthroughs in the sphere of information technology. America's proud "IT revolution" owes a great deal to the creative minds and bold, risk-taking leadership of Asian immigrants and Asian American entrepreneurs. Compare the opportunities for Asian Americans in the year 2000 with the conditions that existed in 1940—the progress has been monumental. America has a stronger economy because it has given Asian Americans greater chances to succeed.

It should be noted that the doors of opportunity for Asian Americans have not swung open automatically. It has taken persistent effort on the part of all minority groups, as well as intense political struggles, a battery of legislative changes in Washington, legal challenges, and the use of the courts to put teeth into the abstract concept of equal opportunity. It also has required a turnabout in America's relationship with Japan. For Japanese American business leaders like George Aratani, the postwar metamorphosis of America's relations with Japan—from archenemy to strategic partner—has transformed the whole climate of opinion with respect to Japan and Japanese Americans. Deep-seated conflicts between the United States and Japan, culminating in the surprise attack on Pearl Harbor and the ordeal of the Pacific War, had contaminated the political atmosphere, hardening and institutionalizing racial discrimination against the Japanese in America.

Viewed in a prewar context, the entrepreneurial accomplishments of Setsuo Aratani are impressive indeed. One reason for his business breakthroughs, as brought to light by Naomi Hirahara, was the capacity of the Japanese community in California to pull together in ways that made it possible for individual entrepreneurs to succeed. Setsuo Aratani built his businesses on the sturdy foundation of the Japanese American community. Japanese Americans served as employees, managers, executives, strategic partners, trusted advisors, investors, lenders, borrowers, accountants, service providers, and customers.

In the prewar structure of discriminatory barriers, Setsuo Aratani's strategy of network building in the Japanese American community made sense. By relying on known friends and trusted colleagues, any concerns about possible betrayal and opportunism could be alleviated. It was easier to develop a bond of trust, a level of honesty, a commitment to reciprocity that obviated the need for constant monitoring, contractual safeguards, and provisions for legal sanctions. Networking with Japanese Americans, in short, lowered transaction costs.

After launching various business initiatives and working assiduously to bring them to fruition, Setsuo Aratani passed his agribusinesses on to his only son, George. George was expected to maintain and expand the businesses and eventually pass the enterprises on to the next generation of Aratanis. However, nearly all of Aratani's assets, the product of decades of extraordinary effort, were confiscated not long after Japan bombed Pearl Harbor and the United States declared war on Japan. George did what he could to salvage the family assets, entrusting several companies to his European American lawyer and his colleagues. But the Aratanis, like thousands of other Japanese American families, lost nearly everything that they had worked so hard to acquire.

In the wake of the upheaval caused by internment, it would have been easy for Japanese Americans to feel embittered and cynical and to come to the conclusion that the fabled American Dream was merely a myth. But instead of giving up and feeling sorry for themselves, Japanese Americans put the setback of wartime internment behind them and moved forward to start anew. Upon their release from camp, a number of Japanese Americans entered new fields of endeavor. Many of the younger generation went on to college and graduate school and entered professional fields that had previously been off-limits; they became doctors, dentists, engineers, architects, and lawyers. Others, like George Aratani, dug down deep to find the motivation and energy to pursue new business opportunities.

Aratani launched business enterprises in new product markets that no Japanese American could ever have imagined entering before the war. He started companies that produced chinaware (Mikasa), medical supplies (AMCO), consumer audio electronics (Kenwood), and even nuclear reactors. Making the transition from perishable foods—agriculture and agribusinesses—to consumer durables such as audio equipment and chinaware must not have been easy, but George Aratani somehow managed to flourish. He succeeded in building a large, diversified, and lucrative complex of businesses.

In his new postwar entrepreneurial endeavors, George Aratani benefited from several advantages related to the Japanese American community. If being a Japanese American in the prewar period meant having to face seemingly insuperable obstacles, membership in the same minority group in the postwar period helped to open up opportunities. Those who had the qualifications and determination to rise to new challenges—like George Aratani, Kay Sugahara, George Ishiyama, Peter Okada, Henri and Tomoye Takahashi, and Martha Suzuki—established highly successful businesses centered on the flow of goods and services between the United States and Japan, and they reaped the rich rewards that came with the opening up of business opportunities across the Pacific.

The first advantage, a carryover from the prewar era, was the extensive human networks that the Aratanis managed to develop among Japanese Americans; in the postwar era Aratani expanded the network to include Japanese colleagues in Japan. Like his father, George Aratani recruited Japanese Americans as executives from among the people with whom he came in contact during the course of his life. Many hailed from three places: his hometown of Guadalupe, California; the concentration camp at Gila River; and the Military Intelligence Service Language School in Minnesota. George Aratani appears to have had a knack for finding Japanese Americans of outstanding character, ability, diligence, and loyalty.

A second factor, alluded to earlier, was the transformation of U.S.–Japan relations following the end of the Pacific War. Not only did the metamorphosis dissipate the dark clouds hanging over the heads of Americans of

Japanese ancestry, but it also created new and expansive entrepreneurial opportunities for Japanese Americans as commercial ties of interdependence between the United States and Japan proliferated over time. By 1975, only thirty years after accepting the terms of unconditional surrender, Japan had become the world's second-largest economy behind the United States. Merchandise transactions between the two economies mushroomed into the biggest trans-Pacific flow of trade in world history: $65 billion dollars in 1980, more than the GDP (Gross Domestic Products) of many nation-states in the world at that time. Such a massive volume of trade meant that there were substantial opportunities for Japanese Americans to establish lucrative enterprises.

While unprecedented riches became accessible, relatively few Japanese Americans cashed in. Many aspired; some enjoyed modest success; only a few hit it big. What set George Aratani apart from other Japanese American entrepreneurs seeking to make a fortune from U.S.–Japan commerce?

His father's business legacy may have helped. It was not so much the cash value of George's inheritance, which incarceration slashed: rather, it was more likely the passed-on business experience, the hands-on knowledge, and the human connections that may have given George advantages that others lacked.

Of greater relevance in explaining George Aratani's success is the time he spent in Japan as a young adult studying at Keio University and immersing himself in the Japanese language, society, and culture. His decision to pass up a chance to matriculate at Stanford University, where he was accepted out of high school, and to go to Japan instead must have been difficult. Today, such a decision would be hard to understand. Why would anyone pass up a chance to earn a Stanford diploma for a degree from a Japanese university? What may appear to be puzzling—even irrational—today is understandable in light of the harsh reality that employment opportunities in the 1930s and 1940s were severely limited for Americans of Japanese ancestry, even for those who might have graduated from Stanford University.

The decision to go to Keio in order to master the language and culture was a wise one, for the objective circumstances—severe job discrimination in the United States—changed for the better in the postwar era. Ironically, the improved climate actually enhanced the value of the practical tools that Aratani had acquired in Japan. His mastery of the Japanese language and business culture yielded far greater value than anyone, including his father, would have imagined. And, as it happened, Setsuo Aratani's illness prompted George to return to the United States after spending only a few years in Japan, and he wound up enrolling at Stanford after all. In a sense, he got the best of both worlds.

The story of George Aratani's life is a window not only into the history of the Japanese in America, but also into the complex and ever-changing relationship between the United States and Japan. Naomi Hirahara skillfully narrates the story of the Aratani family against the background of significant changes taking place in American society and in U.S.–Japan relations. She sheds revealing light on how international factors shaped George Aratani's life experiences and had a major impact on the twists and turns of his business career. Hirahara's book offers a compelling, three-dimensional history: first, of the immigration and assimilation of the Aratani family; second, of American society in the twentieth century; and third, of the turmoil and turbulence of U.S.–Japan relations and its postwar metamorphosis into arguably the world's most vital bilateral alliance.

The story of George Aratani's life and distinguished business career is one that deserves to be told. We have Naomi Hirahara to thank for telling the story, and telling it with such insight and verve. Young Asian Americans probably know little about the formidable barriers of racial discrimination which confronted Asian American entrepreneurs like George Aratani. The young generation may only be familiar with recent Asian American success stories, like Jerry Yang of Yahoo!, who hit the jackpot in the high-tech sweepstakes. Jerry Yang has become a new-age, new-economy hero, a legend in his own time: he is living proof that America is still a land of opportunity. But no one should forget that in his own time and in his own way, George Aratani also followed his dreams, demonstrated resilience and resourcefulness, and blazed new trails for the generations of Asian American entrepreneurs who followed.

Dr. Daniel I. Okimoto
Professor, Department of Political Science
Co-founder and Director Emeritus
Asia/Pacific Research Center, Stanford University

Aratani Family Tree

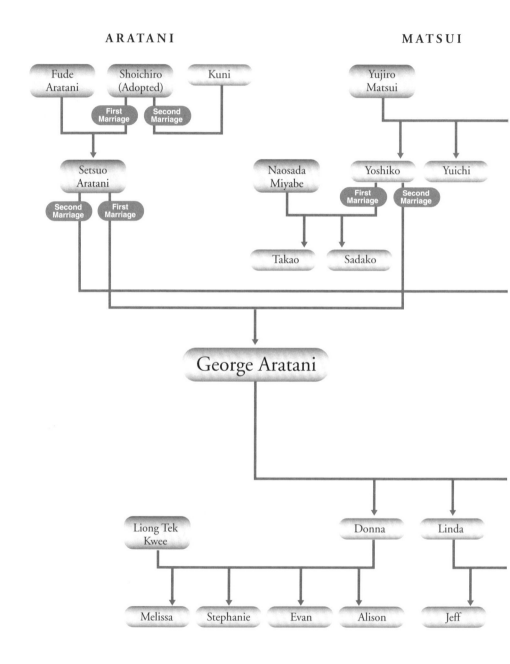

NAKAYAMA

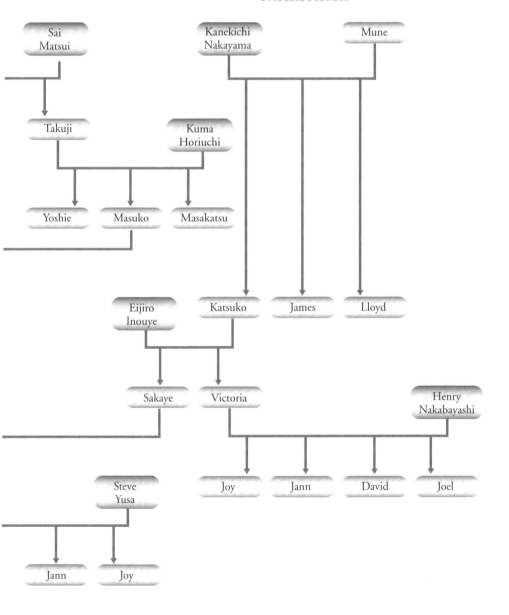

Map of Japan

Major Cities in the Life of George Aratani

Map of California
Communities in the Life of George Aratani

1

Big Boss

Strangers usually don't travel to Guadalupe, and if they happen to stop, they don't stay for long. There's no hotel in this California seaside town located 170 miles north of Los Angeles, and there's barely any mention of it in any tourist books. Of course, there are those who are drawn to such places, those who seek out historic spots lacking neon or fancy signs which contain clues to buried stories. Guadalupe's modest cemetery, surrounded by an iron fence, is one such spot.

The graves of Swiss Italians, Portuguese, and Irish date back to the nineteenth century. A large section of the cemetery, maybe one quarter of its area, has granite headstones marked with such names as Ito, in both cursive Japanese *kanji* characters and English. Among them is a large, simple tombstone with these names: "Setsuo Aratani, 1885–1940," and "Yoshiko Aratani, 1889–1935."

At one time, before World War II, Japanese farmers dominated this region. There were the Big Three—Aratani, Minami, Tomooka—Japanese immigrants who tilled thousands of acres of farmland and harvested tons of carrots, lettuce, peas, and chili peppers; the produce was packed in ice and shipped as far as Texas and the East Coast. In town, boardinghouses were

**Setsuo Aratani, prosperous head of
the Guadalupe Produce Company, in the 1930s.** (99.30.145)

full of bachelors from Hawai'i, their lower arms and faces tanned dark as molasses. Country wives fermented boiled rice in wide, wooden barrels to produce powerful wine for their husbands and friends.

Today, little evidence remains of all this activity. Guadalupe Boulevard, the town's main drag, reveals only remnants of a heyday gone by. Everyone knows the local police chief and the former mayor, who helps operate an ice factory that stands next to the former site of the Guadalupe Produce packing shed.

Before the arrival of the Big Three farmers, Chinese laborers, hoes in hand, broke the arid ground and planted sugar beets for the Union Sugar Mill in Betteravia, established in 1899. "All that's left of that era is a line of old tin buildings," explains Jose Rubalcaba, the co-founder of the Rancho de Guadalupe Historical Society.

Jose, who is past 70, is the resident historian, with keys to all the important spots in town. He unlocks an old adobe jail that his group has restored and proudly points to bricks with donors' names at the top of the building. Later he guides us into the empty senior citizen center, where he takes from his briefcase colorful crate labels touting "Home Run King" and "All Star" vegetables. "These came from Guadalupe Produce," he says, "Aratani's place."

All the old-timers know of Setsuo Aratani and his son George. Of the Big Three farmers, Setsuo was probably the most ambitious. He began one of the first packing operations, and he always thought big. He diversified his crops and his businesses, dabbled in the sale of sake (rice wine), from his hometown, and he launched a hog farm, a chili dehydrating plant, and a fertilizer plant, as well as investing in a wholesale produce market in Los Angeles.

While other farmers had wood-framed homes with peeling paint battered by the weather, Setsuo resided in a Spanish-style house complete with a Japanese garden and goldfish pond. He was known as "Ace," both for his golfing and poker expertise. He played with the Japanese and he played with European Americans, and his passion for sports was infectious. Soon the whole town was baseball crazy, and everyone participated in golf tournaments held at the Santa Maria Country Club. For two decades in Guadalupe, the town—at least superficially—disregarded color barriers and joined together for picnics where Japanese, European Americans, Mexicans, and Filipinos sat together to eat mesquite barbecue and watch performances by locals.

Setsuo was responsible for farming close to 5,000 acres in both the Santa Maria and Lompoc valleys, and he operated two packing sheds, including Guadalupe Produce. Poised to inherit this agricultural kingdom was his only son, George Tetsuo, but the glory days of Guadalupe proved to be fleeting. It was then up to the son to take the lessons of Guadalupe and apply them to an arena that involved factories rather than fields.

—◆—

George Aratani, now in his eighties, lives 200 miles away in a home tucked into the Hollywood Hills, a five-minute drive from Universal Studios and the Hollywood Bowl. His presence is most visible in Little Tokyo, a district of downtown Los Angeles adjacent to City Hall and bordering commercial areas where discount toys, fresh flowers, wholesale produce, and clothing are sold. In this same Little Tokyo, a renaissance is taking place as community institutions, a museum, low-income and senior housing, and a theater have recently been built alongside historic storefronts, hotels, churches, and temples. The names of George and his wife Sakaye are stamped on plaques in many a courtyard and community meeting place, including the Japanese American National Museum, the Union Center for the Arts, and the Little Tokyo Service Center. Close associates have honored and roasted the couple at dinners attended by thousands of friends and colleagues.

In spite of the differences between the Guadalupe of old and the Little Tokyo of today, one thing remains constant for George: he has carried the entrepreneurial spirit of his father, Setsuo Aratani, inside him. This spirit has given birth to three international companies—Mikasa, Kenwood, and AMCO—and it has provided direction during times of turmoil on foreign soil in Japan, in scorched desert camps in Arizona, and on the congested streets of Manhattan.

To examine the life of George Aratani is to understand how an only child was always part of a larger community and how his family and friends, once forcibly separated from that community, found each other again. And through their reunion, George and his associates have challenged stalwarts in the dinnerware and electronics industries, changed ways of doing business, and even impacted cultural identity. Much of this was first nurtured in the now-sleepy town of Guadalupe.

George once sought to move his parents' ashes from the quiet Guadalupe cemetery to a location closer to his Hollywood Hills home, but a dissenting cry went up from Guadalupe's diminishing Japanese American community.

Setsuo Aratani belongs in Guadalupe: he will always be a part of the town and its soil. In much the same way, however, Setsuo and Yoshiko can never be separated from their son. To know his parents is to know George Aratani. Before we can comprehend the twists and turns of the Aratani family in Guadalupe, we must start at the beginning, in Japan.

Setsuo Aratani was born on August 26, 1885, in the lush green village of Saijo in the Hiroshima prefecture. His father, an herbalist, died before Setsuo's birth. His mother remarried a man named Shoichiro, who adopted the Aratani name. When Setsuo was two years old, his mother, Fude, passed away, leaving the boy in the care of wealthy relatives who had made their fortune producing soy sauce.

During this time, Japan was undergoing a political and cultural transformation. After centuries of isolating the country from outside influences, the government was finally opening its borders to the West. With the weakening of the Tokugawa shogunate, which had ruled the nation since the seventeenth century, powerful forces called for a more modern Japan. Moreover, America, Britain, and Russia were all pressing for trade relations.

Consequently, the Japanese were wrestling with new cultural influences from the United States and Europe while still holding fast to feudal customs within their homes. Shoichiro, the only father that Setsuo had ever really known, eventually married a charming, energetic cousin who practiced traditional etiquette. Her given name was Kuni, but on the advice of a fortune-teller she changed it to Asae, meaning "Shallow River."

Most Hiroshima boys attended high school or pursued farming. Farming was an honored profession in feudal Japan, but Setsuo's immediate family did not own any agricultural land. The family was educated and even literary, but books and social status alone could not put food on the table. Thus, commerce seemed to be Setsuo's best option as a profession, and so he was sent to a nearby trade school, the Onomichi School of Commerce.

At Onomichi, Asae introduced him to the beautiful Yoshiko Matsui, who had large dark eyes filled with playfulness. A talented seamstress, she made lacy Western-style outfits for her relatives and friends. As soon as Setsuo graduated, stepmother Asae was eager for him to marry Yoshiko.

But Setsuo had other ideas. Like many other young men in the western coastal prefectures, he burned with ambition. He wanted to cross the Pacific and see what riches awaited in the land called Beikoku, or "Rice Country."

More than 21,000 adventurers from Hiroshima Prefecture had already traveled over the Pacific Ocean to settle in Hawai'i, California, and Washington.

"I'll go to the United States first," Setsuo told Asae. "I'd like to see what the people of Hiroshima are doing over there." He promised her that after he had accumulated some wealth he would return to wed Yoshiko, who was headed for a trade school in Tokyo.

With money from the family's savings, Setsuo sailed for San Francisco in April 1905. He was only 19 at the time. He wore a dark suit and tie, and his hat brim was angled over his oval face and prominent nose. Seeking more than riches, Setsuo Aratani was in search of a place of his own, a place where he could be free to exercise all his ingenuity and creativity.

<hr />

San Francisco, long established as a port of entry for Chinese laborers, became Setsuo's new home for three years. By 1906 8,000 Japanese immigrants had settled in this picturesque seaside town so reminiscent of Japan's Nagasaki. Setsuo enrolled in an English-language school at one of the Christian missions sponsored by the Methodist and Presbyterian churches. In addition to providing English-language classes, both missions also offered room and board. Although most students never graduated and very few enrolled in public institutions, the mission schools eased the Issei into American life while serving as centers for social networking.

Baseball had been introduced in Japan in the 1870s, and Setsuo became an avid sports fan who fell in with a crowd of baseball enthusiasts. These men—including Chiura Obata, who later became a professor of art at UC Berkeley—launched a baseball team, the Fuji Athletic Club of San Francisco.

While the members of the Fuji Athletic Club identified themselves as Californians, Californians did not prove particularly hospitable toward the Japanese. Although a small island country, Japan had already demonstrated its military might in the Russo-Japanese War. Suspicions about Japan's growing strength coupled with xenophobia sparked a backlash against Japanese laborers in the United States. Both Chinese and Japanese were the targets of the *San Francisco Chronicle's* inflammatory headlines: "Crime and Poverty Go Hand and Hand with Asiatic Labor," "Brown Men Are an Evil in the Public Schools," "Japanese a Menace to American Women," and "Brown Asiatics Steal Brains of Whites." A legislative act dating back to 1790 barred non-European immigrants and even American Indians from naturalization. A San Francisco Board of Education resolution in May of

1905 decreed that Chinese and Japanese children should be sent to separate schools. The message was clear: No Asians welcome.

On April 18, 1906, the Great Earthquake shook San Francisco. Fires swept the city, destroying homes and businesses; looting and violence soon followed. Once the embers cooled, the immigrant communities unfairly took the brunt of residents' frustration and fury, so thousands of Japanese left San Francisco and headed south to Los Angeles. During the following four years, the Japanese population of Los Angeles would double to 8,000. Among those making the exodus in 1908 was Setsuo Aratani.

The move was a setback to his plans to make his fortune; this in turn meant no return to Japan, and consequently, no marriage in his immediate future. Setsuo simply refused to return with empty hands, for the people of Saijo would undoubtedly ask, "Where's all the wealth that you were supposed to bring back?" He could imagine Yoshiko's face, her large eyes filled with expectation. Although it would be easy to blame the anti-immigrant mood he'd encountered, it would be *haji*, shameful, to come back to Japan with only a Fuji baseball uniform to show for his efforts. To attain financial independence, Setsuo followed the lead of other Issei: putting away his stylish suits and jaunty hat, he learned to work the land.

***

Until the late 1800s, the majority of farm laborers working in California's vegetable and fruit fields were Chinese. West Coast miners and railroad workers needed food, which had spurred Chinese immigrants to develop "truck gardening." But California politicians implemented the Exclusion Act of 1882, which barred any more Chinese immigrants from entering the country. With their primary labor source cut off, Chinese agriculturalists' profits rapidly withered. Soon Issei replaced the Chinese in the fields of both Japanese farm operators—who numbered approximately 3,000 by 1909—and European American landholders.

Setsuo quickly found employment with a European American strawberry farmer in El Monte, near the San Gabriel and Rio Hondo rivers at the end of the Santa Fe Trail. There he learned how to grow strawberries, a labor-intensive crop that sold for higher prices than such vegetables as beans and onions. Why farm cheaper vegetables, he reasoned, when you could take the same land and plant more profitable crops? As he bent to pick the red berries, his mind whirled with plans and ideas to utilize and optimize resources. His pale skin grew tanned and ruddy, and soon he

**In 1914 Setsuo Aratani (center, wearing tie) leased nine acres
in Moneta, California, to grow strawberries.** (99.30.142)

began to look the part of a genuine farmer.

After three years, Setsuo was ready to establish his own operation. It
didn't need to be especially large—in fact, most berry farms owned by Issei
were only between one and ten acres. Approximately $1,500 was necessary
to start up a three-acre strawberry farm, one acre of which could be expected
to produce an annual profit of $500. The yield per acre of strawberries was
higher than that for any other crop. Setsuo could expect to regain his initial
investment in one year. The only problem, as he would learn later, was the
fact that strawberry plants quickly contaminate the soil with pathogens—
within two to three years he would have to move on.

For his first piece of land, he looked to Moneta, a green fertile area
south of downtown Los Angeles in the Gardena Valley. The leading strawberry growing area in Southern California, Moneta (which means "coins" in
Italian) had attracted a number of Japanese farmers, who formed a
Strawberry Growers Association.

However, another obstacle threatened Setsuo's plans: the proposed Alien
Land Law, which would prohibit anyone ineligible for citizenship from buying farmland; leases were also restricted to a maximum of three years. The
law, which took effect in 1913, was carefully crafted to avoid mentioning
any particular ethnic group, but it was clear that its intended targets were
Asian immigrants, who continued to be barred from citizenship.

Once again faced with racism, Setsuo could have returned to his birthplace in Hiroshima. Instead of getting discouraged, however, he examined the 1913 law for loopholes. Such loopholes included the fact that immigrants with children born in the United States could purchase land in the names of their sons or daughters; the Issei also bought land by simply borrowing the name of an American friend of legal age; and some formed dummy corporations owned by second-generation Nisei stockholders. Setsuo observed these legal subterfuge tactics with the knowledge that they might be useful for his survival and success in California.

In 1914 Setsuo leased nine acres in Moneta for his own strawberry operation. He was among 240 other Japanese farmers in an area that supported four Japanese-operated grocery and dry-goods stores, two tofu shops, two barbershops, and five bathhouses. The same year he arrived in the area, the Moneta Cooperative Association was organized to provide mutual aid to local farmers and to collectively market their produce, as was commonly done in Japan. Setsuo was quickly learning that, in California as well as Japan, it was better to combine efforts with others than to stand alone.

Setsuo had been in the U.S. for 9 years, and as he approached the age of 30, his concerns about marriage grew. He watched other Issei men send for "picture brides" from the homeland: after marrying by proxy in Japan, these young women, usually from farm families, would travel to the United States to join husbands they had never met. Setsuo didn't want to follow this popular practice, for he still dreamed about Yoshiko Matsui, the beautiful woman with the streak of playfulness. He had made her a promise years ago, a pledge he had not yet been able to fulfill.

Back in Japan, however, even his stepmother Asae was advising Yoshiko to marry a more likely suitor. A single woman in her mid-twenties would be considered an old maid with little chance of making a good match. "It does not look as if Setsuo will return," Asae told Yoshiko, now working as a home-economics teacher. Yoshiko understood the underlying message: Don't let these crucial years pass by in hopeless waiting.

So while Setsuo was learning how to cultivate strawberries in the fertile El Monte soil, Yoshiko married and bore two children: a son, Takao, and a daughter, Sadako. A few years later her husband died, leaving her a young widow with a meager income. Relatives helped care for the children, but Yoshiko's prospects nevertheless looked dim.

**Setsuo and Yoshiko Aratani in a formal portrait
shortly after they married, ca. 1915.** (99.30.39)

During the feudal period, Japanese men married as many times as they could afford, and some sired children with concubines. A woman—whose identity was dependent on her father, husband, or brother—typically married only once. What eligible bachelor would want to marry a widow with two children?

Hearing of Yoshiko's plight, Setsuo wrote to his stepmother and made some preliminary inquiries about marrying Yoshiko. Asae Aratani advised against it, for she knew about the conventions within the Japanese community. Tongues would wag if Setsuo Aratani married a woman with children, and her stepson didn't need any additional hindrances to his progress.

The machinations of family politics ultimately served to facilitate Setsuo's decision. The relatives who were caring for Yoshiko's children had no sons to carry on their family name, so they needed a *yōshi*, a male, to adopt. Takao, a young boy with his hair in a crewcut, would be adopted by one family, while another would raise Yoshiko's daughter, Sadako, a thin girl with a delicate face. Yoshiko would thus be free to go to Setsuo Aratani.

In a photograph taken at Yoshiko's engagement party before she sailed for California, she wears a heavy brocade kimono, and her face is powdered white. She faced the camera alone, without her new husband and without her children. For this marriage, Yoshiko had made the ultimate sacrifice.

The newlyweds made their home in South Park, a community near Moneta, where Setsuo continued plying his agricultural skills. Within two years Setsuo was elected president of the area's Japanese Association of America, the Issei organization with the greatest influence within the ethnic community. Although these associations also served as a vehicle for communicating Japanese government policies to Japanese immigrants, they primarily addressed the needs of an embattled minority community in the midst of a growing racial hostility manifesting itself up and down the West Coast.

As he built the foundation for his new family, Setsuo was also refining his own personal style as both an entrepreneur and a community developer. Now sporting a small straight mustache, he had a comfortable paunch and preferred bow ties. Although he had never attended one of Japan's illustrious universities, he was highly literate. He saw the need for Japanese immigrants to band together for economic power, so with other growers he launched a co-op where farm equipment, seeds, and fertilizer were purchased in bulk and sold to members at cut-rate prices.

Setsuo also concerned himself with the general welfare of Issei in various realms beyond the agricultural. Although his English-language abilities were limited, he was not deterred from dealing with European Americans in the produce market. In the evenings he attended dinners where dignitaries, flushed with sake, sang folk songs brought from their hometowns back in Japan—for a moment, they could forget about combative California race politics.

Meanwhile, across the Pacific, Setsuo's rising stature in his community was being observed by Japanese government officials, who noted that this thirty-something Issei seemed innovative and resourceful. Only 10 years after arriving in the United States, Setsuo was recognized by the governor of Hiroshima for his efforts in spearheading Issei interests. Japan's Prince Fushimi later rewarded him for his achievements in agriculture. However, perhaps his greatest achievement occurred on May 22, 1917, with the birth of his first and only child, George Tetsuo Aratani, at the family home in South Park.

———— ◆ ◆ ◆ ————

Ever since her arrival in California, Yoshiko Aratani had sometimes found it hard to breathe. She didn't know if her difficulty was caused by the ocean breeze that blew into the Gardena Valley during the winter evenings, or whether it could be traced to the bouts of loneliness she felt when Setsuo was out at community functions. She tried not to think about the two children she had left behind, instead keeping busy sending parcels to them in Japan or meeting with friends she made through the Nishi Hongwanji Buddhist Temple in Los Angeles's Little Tokyo.

The birth of her third and last child finally eased some of her regret and sadness. The Aratanis named their son after George Washington, the first president of their new homeland, while his middle name, Tetsuo, would forever connect father to son. Yoshiko would always call her son by his American name, pronouncing it "Joji."

With George, Yoshiko did not have the jitters of an inexperienced mother. She knew how to nurse and bathe him, and she sewed him fashionable outfits. She was amazed by how chubby and fat he became and wondered if it was the California air that produced such healthy, large people.

In 1919, when George was two years old, the family moved more than thirty miles from South Park to Pacoima, in the San Fernando Valley. While a giant aqueduct had just been built to bring water from the Owens River, about 250 miles to the north, Issei had already been farming in the area for years. Moreover, the availability of land uncontaminated by pathogens in the Moneta region was limited, and with the end of World War I farmers saw the potential of growing fresh table vegetables instead of a cash crop like strawberries.

Yoshiko supported the move—provided she was able to keep in touch with their friends in Little Tokyo. Secretly, she also hoped that the drier inland climate would relieve the persistent congestion in her chest. One day, while sweeping the dirt floors of the family home, she collapsed in a chair and put her head down on her folded arms.

She then traveled to consult with Dr. Kikuo Tashiro, a native of Nagasaki, in a Little Tokyo hotel. "Asthma," he diagnosed, as he took out a syringe. Yoshiko closed her eyes and felt the needle prick her arm. Within minutes, she felt better. "Adrenaline," Dr. Tashiro explained. Adrenaline

George Aratani with his mother, Yoshiko. (99.30.6)

shots were a popular treatment for asthma at the time.

George was always by Yoshiko's side in Pacoima. Energetic and curious, he was also a respectful child. On the rare occasions when he was disobedi-ent, Mama would use *yaito*, or moxa, an incense punk the shape of an oblong piece of chalk. *Yaito*, made of shredded dried vegetables, alleviated Yoshiko's pain in her neck and shoulders. Lighting the end of the *yaito* with a match, she warmed her skin for a few minutes until she felt relief. To dis-cipline George, however, Mama brushed the *yaito* against his delicate skin for barely a second. He felt a flash of heat and knew not to disobey again.

Walking hand in hand, mother and son passed fields of Setsuo's water-melon and corn, and pastures where horses grazed. A friend approached them in the distance. "Behave," she told George as she released his small hand.

George nodded, his chubby cheeks tanned by the summer sun. The wind whipped dust from the dirt road, and as he ran after his friend, like his mother, he began to wheeze like a squeaky door.

Setsuo was experiencing his own struggles of a more political nature. A second Alien Land Law, approved in 1920, was enacted to close loopholes in the 1913 legislation—now Setsuo and other Issei were prevented from even leasing farmland. Corporations with a majority of Japanese stockholders were prohibited from leasing or purchasing land, and Issei parents could no longer act as guardians of property for their minor children. Furthermore, if the state proved that Issei money was being invested in land under a Nisei's name in order to circumvent the Alien Land Law, the property could be confiscated.

In response to such harsh legislation, Setsuo became more deeply involved in the Japanese community. Having organized the San Fernando Valley Sangyo Kumiai, or farmers' association, he became its manager in 1921. That same year, Pacoima won a first-place prize for farm products at the Los Angeles County Fair in San Fernando.

In spite of such accomplishments, Setsuo was becoming disenchanted with the San Fernando Valley, and drought threatened his tilled acreage. As he looked over his fields of wilting lettuce, he listened to other men speaking of a place up north by the ocean. It had a Spanish name: Guadalupe.

Guadalupe was more than 100 miles away, in Santa Barbara County. Located on the delta of the Santa Maria River and neighboring the city of Santa Maria, Guadalupe was known for its fertile land rich with alluvial deposits. "A grower can plow all day and never touch a rock as large as a pebble," a local European American grower had said.

Guadalupe's land had originally been almost exclusively devoted to sugar-beet production, though Swiss Italian immigrants did operate several dairies in the area. After the decline of the Gold Rush, the Union Sugar Mill in Betteravia had replaced Chinese tenant farmers with Japanese laborers. Sugar-beet farming had transformed the wind-beaten land into a prosperous, soil-rich region, but this success came at a cost to the Issei laborers.

Workers were housed in stables and fed so poorly that many eventually developed beri-beri. Their collective spirit, however, rescued their future. In 1906 Japanese workers formed the Guadalupe Japanese Association, a *kyōwakai* (cooperative organization) "to develop friendship among the Japanese, to help each other in emergencies, to preserve the strength of each, and to promote the welfare of all," according to Masakazu Iwata's *Planted in Good Soil.*

In Guadalupe, the Aratanis first settled in a small labor camp that supported a few homes for Japanese families as well as smaller dwellings for Mexican farmworkers. A barn full of horses and several tractors stood about 100 yards away. Other structures included a wooden outhouse and a Japanese-style bath.

For two years George walked to and from the elementary school with his Mexican neighbors. Many times after school he played with these same friends. Around five o'clock in the evening, his friends' father would come home, dirty and dusty from his work in the fields. While the father washed up, the mother would call the children into the house. "Sit down," she told George in Spanish, as she dished out pork and beef simmered with bell pepper, potato, and tomato.

This happened every night, so George routinely ate two suppers for a couple of years. He mentioned nothing about his extra meal to his mother, because somehow he sensed that Yoshiko would put a stop to it—after all, she had always stressed that he should not be a burden to others. But the lure of food was too much. Yoshiko noticed how quickly her little boy was growing, but she never suspected that it was due to nightly extra servings of tortillas and pork.

While George grew strong physically, Setsuo was growing his business. Throughout the town's history, Japanese, flush with ambition and vision, had come to make their fortunes in the Santa Maria Valley. Setsuo had the capital and knowledge, but he needed to find employees; even more importantly, he needed to obtain land at a time when the legal cards were stacked against him. In fact, in 1922, shortly after his arrival in the area, the United States Supreme Court ruled that Japanese were indeed "ineligible for citizenship" because they were not "free white persons," as stipulated in the naturalization laws.

Absentee landowners, however, especially those connected to the Union Sugar Mill, were only too happy to make flexible arrangements with the enterprising Japanese. And Setsuo—who would not be deterred from his vision of a burgeoning agricultural empire—had a plan that depended on a friendship developed earlier in Los Angeles. The Aratanis had befriended the Tamuras, an older couple from their Buddhist temple, who lived with their two grown children on the east side of downtown Los Angeles. Their son Yoshizumi, nicknamed "Butch," played basketball and baseball with the Wanjis, a team sponsored by Nishi Hongwanji Temple.

Butch was a quiet person with high cheekbones, an open face, and the muscular build of a natural athlete. Two years earlier he had dropped out of UCLA to help support his family by working at Sumitomo Bank, where he experienced the rigid Japanese work ethic: for example, employees were even required to report the number of postage stamps they used during the course of a day.

Setsuo wanted Butch to manage his accounting section and also lead a new baseball team sponsored by the Young Men's Buddhist Association (YMBA). He needed the younger Tamura for a much more important reason, however: Butch had been born in the United States, and on official documents he would be listed as a co-partner of Central Produce, the 600 acres Setsuo leased for his farming operation.

Setsuo knew he was taking a risk by placing his lease in someone else's name—especially when the law prohibited such practices—but his American-born son, George, was still too young to be named on real-estate documents, and Butch Tamura, steadfast and honest, was like a member of the family. In addition to Butch, Setsuo also hand-picked other American young men of Japanese ancestry—most of them baseball players—to work for this company. He also paid for the whole Tamura family to relocate to the Santa Maria Valley. For Setsuo, a man without siblings and no adult relatives in his adopted country, the loyalty of friends would hold the key to the future of his company.

———•◆•———

To handle the shipping-and-packing end of their agriculture business, Setsuo and his Issei friends Naoichi Ikeda and Reiji "Ben" Kodama started Guadalupe Produce Company in 1923. Key to their operation were not simply healthy crops, but also ice.

At the time, vegetables could be sent "dry pack" from Santa Barbara County to the Los Angeles produce markets. "Dry pack" meant that crates of fresh vegetables were loaded right from the field into trucks without refrigeration. "Ice-pack" transportation, on the other hand, was via railroad cars loaded with ice.

The Puritan Ice Company had opened in 1921 on the corner of Guadalupe and Santa Maria roads, right next to the Southern Pacific rail line; its primary business was icing down cars of salad greens. But crop failure caused one of the ice plant's partners to close its packing shed, thus creating an opportunity for Guadalupe Produce, known to the locals as "G.P."

Setsuo set up a packing shed immediately northwest of the ice plant. In the early days, 300-pound blocks of ice were unloaded at the packing shed, and icemen—usually muscular Irish Americans—chipped the blocks into ice chips with metal mallets.

The ice chips would then be quickly placed on a conveyor belt to be packed in with fresh vegetables in crates lined with waterproof oiled paper. Later, the process became more sophisticated with the introduction of a mechanized ice crusher.

Ice packing made it possible for Guadalupe-grown vegetables to be transported east, beyond the state border. Once Guadalupe Produce and other packing companies arrived on the scene, the transportation of ice-packed lettuce quadrupled. Setsuo Aratani shipped the first carload of lettuce from Santa Maria Valley to Texas. A pioneer among the Japanese large-scale farming enterprises, Setsuo's packing shed was soon the model for another thriving operation, Minami Farms, as well as other Issei farmers.

Once lettuce growing had been introduced to Guadalupe, Setsuo experimented with carrots and cauliflower. It was Setsuo's idea to mix vegetables, not only on his land but also in refrigerator cars, a practice that distinguished him from other Santa Maria Valley farmers. Eastern buyers were wild about G.P. vegetables, which were sold under multiple brand names such as Home Run King and All Star, all chosen because of Setsuo's love for baseball.

Yoshiko, who continued to suffer serious bouts of asthma, found her place in the Guadalupe women's social scene. As the wife of one of the valley's top growers, she served as president of the Japanese Fujinkai, called the "Women's Auxiliary" in English; this group supported the Guadalupe Buddhist Church, and more importantly, it provided a place for Issei women to gather and exchange information.

The farm women were a tight-knit group who could be counted upon to lend help in times of crisis. One of Yoshiko's close friends was Toyoko Kodama, a jovial woman who seemed to always have the ability to make the more reticent Yoshiko laugh. The Aratanis had met Toyoko and her husband Reiji, known as Ben, back in Los Angeles, and they recruited them to come to Guadalupe. Ben, an experienced produce man, played a vital role at the packing shed, while Toyoko ran one of the boardinghouses in town.

One day, after the Buddhist temple's *Obon* festival, an envelope addressed to a blind man and his impoverished family was found in the offering box. Once delivered, the envelope was opened to reveal $300, a small fortune at that time. The minister, entreated by the blind man to discover the identity of the donor, finally ascertained that it was Toyoko, the proprietor of the Kodama Boarding House, who insisted that the gift be given quietly to preserve the "purity of the children."

In addition to organizing festivals and practicing mutual aid, the women also shared in another important activity during the Prohibition years of the 1920s: the brewing of rice wine. It was not produced for sale but for their household's own consumption, and it was made with the full knowledge of the local authorities. George even assisted his mother Yoshiko in making sake. After boiling *mochigome* (sweet rice), she poured the mixture into a large wooden barrel and fastened the lid. Then George carefully placed a large rock on top to ensure that the barrel was properly sealed as *kōji* (malted rice) fermented the contents.

"Mrs. Aratani, ready?" Sheriff Tognazzini would inquire on a regular basis. When the sake, brewed in a special barrel from Japan, had attained its full flavor, the sheriff, who liked his sake cold, sampled a fresh batch in a glass cup. "Very good!"

———◆———

Although Setsuo had abandoned formalwear during his early years as a strawberry farmer in El Monte, he soon returned to wearing three-piece suits in his role as an agricultural magnate. His felt hat pushed back on his forehead, he would wander through the packing shed, his dress shoes crushing discarded lettuce leaves as the sun filtered down through the gaps in the wood roof. The 30 workers, their faces shining with sweat, illustrated the diversity of Guadalupe Produce's employees. Japanese Hawaiians, mostly bachelors who lived in boardinghouses on Guadalupe Boulevard, worked alongside Swiss Italian dairy farmers.

Half of the men worked as trimmers, who quickly sliced off the thick stem of the lettuce with a hooked knife, while the other half packed the trimmed heads in crates. An Irishman then nailed the crates shut with a hatchet before sending them up a crude conveyor belt to an open railroad car.

Among the first of Setsuo's summer hires was a 16-year-old Nisei, a student at Palo Alto Union High School. Ken Kitasako had been recruited by a friend at Stanford University who claimed that workers could make three times as much in this new packing shed as they could picking apricots and prunes during the summer.

Guadalupe was more than 200 miles away from Ken's Palo Alto home, where his father, a gardener, was single-handedly raising Ken's two younger brothers; as a result, he stayed in the Kodama Boarding House run by Yoshiko's friend Toyoko. Small-framed and with a bright smile, Ken won the favor of Setsuo, who called him "Youngu" because of his youthfulness.

The work was demanding, especially during harvest time. Arriving at the shed by seven in the morning, the laborers worked until seven in the evening, sometimes until midnight because trains en route to Texas and the East Coast needed to be loaded as soon as possible to ensure the freshest vegetables on delivery. When the packers returned to work after supper, Setsuo called the local Japanese restaurant to order sandwiches and coffee cake for a midnight snack for his crew.

One evening while Ken was waiting for a friend to get off work, he noticed that some nails had spilled onto the floor from a crate-lidding machine. Getting down on his hands and knees, he picked them up and put them in a container. It was a simple act, but one witnessed by the man standing in the shadows of the packing shed.

At the end of the week, the 16-year-old found a larger-than-usual figure scrawled on his paycheck. Ken called his friend over. "There must be some mistake here. I didn't put in any extra hours."

"You were compensated for salvaging those nails," his friend said. "Aratani-*san* saw what you did."

———— ·◆· ————

Setsuo, with his engaging personality, easily fit into Guadalupe's social scene. He was by no means loquacious, and in fact he was described as a man of few words, or *kuchi kazu sukunai* (literally, "small-numbered mouth"). However, when called upon to speak at banquets and meetings, Setsuo could masterfully weave an impromptu speech that was succinct and to the point.

Sometimes George would accompany his father down the main street in town, Guadalupe Boulevard, which was lined with boardinghouses and grocery stores stocked with seaweed, pickled plums, and dried abalone. They could barely take 10 steps before Setsuo stopped to chat with someone.

"How come we have to keep stopping?" George complained to his father.

And Setsuo was a busy man: he attended community functions three or four nights of every week. After sundown Guadalupe Boulevard was a lively place, full of bright lights and raucous male voices emanating from the *ryōri-ya*, eateries where the Issei relaxed and drank after a full day's work in the fields. Many times Setsuo would join them and exercise another of his skills—his ability to hold his liquor. An article in the Buddhist journal *Bhratri* once described him as "the man who could outdrink any other person in the state of California."

Guadalupe's sense of community was not just about celebratory camaraderie, however. The year after the Aratanis arrived, Setsuo observed firsthand the strength of the town's Issei network. One cool evening a fire started in a Chinese joss house on Guadalupe Boulevard and quickly swept through a block and a half of the downtown area. Families ran out of their homes, watching as the buildings collapsed in flames. Lucky ones were able to drag their household belongings or store inventories and fixtures out into the street.

The fire left 200 people homeless and destroyed 18 buildings in the small town. Among the victims was Zentaro Yamada, a Hiroshima immigrant. His family not only lost their grocery business but also their home. Other victims were the Nakases, Wakayama immigrants who ran a dry-goods store and were raising three young sons.

Setsuo was one of the local leaders called to an emergency meeting that night. A total of nine Japanese businesses had been wiped out, Setsuo learned. The group, many of whom were members of the Japanese Association, met again the next morning in the Nakano Hotel. Setsuo, still a newcomer, watched as the senior members called for donations to help the fire victims; others volunteered to make fund-raising appeals to the neighboring communities of San Luis Obispo and Lompoc. What moved Setsuo most were those who opened their doors to the homeless families. Guadalupe, he saw, was a town where people came together in times of trouble.

Within a week, Zentaro Yamada announced that he would be rebuilding. Among those lending a hand was Setsuo Aratani.

---

*"Guadalupe Baseball Team Now Ready
to Invade Japan"*
—**Headline in *The Rafu Shimpo*, 22 July 1928**

Almost as strong as Setsuo's passion for business and community building was his enthusiasm for sports, especially the all-American pastime of baseball. He always made time to cheer on the Guadalupe Buddhist Church's YMBA baseball team as they faced such opponents as the Santa Maria Elks, Cambria Pines, and Santa Maria Athletics.

In 1927 Setsuo formed a company baseball team that competed in the semipro Central Coast League. Unlike other popular Nisei teams, the Aratanis, echoing Setsuo's employees, were ethnically mixed. There were only three players of Japanese descent on the team; the rest of the Aratani team were either European American or Mexican. Within a year they had captured the league championship with victories over a team in the Negro Leagues, the San Luis Obispo County All-Stars, and the Fresno Nippons.

By 1928 Setsuo's business was doing so well that he prepared to send the team to Japan. "They are going on their own 'hook,'" reported *The Rafu Shimpo,* a Japanese vernacular newspaper based in Los Angeles. "The strong team will not have much trouble booking games."

Goodwill baseball tours were not a new phenomenon in Japan, with both college and professional teams from the U.S. having played there. Casey Stengel's All Stars had arrived in 1922, and the same year as the Aratani tour Ty Cobb came to Japan to teach "batting secrets." Flourishing Japanese American teams such as the Alameda Kono All Star Team made overseas goodwill trips as well.

Wearing their baseball uniforms as they posed for group photos, the Aratanis sailed from San Francisco on the *Korea Maru* on August 1, 1928. The youngest member of the tour was the team's 11-year-old bat boy, George Aratani, who was outfitted in an authentic Aratani uniform.

As they traveled throughout Japan, Yoshiko, who also accompanied the team, would occasionally mention to George, "Soon you'll be meeting your *Nīsan,* your *Nēsan.*"

The Aratani baseball team traveled in Japan from August through November 1928 (Setsuo Aratani, second row, center; George Aratani, age 11, first row, center). (99.30.144)

George brushed her comments aside. An older brother and sister? He knew other people had siblings, but he didn't know how it felt to have them. He was content serving as the team mascot and running after loose bats and balls.

In Hiroshima the entire baseball team and its supporters stayed at a grand house with a huge garden pool filled with carp. This was the home of wealthy Aratani relatives who had made a fortune in the soy sauce business. In anticipation of the team's visit, the family had even remodeled the home and added Western-style showers to accommodate the baseball players from America.

Yoshiko introduced George to two teenagers.

"This is Sadako." She placed her hand on the shoulder of a thin girl. "And this, Takao." George studied the two strangers. They bore little resemblance to him. They stood together quietly at the edge of a pond, feeding dry bread to hungry carp.

Yoshiko went to sit on a *tatami* mat with the adults, thankful to have this brief, rare moment to observe her three children together. She knew that in a few weeks she would again be thousands of miles away in California, but for now, all of her children were with her. She was happy to see that both Sadako and Takao had grown to be healthy young people. The relatives had raised them well, yet she yearned to know what it would have been like to have shared those missing years.

Setsuo Aratani and son George in Guadalupe Produce vegetable fields in 1928. (NRC. 1998.575.3)

Before leaving Japan in the middle of November, the Aratanis had another unforgettable experience: they attended the coronation of Emperor Hirohito in Kyoto. The coronation was meant to herald the beginning of the Showa, or "Radiant Peace" era in Japan. Masses of people gathered along the train track as the emperor and empress traveled from Tokyo to Kyoto. The Aratanis watched as the royal couple, riding in a horse-drawn carriage from the railway station, made their way to Kyoto Palace.

Everyone in the crowd bowed as the carriage passed by. "Look down," Yoshiko told George. "No one is allowed to gaze directly at the emperor and empress." George, however, sneaked a peek. They looked just like ordinary people in fancy costumes, he thought.

When the Aratanis arrived home again, the team was greeted with accolades from all quarters. *The Rafu Shimpo* trumpeted their "splendid record" of twenty-five victories, one tie, and four losses. The *Guadalupe Gazette* welcomed the club back with the headline, "They Taught the Orient How!" The newspaper claimed the team's "walloping three months' barnstorming tour of Japan" had "brought many baseball laurels to Guadalupe."

Setsuo had spent $3,000 on the tour, a small fortune at that time. Weeks later, when he took George for a walk through fields of cauliflower and broccoli, he explained his business philosophy to his son. "Joji, if you want to get into business and continue to grow, you have to surround yourself with capable people," Setsuo said. "You must treat them as part of the company. There are only 24 hours in a day. When the business gets bigger and bigger, there are so many things to do. You need good people to take on various important responsibilities. Then you can continue to make progress and grow bigger. But first you have to work as a team, just like the team that went to Japan." This philosophy, which had been crucial to the success of the elder Aratani, would become the foundation of George's future empire.

Let It Roll

To business men, trying to crack the depression,
the New Year's calls not
so much for resolutions as re-solutions.
—Guadalupe Gazette, 1 January 1931

When a bitter cold wave hit the South in 1927, sales of Guadalupe carrots reached a record high. Housewives preferred carrots with their green tops intact, in contrast to the trimmed ones from Louisiana. As a result, business boomed for Guadalupe Produce and the other Issei-operated farms (which were usually referred to as ranches). Setsuo soon opened a second packing shed in Lompoc, another farming town about an hour's ride away in the Lompoc Valley. Santa Maria Produce, a packing shed launched by two Tomooka brothers, hired Ken Kitasako, Setsuo's former summer worker who had returned to the valley after graduating from Stanford University with a degree in economics.

Guadalupe had grown up from its sugar-beet days of the early 1900s. The Swiss still dominated the dairy industry, while the Portuguese and Italians were the primary landholders. Mexicans and Filipinos tended the fields, but now the Japanese operated the large ranches and the packing sheds. Then the Depression hit, and the farmers faced days when they couldn't sell anything.

The Aratani family and a neighbor child traveling
by automobile, early 1920s. (99.30.27)

Train cars filled with produce started for the East Coast. If the produce wasn't purchased at its first destination, the salesman would instruct the railroad company to "let it roll," or go on to the new city.

Salesman Ken Kitasako experienced this firsthand. He wired buyers across the country, notifying them of the incoming produce, then he would make his calls: "I got a roller of cauliflower, two rollers of lettuce."

"How much?" the buyer would ask. Then began hard-core negotiations between the salesman and buyer. If Ken could recoup his costs, he usually sold his produce. If not, he would "let it roll" to Chicago, and maybe on to New York. This strategy was risky, because at times it reached its last destination without finding a home.

* * *

Whether they were large shippers or itinerant farm workers, Issei parents attempted to shield their children from their financial problems and their daily toil in the fields. Some children even were sent to live in Japan. Other families in such remote areas as Arroyo Grande, Pismo Beach, San Luis Obispo, and Morro Bay chose another option—the Guadalupe Children's Home at the Buddhist church. Desiring a good education for their American-born children, these immigrants believed that the Children's Home would provide a more nurturing environment than they were able to offer.

Approximately 20 children at a time lived under the guidance of the Reverend Issei Matsuura and his wife Shinobu. The children attended Guadalupe public school and also received Japanese-language instruction and religious training at the church. Quite frequently, illness spread among the children; on one occasion the home was even quarantined during the holidays because of an outbreak of scarlet fever.

Every Sunday morning Reverend Matsuura would speak to all the children in his congregation, including George. He explained how a prince grew up in a protected paradise only to be awakened to another reality when he witnessed suffering and poverty beyond the walls of his palace. "This prince," Matsuura explained, "became Buddha." The minister would inevitably close the sermon with his favorite saying: "*Jinsei wa ku de aru*" (Life is full of hardship).

George glanced over at his friends—not that again. Soon, the saying became a running joke. "*Jinsei wa ku de aru*," the children would yell out as they ran in the playground.

Later, George would come to understand the meaning behind the minister's mysterious saying, but for some in the Children's Home, hardship had already been experienced at a tender age.

———— • ◆ • ————

As the only child of one of Guadalupe's prosperous growers, George was barely aware of the economic hard times that had hit the United States. Occasionally he overheard friends talk about how their parents had to work all the time, but the Depression still remained a distant topic.

Life in the Aratanis' comfortable Spanish-style home on Peralta Street remained unchanged. The ailing Yoshiko, seeking help with household chores and entertaining duties, elicited the help of young single Nisei women, who stayed at the house until they eventually married. Among these helpers was Butch Tamura's younger sister Mutsuko, nicknamed Muts, a former Sunday School teacher at the Nishi Hongwanji Temple in Los Angeles's Little Tokyo.

The door to the Aratani home was always open, and George's friends often stayed for lunch and supper. His best friend and neighbor, Tets Murata, was born in San Jose in 1917, the same year as George. Tets and his parents, who were farm laborers, had moved to Guadalupe when Tets was 10 years old.

Tets practically lived at the Aratani house, and he was viewed as the family's second son. He enjoyed the delicious Japanese food prepared by Yoshiko and Muts, while George's favorite food was hot dogs (although for breakfast he ate broiled fish, either sea perch or bass).

George and Tets played baseball at the local playground across the street, and on occasion they went to the sand dunes to see the props left there after the filming of Cecil B. DeMille's *The Ten Commandments*. The sand dunes, whose shapes constantly shifted from the constant winds, were a popular destination for picnics and impromptu outings.

One day George and his friends heard that the dunes were to be transformed into the Sahara Desert for an upcoming movie called *Morocco*. Hoping to spot some movie stars, they gathered on the outskirts of the shoot, watching as giant lights and sound booms were set up in the sand.

"Hey," a film crew member called as he motioned them over. "How would you boys like a job?"

The job consisted of taking care of a flock of sheep when the animals were not being used in a scene. As they sat back by the sheep pen, George spied a striking barefoot woman dressed in a sarong standing in front of the camera. Her makeup was applied to make her look "roughed up" by the desert, but that could not conceal her beauty. "Who is she?" he asked one of the older boys.

"A foreign actress. I think her name is Marlene Dietrich."

"A looker," another boy chimed in.

"Yeah," George agreed.

For the most part, however, life was not filled with glamorous Hollywood stars. During their summer breaks, most of the Guadalupean children were out in the fields earning extra money alongside their mothers during the lean years of the Depression.

At Guadalupe Produce, many participated in seasonal celery "panning": after acres of young celery plants were freshly plowed, the field workers tossed them into large piles. The children and women then would peel the dead leaves off, cut the tops off, and place the six- to seven-inch plants in a shallow pan of water. For each pan the worker received 12 cents. Issei women also worked at broccoli "bunching," the tying together of broccoli with raffia.

George had his own household chores at home on Peralta Street. From age 12 he was assigned the jobs of mowing the lawn every Saturday and cleaning out the Japanese koi (carp) pond, which was lined with rocks. For this work he was handsomely rewarded with two dollars a week.

One year, without any prompting from Setsuo, George and Tets decided to ask him for work. Setsuo made no promises. Instead, he sent the two boys to the packing-shed manager, Ben Kodama, a tough, strict Issei who could express displeasure or approval with one simple look.

"What can you do?" Kodama asked. Most young boys worked out in the fields, not in the packing shed.

"I think we can do whatever those people are doing over there," replied George, pointing to the trimmers.

"You sure?" Kodama folded his arms. Finally, he agreed to let them try.

Eventually the two boys were on the line trimming lettuce, celery, and cauliflower. They worked hard, loading crate upon crate of vegetables until eight in the evening. Soon the rest of the employees were telling them, "Hey, you guys are too fast. Slow down like the rest of us."

When the boys received their first checks, George felt truly rich.

European American and Japanese American farmers in Guadalupe in the early 1920s. Among them was Setsuo Aratani (first row, center). (99.30.136)

While George and Tets were laboring at the packing shed for the summer, Setsuo and the other growers banded together to put food on their families' tables. One such grower was Yaemon Minami, who was referred to as the "pride of Wakayama prefecture" even though he had been living in Guadalupe since 1905. Minami was regularly observed quietly leaving a bag of groceries at the door of an impoverished family on the edge of Betteravia. The Aratanis also helped their friends and neighbors. When a friend from Onomichi had a difficult time farming in the Sacramento Valley, Setsuo moved the whole family to Guadalupe and even provided some capital for an asparagus operation. This spirit of mutual aid marked the way the Issei survived during the Depression years.

Cooperative approaches had been encouraged in Japan since the beginning of a rural movement that developed during the 1910s. Facing the additional hardship of discrimination in California, Issei immigrants depended more than ever on forming alliances within their ethnic community. Farmers could independently produce ample crops, but selling their goods was an entirely different matter, and many immigrants fell victim to unscrupulous dealers and commission merchants. While many of the Issei primarily socialized with those from their home prefectures in Japan, they put aside any regional or cultural differences when it came to business.

Setsuo put this philosophy of cooperation into practice time and time again. He served as the inaugural chairman of the Guadalupe Agricultural Association, which sought to counteract falling prices on agricultural products and successfully negotiated to lower fees charged by brokers of farm products from 12 to 11 percent.

Such agricultural organizations served their purpose not only in collective bargaining, but also in controlling their members' production to meet consumer demands. In 1930 lettuce production in the Santa Maria Valley and outlying areas exceeded expectations: instead of shipping 2,000 crates per day as they had the previous year, the farmers produced 6,000, but Los Angeles's daily demand ranged from only 3,000 to 3,500 crates. Prices plunged. The farmers lost more than half a million dollars that year. Setsuo and the other growers knew that they could not sit passively and watch their profits go down the drain. Later that year they gathered to form the Central Coast Farm Federation. With Setsuo as their leader, they made an agreement with the Japanese-operated Produce Dealers Exchange in Los Angeles: all dry-pack lettuce would be shipped to the produce market through the association, which would carefully monitor supply and demand. Voluntary quotas—based on each farmer's selling capacity—would be administered.

The state of California also approached both Setsuo and Yaemon Minami to serve on the regulatory board that limited the production and shipment of lettuce. Such regulatory activities were in line with President Franklin D. Roosevelt's New Deal policy, which sought to reduce agricultural production to stem falling farm prices.

Setsuo also practiced personal philanthropy, which George witnessed most evenings toward the end of his dinnertime. Someone would knock on the door, usually Issei men dressed in suits, with their hair freshly combed. Yoshiko and Muts served refreshments while Setsuo and the men talked; inevitably the conversation turned to money, usually a request for financial assistance.

"*Ōrai, ōrai* [All right, all right]," Setsuo always said without hesitation. No money was exchanged at such meetings, just an understanding that on the next business day money would be transferred or sent where needed. These were not loans, but rather outright gifts. Setsuo didn't want to lose friends over money, a philosophy that Yoshiko also supported.

Later, when he was even more financially successful, he delivered a shiny new car to the Buddhist temple. When the minister came to thank him, Setsuo responded in his unaffected manner: "You *enryo* [hesitate] so all the time. Old cars are dangerous, and it will also wear you down. This is given so that it may help you with your work."

Setsuo's generosity was not limited to the Japanese American community. He also served as director of the Santa Maria Rotary Club and the Santa Maria Valley Chamber of Commerce, and he donated money to the Red Cross. And his G.P. picnics were well known throughout the valley. Four whole beef carcasses from the local butcher would be ordered for mesquite barbecue, and a hundred dollars worth of soda and ice cream were served. He even made arrangements for local sumo wrestlers to entertain his 2,000 guests.

Most notably, Setsuo reached out to the community's population at large with his work as president of the Japanese Association of Guadalupe. Based on the *kyōwakai* (cooperative) concept developed in the early 1900s, the association sought not only to "further the economic welfare of its members," but also to support better relations between the Japanese community and the larger European American population. Under Setsuo's leadership, the association constructed exhibits for the Santa Barbara County Fair and sponsored a colorful float in the Armistice Day Parade.

The *Guadalupe Gazette* lauded the association's financial campaign to consolidate four elementary schools under one roof. Because 45 percent of the students—or 450 children—were in fact Japanese Americans, the Japanese Association of Guadalupe was able to raise thousands of dollars within just days.

The *Gazette* editorial stated,

> Such a spirit is hard to duplicate. Realizing that their children receive great benefits at the local institution, these Japanese, all along the line, have indicated that they are willing to cooperate with every agency to insure continued development and advancement.
>
> By such generous acts they have endeared themselves to the hearts of every Guadalupean.
>
> They are REAL citizens, the Japanese of Guadalupe.

While the Issei men who visited the Aratani household were typically middle-aged, sometimes young couples would come to the door. George, more interested in baseball, didn't care to sit around and listen to talk about weddings and receptions, but for both Setsuo and Yoshiko it was a different story. While some prominent prewar Japanese leaders approached their role as a *baishakunin*, a marriage go-between, as a purely perfunctory duty, the Aratanis relished it.

"You better think about getting married," Setsuo one day told Muts Tamura, Butch's sister, who lived with the Aratanis. Muts was a pretty, round-faced young woman with an easy smile. In addition to assisting Yoshiko around the house, she also taught George etiquette and social dancing, skills she had learned from the Olivers Club in Los Angeles. (The Olivers Club was started by a European American schoolteacher, Nellie Grace Oliver, to engage Japanese American youth in character-building activities such as sports.)

Shortly after Setsuo's comment to Muts about marriage, the Aratanis hosted a sukiyaki dinner for the Japanese American Citizens League in Santa Maria. Setsuo made a special point to invite Ken Kitasako, the general manager of Santa Maria Produce. Little did Ken know that he was being considered for good-husband material.

At the sukiyaki party, then-25-year-old Ken met Muts, but he failed to ask her for a date. Soon afterwards he was approached by the Reverend Gisei Motoyama, the Guadalupe Buddhist Church minister. Reverend Motoyama had replaced Reverend Matsuura, who had been transferred to Fresno for four years.

"Ken-*san*, what are your plans for your future?" Motoyama asked.

"What do you mean, Sensei?"

"Well, you've got to be thinking about getting married. You're single now, but you're not going to be single forever."

"I'm working, but I can just barely support myself; I can't be thinking about marriage. If I marry, then it's going to cost me some money, and after that I'll have a family coming. If I can barely support myself, how can I marry and support a family?" Ken asked.

Reverend Motoyama's response was far from understanding of Ken's logic. "As a young man," the minister said, "if you worry about these things, how are you going to be able to tackle life? Whether in a depression or good times, people have to go on. If they didn't, everything would stop. There would be no more babies."

Within two years Ken and Muts were married at the Guadalupe Buddhist Church, and they held their reception at New York Cafe under the guidance of their faithful *baishakunin*, Setsuo and Yoshiko Aratani. Later Muts would be able to return the Aratanis' favor by playing a role in George's love life.

George's chronic childhood asthma had all but disappeared by the time he entered his teens. A star on the Guadalupe YMBA baseball team, he had been instructed by Setsuo to drink a concoction of *shōyu* (soy sauce), two raw eggs, and Worcestershire sauce before each game. "It'll give you energy," Setsuo said. George eagerly complied—if Papa said it, it must be true, he thought.

During his sophomore year the whole family moved to Santa Maria for a short time so that George could be closer to school and his many extracurricular activities. Moreover, because Santa Maria was about 10 miles east of Guadalupe, it was hoped that the area's drier climate might ease Yoshiko's asthma attacks.

By the time George entered Santa Maria Union High School, he was primed to excel in athletics. Even Setsuo and Yoshiko agreed that their son could miss the six-days-a-week Japanese-language classes so that he could pursue team sports. He played baseball and football, as well as swimming, judo, kendo, and the shot put.

Setsuo continued to dote on his son: when George turned 15, he was presented with a two-door Chevrolet to use for his high-school commute, and he became the envy of his Guadalupe schoolmates who had to rely on the bus. (The Aratanis also loaned out the same Chevrolet to newlywed couples on their honeymoons.)

High-school life was simple, and most boys were obsessed with sports, not romance. George—nicknamed "Babe" by his high school classmates—in fact was barely aware at this time of his female admirers, who were smitten by his good looks, athletic prowess, and confidence.

George was the baseball team's star shortstop. With an impressive batting average of .500 one year, he was even being scouted by pro teams, including the Pittsburgh Pirates, who held their spring training camp in nearby Paso Robles. Every year two outstanding boys from the Santa Maria High School baseball team were selected to assist the team, and George was chosen for this honor two years in a row.

Before the 1933 spring training began, all of the valley was abuzz. The Pirates had a new coach, the legendary "Flying Dutchman," Honus Wagner, who was regarded as the greatest shortstop of all time. Setsuo told George that he had followed Wagner's career with the Pirates in the early 1900s. Now Wagner was coming to a nearby town, and even more importantly, he would be crossing paths with George.

"Hey, Aratani, shag the ball." Wagner pointed to a fly ball coming George's way. George caught the ball easily and threw it back home. Wagner, now graying, was still an imposing figure with piercing eyes and a thick nose. Sometimes he even filled in for a player at first base.

As spring training came to a close, George was called in by his high-school coach, Kit Carlson. "George, I spoke to Honus Wagner the other day. He says if you continue to get bigger, he'll sign you up in the minor leagues. What do you think about that?"

George was speechless. That had been his dream, and Setsuo's, as well. All he needed to do was stay in shape.

George was even more determined than ever to excel in sports. That same year—1933—he helped the Santa Maria Saints capture the California Interscholastic Federation (CIF) state championship. One team they faced on the way to the championship was Hoover High School in San Diego, whose star player was a lanky teenager named Ted Williams. He was a year younger than George, and after the war he would prove to be one of the greatest hitters of all time as a Hall of Famer with the Boston Red Sox.

Although George had a bright future in baseball, his true love was football. He was first introduced to football through a radio broadcast of a University of Southern California game. He was immediately excited about the game, but he was discouraged from playing by his parents.

"My parents never approved of me playing football," he remembers now. "The Japanese kids are not as big as the Caucasians. My father knew that; so did my mother." At 5 feet 9 inches and 150 pounds, he was large for a Japanese, but still small compared to his classmates. Indeed, rosters printed in the *Santa Maria Daily Times* listed the size of Santa Maria's starting line-up, who averaged more than 170 pounds. That didn't stop George from joining the Santa Maria Union High School varsity football team. He was selected to play second-string quarterback and punter, and there were also a handful of other Nisei on the team.

On Armistice Day in 1933, Santa Maria played against their rivals, the San Luis Obispo Tigers. A win would definitely send the Santa Maria Saints on their way to compete in the Southern California CIF playoffs. Amidst the cheering in the stands, the coach called George over. "Kick off, Aratani," he said.

George pulled on his helmet and ran onto the field. He kicked the ball well down into the Tigers' territory. Then tragedy struck: as George and his teammates rushed forward, a Tigers player fumbled, and everyone went for

George Aratani, on crutches, sustained a football injury that ended his dream of a professional sports career (standing left of George is Tets Murata), 1933. (99.30.73)

the ball. George saw a blur of color from the right side. As he fell to the ground, he heard a snap in his knee. He tried to stand up but couldn't.

George's friends stood frozen in the stands as he was carried off the field on a stretcher. "What happened to George?" they asked among themselves. "Looks pretty serious."

Neither Yoshiko nor Setsuo were at the game. They didn't understand football, and Yoshiko especially abhorred watching her son get tossed about the field. As George was laid out on a bench, he remembered his father telling him, "Take care of yourself. Be responsible. I can't always be around, so you have to watch yourself." There was no team doctor at the time, so George had to withstand the pain as he sat on the sidelines for the rest of the game.

After the game, George was driven to his house in Santa Maria and helped to the front door.

"What happened?" Yoshiko had a stricken look on her face. Her worst fears were realized.

"I'm able to move my leg; I don't think it's broken. But my knee—it's real sore."

Setsuo didn't waste any time. He wasn't going to take his son to the local doctor. Instead they would travel to the Japanese Hospital in Los Angeles, where Dr. Tashiro and Dr. Crow, an orthopedic surgeon, examined George's leg and took an X-ray. The diagnosis: torn cartilage.

"You'll be okay," said Dr. Crow, who explained that surgery was necessary to remove the damaged cartilage. However, there was one catch—George would no longer be able to participate in any physical activity that required vigorous lateral movement. This meant no football, and no baseball. There would be no pro career with the Pittsburgh Pirates. George felt hot tears come to his eyes, but he knew his father must be feeling even worse.

They returned to Santa Maria a week later. George was in a full cast up to his hip and was relegated to crutches for two months. Once the cast was removed, he could not move his knee easily, and he underwent physical therapy supervised by his mother. Under instructions from the orthopedic surgeon, Yoshiko purchased a large metal garbage can. Every day she filled it with steaming hot water, and George soaked his injured leg in order to loosen his sore ligaments. Immediately afterward he bent his leg towards his chest. The pain was fierce, but he knew it was necessary to withstand it as part of the healing process.

<hr />

As George recovered from his football injury, Setsuo and the other growers were facing labor problems. "Be kind to the Mexicans and Filipinos," he had told his family. "Treat them with respect. It's because of them that our business has been able to grow."

In spite of such tolerant comments, the valley was not devoid of conflict. In order to mitigate losses suffered during the Depression, the Central Coast Farmers Federation, which had taken complete control of a trucking group, reduced the hourly wage of farm laborers by five cents in 1934. Other growers followed suit.

By this time three labor unions representing local agricultural workers had been formed: the Filipino Labor Union, Inc.; the Mexican Labor Union; and the Fruit and Vegetable Packers' Union. During that same year, a widespread textile strike in the East had commanded headlines in the nation's newspapers. Now the field workers of Santa Maria Valley refused to passively accept the news of reduced wages, and the shed workers had other issues as well.

As a result of unresolved conflicts, approximately 3,000 field workers and packers went on strike for 10 days in November of 1934, virtually paralyzing the produce industry in Santa Maria, Guadalupe, Lompoc, and southern San Luis Obispo County. As a result, growers and packers could not harvest or transport their crops. They were also prevented from unloading "shook," material used to make crates, at train depots.

Before the situation became even more serious, the growers, labor leaders, and authorities in the Santa Maria Valley decided to act quickly; they sought the services of an arbitrator, Dr. Towne Nylander, a director on the Federal Regional Labor Board. In this situation, the large Japanese farm operators deferred to their European American counterparts.

According to newspaper accounts, violent incidents during the strike were few. Two Filipino men, who were arrested in Oceano for stopping and overturning a lettuce truck, were held in the San Luis Obispo jail. In another incident the manager of a packing company tussled with a sheriff's deputy who had advised him not to make attempts to unload shook. "Later," reported the *Santa Maria Daily Times*, "the two were said to have shaken hands and called it a day." For the most part, the strikes and businesses' responses to them were peaceful.

Civil-rights advocate and labor attorney A. L. Wirin, and Ernest Besig, both legal counsel for the American Civil Liberties Union, came to the valley to review the situation. "They found 'everything quiet and no apparent attempt to intimidate the strikers or interfere with their picketing,'" reported the *Santa Maria Daily Times* on November 20, 1934. Wirin was quoted as saying, "We find things here much better than we had found in any other district where similar strikes have taken place, and that is a high compliment for your county and its peace officers, coming from a representative of the Civil Liberties Union." He was referring to his previous treatment in Imperial Valley, where he claimed that he was "kidnapped" and kicked out of the region during a strike by pea pickers.

Finally, on November 25 representatives of the growers and labor unions met in the Superior Court courtroom in Santa Maria's county office building. After three hours a decision was reached: an arbitration team would start negotiations in early December, and striking employees would return to work. In the meantime, the field workers would receive 30 cents an hour, their wage before the growers' 5-cent reduction. Shed workers would be paid at the prevailing rate prior to the strike.

"I think you all have been remarkably fair," stated chairman C. L. Preisker of the county board of supervisors, "and I think you have shown an unprecedented spirit of cooperation in agreeing to arbitrate." He also assured the spokesman for the Filipino union that the two arrested strikers would be released from the San Luis Obispo jail. After details of the arbitration board meetings were finalized, the agreement was ready for signatures. Among the Japanese signers—all growers or shippers—were Yaemon Minami, C. M. Otoy, S. Akahoshi, and Setsuo Aratani.

A day later, the local newspaper reported that the packing sheds in Santa Maria valley were open again and "laborers were busy in the fields, cultivating, planting and harvesting."

———◆—◆◆———

Setsuo was never still; he constantly sought new investments and entrepreneurial opportunities. For example, he opened his own fertilizer plant and chemical company, Guadalupe Fertilizer and Chemical Company, so that the ranch didn't need to buy fertilizers from outside sources.

Santa Maria Valley continued to be an important pocket of Southern California agriculture. Guadalupe specialized not only in lettuce, but also carrots, cauliflower, broccoli, and celery, while the Imperial Valley, located near the California-Mexico border, was known for both its cantaloupe and lettuce production.

Setsuo was aware of each region's strengths, so in 1933 he teamed up with farmers in the Imperial Valley to launch Los Angeles Vegetable Exchange, Inc., five produce stalls within the Seventh Street Wholesale Market in downtown Los Angeles. With the different planting and harvesting seasons possible in the two agricultural regions, investors could be sure that stalls would be constantly stocked with produce throughout the year.

Even non-Japanese were aware of Setsuo's success. In fact, when the Aratanis traveled to San Diego, they rode in a limousine and were greeted by a bevy of reporters and photographers. At night they attended dinners with San Diego dignitaries and community leaders.

Setsuo also invested in the Olympic Hotel in Little Tokyo, and during the 1932 Los Angeles Olympics the entire family and their friends from Guadalupe stayed in the impressive hotel. During more leisurely trips to Los Angeles, the Aratanis would stop along the shore, collect shellfish, and cook it over an open fire. As they extracted the meat with one of Yoshiko's long sewing needles, they delighted in their seaside feast.

As George entered his last years of high school, Yoshiko suffered more frequently from asthma attacks, and he often drove her down the coast to see Dr. Tashiro in his downtown L.A. clinic.

In spite of her health problems, Yoshiko loved to socialize with the people of Guadalupe. While Setsuo was often the center of attention, Yoshiko

The Aratanis and friends enjoying a picnic at Pismo Beach, ca. 1930s. (99.30.10)

was more of an observer. When she attended functions, she was delighted by the men who sang folk songs and the women who danced on stage. She wanted to participate as well. "I'm thinking about learning the *shamisen*," she told Setsuo one evening. The *shamisen*, a stringed instrument shaped like a banjo, was popular among female entertainers.

He wrinkled his forehead. "What, you want to be a geisha?"

Yoshiko, unamused, grew quiet. Realizing that she was quite serious about this undertaking, Setsuo tried to discourage his wife. "There's no one in Guadalupe who can teach you. You better give up that idea."

"No." Yoshiko shook her head. "I've already sent for a *shamisen*. I'll teach myself."

And so she did: using books sent from Japan and Little Tokyo, Yoshiko twanged the *shamisen* in the solitude of her Guadalupe home. Later she received more advanced instruction from Japanese musicians who traveled through Guadalupe on their way to or from Los Angeles.

During one of the G.P. picnics, Yoshiko took the stage. Dressed in a kimono, she began to play, and after her performance everyone in the crowd clapped, hooted, and hollered, including her amazed husband.

Even as Setsuo attempted to discourage Yoshiko from playing the *shamisen*, he pushed 15-year-old George to play golf. George was less than enthusiastic.

"Hey, Papa, that's not for me," he said. "That's okay for you. But golf is for old people."

"Well, that may be," replied Setsuo. "But it's a good sport, and I'll buy you golf clubs."

George tried to fabricate more excuses. "Listen, I think I should wait two, three years before I take it up."

"No," said Setsuo, and so it was final. George was set up with golf clubs and a golf "pro" by the name of Arthur Sato, a public relations man who did business with American companies. A skilled golfer, Sato had reached the finals of the California State Golf Amateur championship. He traveled up and down the coast and was a frequent houseguest of the Aratanis.

Setsuo, known by his nickname, "Ace," was one of the first Issei members of the Santa Maria Country Club. He understood the important role of golf in establishing relationships with European Americans, many of whom were his customers. "Big buyers of produce come in all the way to the West Coast and buy carloads of vegetables: two cars of lettuce, three cars of carrots. These buyers were very precious to the company. They were his customers. Naturally, he wanted to be friendly. He had a way of making friends in his own style," recalls George.

Setsuo pioneered the local Japanese community's involvement in both the country club and the game of golf. Before Setsuo came on the scene, Santa Maria's high society viewed the Japanese as "less than human," one Nisei observed. But Setsuo opened doors. In fact, when he donated a thousand dollars for a remodel of the clubhouse, the established elite murmured amongst themselves. How could a Japanese man afford to give so much? Surely he had some connection to the Japanese government. They were in awe of Setsuo, but fearful, too—this was clearly a man who could affect the status quo.

Indeed, changes began to take place. A number of Issei, even the Buddhist minister, became avid golfers, and the Japanese Consulate eventually sponsored its own golf tournament involving both the Japanese and prominent city leaders, including the mayor of Santa Maria.

Setsuo foresaw the important role that golf would play in his son's life, not just in terms of the pleasure it would provide, but also in the context of the corporate business world. "You know what I had to do," says George. "I had to play golf very secretively so that my friends wouldn't hear about it, because I didn't want the guys to say, 'Hey, did you know that George Aratani is playing golf?'"

———◆·◆·◆———

Hardships and troubles arise like rocks.
It is between the rocks in a garden that the loveliest
flowers grow.
—*The Review* (Santa Maria High School yearbook), 1932

For George, life in Guadalupe during the 1930s was largely innocent, but he was not entirely isolated from the more passionate activities the town had to offer. Gambling had always had its place on the main boulevard, first appearing in Chinese establishments. George himself once wandered into a gambling den; he watched as men laid down bets and guessed the number of dried beans hidden underneath overturned rice bowls. Japanese pool halls where Issei and Nisei gathered to play poker were also popular.

Later, gambling became more sophisticated and dangerous when criminal elements from Los Angeles opened a Tokyo Club in Guadalupe. Rumors circulated about gang killings, furthering Guadalupe's reputation as a rough-and-tumble town (in contrast to the more pristine image of nearby Santa Maria).

Guadalupe also had its house of prostitution, and the women who worked there could often be seen walking past the open front door. And it was not uncommon to hear about drunken Issei being involved in serious automobile accidents.

During his senior year, George relaxed the high health standards that had been necessary while he was in training. He was still on the swimming team but he no longer had football and baseball games to prepare for, and he began drinking sweet concoctions made with alcohol and soda.

He took his Chevrolet and went on short excursions, often accompanied by Tets and another good friend, Yoichi Nakase. George would frequently wear a knit skullcap, fashionable at that time, while the slim Tets usually combed his thick hair back with some oil.

Once they stopped at a swimming pool. "Sorry, the pool's full," reported the attendant, but Tets noticed that a lot of other teenagers were entering the property while they were leaving. "We were still young and naive about that kind of discrimination," he says. "That was one of the first times I knew that we were being discriminated against because we were

Japanese." In another incident, Tets and George took a trip around Visalia towards Sequoia National Park. "We stopped at a restaurant, and they didn't serve us," Tets remembers.

For the most part, however, George remained ever optimistic: his father was a wealthy farm operator, and his own future seemed secure. As a member of Santa Maria Union High School's Senior A Class, he graduated in June of 1935. Both he and Masato Inouye, a champion orator, were among the graduating class's 12 outstanding students. In addition to belonging to the Block Letter society (a lettermen's group), he was also a member of the California Scholastic Federation and the Forensic Club.

Like many other college-bound Nisei in the valley, George planned to attend Stanford. The university, founded by railroad magnate and former California governor Leland Stanford in memory of his late son, was located approximately 300 miles north in Palo Alto, south of San Francisco. Nisei and Japan-born students often congregated on campus at the Japanese Student Association clubhouse on Santa Ynez Street.

George applied to Stanford, and he was elated when he received his acceptance letter. But then his parents stepped in.

"You go to Japan first," said Setsuo.

What? thought George. After his football accident, he had set his sights on Stanford. How could he go off and live in Japan? Then Yoshiko spoke to him in her gentle way. "I beg of you," she said. "Go to a Japanese university first."

In the 1930s 1,700 Nisei were already studying in Japan, including Guadalupeans Tad Yamada and Paul Kurokawa. Setsuo and Yoshiko did everything possible to make the decision easier for their son. They made arrangements for a former Guadalupe Produce packing-shed worker who had attended St. John's law school to serve as a private language tutor for George in Japan. They even contacted the parents of some of his upper-middle-class classmates and offered to send them to Japan, too. Masato Inouye was one of them. "In those days, it was pretty hard for a college-educated Japanese American to get a job," explains Inouye. "My parents thought that if I got an education in Japan and at the same time learned about the culture, I would be in a better position to be employed."

Again, Yoshiko entreated her son. "If it doesn't work out, you can come back and then go to Stanford," she said. At the time, George didn't understand why it was so important for him to attend a Japanese university. But looking at his mother's face, still bright in spite of her battle with asthma, he nodded.

3

Japan Journal

Masato Inouye, 4A, George Aratani, 4A, and
Jimmie Hamasaki, '33, will enroll in a Japanese university
this fall. Bob Ishii may enroll also, but he is not
yet positive. All of them have been high in their classes, with
Inouye and Hamasaki life members of the
California Scholastic Federation.

The boys intend to sail some time in July and have not
yet made any definite decisions on their courses or the
university to which they will enter.
—*The Breeze* (Santa Maria Union High School newspaper), 1935

They were 4 young men, each either 18 or 19 years of age, healthy, and athletic. Growing up in the wide-open valleys of Guadalupe and Santa Maria, they had played some community baseball together and perhaps sat next to one another at Guadalupe Buddhist Church. They weren't necessarily close friends, but now, sailing aboard the *Tatsuta Maru* to Yokohama, they were on their way to becoming what one described in his travel diary as the "four musketeers."

Masato Inouye was quiet and soft-spoken in private, but he had garnered dozens of high-school oratorical awards, even competing in a contest at the Southern California Festival of Allied Arts in Los Angeles. Though

The "four musketeers" (as they came to be known) in school uniform in Japan.
From left to right: Masato Inouye, George Aratani, Jimmie Hamasaki, and Bob Ishii.
(99.30.20)

small, he excelled in basketball and played on the lightweight football team. Masato's thick hair was usually slicked back, and he was a snappy dresser, wearing red and yellow shirts and sweaters with his corduroy slacks. In Japan he would replace those colorful outfits with a navy blue uniform and square cap. During the next four years Masato would keep a daily log of his activities in Japan, and he made frequent mention of the other three "musketeers."

The oldest of the four travelers was Jimmie Hamasaki, who had graduated from Santa Maria Union High School a year earlier as valedictorian and had served as the sports editor of the school newspaper. Jimmie, a strong boy with a wide face and arching eyebrows, had played alongside George on the Saints' championship baseball team. Bob Ishii, who usually wore glasses, had once been the first-string quarterback on the Santa Maria football team.

By Depression standards, all four boys came from comfortably well-off homes. Masato's father was a successful farmer, Jimmie's family ran a hotel for single agricultural workers, and Bob's father owned a general store in Santa Maria and was chairman of the powerful Japanese Association. Bob's mother, Futaba, accompanied the group to Japan, but while she and the four boys shared a small room in the third-class section, Setsuo and Yoshiko Aratani had a stateroom on the first-class deck.

Although George had acquiesced to his parents' desires, once on board the *Tatsuta Maru* the 18-year-old had second thoughts: "Why should I go? I live in the United States. I'm not going to use Japanese. I don't know what good it is to pick up culture."

The boys sneaked up to the first-class deck to play shuffleboard and watch movies. "Felt like a million today," wrote Masato Inouye in his diary. They met Nisei girls and gawked at Joe Teiken, a professional boxer from Korea. Later Masato would even play the trumpet in an amateur entertainment program aboard the ship.

Mr. Nakamura, the boys' tutor, was also on board. In his early thirties and easygoing, he nevertheless wasted no time starting his charges' studies. They had sailed from San Francisco on July 16, 1935, and within three days he had conducted his first lesson. "Get these four guys into college," Setsuo had told him.

But George had his own secret plan: in six months he would send a letter poorly written in Japanese back to his parents. That would convince them he was wasting his time in Japan. Maybe then they would let him return to the United States to go to college.

Veddy veddy exciting day. All aflutter
over landing in Yokohama tomorrow. Pleasant dreams
until tomorrow.
—Diary of Masato Inouye, 29 July 1935

When the Aratani group sailed into Yokohama harbor, they were greeted by some familiar faces, including the Reverend Motoyama, formerly of Guadalupe Buddhist Church, and another Guadalupean, Tadao "Tad" Yamada. Like many other Nisei, Tad had opted to attend one of the Tokyo "Big Six" colleges, Meiji University. (The other members of the Tokyo Big Six included Waseda, Keio, Rikkyo [St. Paul], Hosei, and of course, the most prestigious, Tokyo Imperial [also known as Todai].)

Masato, Bob, and Jimmie were also planning to enroll in Meiji University with the help of one of Setsuo's friends, Frank Takizo Matsumoto, a well-known Nisei leader from Fresno. Meiji was located near the Kanda District, an area full of quaint used bookstores. It was popular with Japanese Americans because of its affordability; while the tuition for Tokyo University was also reasonable, only top students were admitted.

Setsuo Aratani's goal for his son, however, was Keio University. Prestigious and exclusive, the school had a cosmopolitan flair. Its founder, Yukichi Fukuzawa, began the school during the Meiji Period, when Japan was opening up to the West. Fukuzawa's intent was to expose Japan to other cultures of the world.

"Keio is the best place," Setsuo had told George. Now the challenge was for George to get accepted.

The four musketeers' first order of business in Tokyo was study, and lots of it. The Aratani party—including the tutor Nakamura—intially lodged at the spacious home Setsuo had financed for Asae Aratani, his stepmother. The large Western-style house was located in Suginami-ku, a suburban area west of the center of Tokyo. Built especially in preparation for George's arrival, it had Western-style toilets and required the service of at least three maids under the supervision of Asae, also called "Grandma Aratani." In the beginning George addressed the maids in the *keigo* language form, which was reserved for dignitaries and superiors. This was soon corrected by Grandma Aratani. "Don't talk to them like that," she informed him.

For three or four hours every morning, the boys participated in language sessions with Nakamura-*sensei* (teacher). Nakamura had a difficult task ahead of him. In six months he had to raise the boys' knowledge of Japanese to a high-school level and also prepare them for the college-entrance exam in March. Their knowledge of *kanji* (Chinese characters) was minimal—they had learned perhaps a hundred *kanji* during several years at the Guadalupe Japanese school. Now, in six months, the boys had to master at least one thousand characters.

By September Bob had moved with his mother to a rented house a short walk away, while Masato and Jimmie moved to the Nichibei Home, the boardinghouse where Tad Yamada lived. They continued to meet with Nakamura-*sensei* every morning at the Aratani home. The sessions began with simple Chinese characters and concluded with *kanbun* (Chinese classical literature). The four teenagers even engaged in some friendly competition. "Got 92% in 'exam' today but took only 3rd behind Jim and George. Well maybe next time. Study hard and you can't lose," wrote Masato in his journal on October 17, 1935.

The boys did enjoy some fun in between cramming sessions. Asae was always ready for a lively game of *hanafuda*, played with small colorfully decorated cards which fit in the palm of one's hand. A *shamisen* player, she tried teaching George to sing, "so you can do well with the geisha girls," she told him.

George referred to Asae as his "Modan," or modern, grandmother, and he appreciated her straightforward advice. "Once you get into Keio," she said, "you and your classmates will be going to a *nomiya* [bar]—so you'll have to learn to be a good drinker. You'll have to hold your liquor; don't be boisterous." Before the samurai engaged in battle, she explained, they always drank sake. Similarly, in the corporate world businessmen were expected to drink liquor before any serious negotiation.

Yoshiko Aratani, on the other hand, seemed to be suffering some ill effects from traveling. When she wasn't accompanying Setsuo, she was often bedridden with her chronic asthma, which was aggravated by Japan's humidity. Her doctors in Los Angeles had supplied her with adrenaline so she could give herself injections whenever the bouts occurred, but they had warned her to not use it too frequently.

In spite of Yoshiko's increasingly poor health, Setsuo continued to reach out to help others. The father of his ranch foreman in Lompoc had been diagnosed with cancer and was given only six months to live, so Setsuo made arrangements for the whole family to come to Japan. In addition to securing top doctors for a second opinion, Setsuo began construction of a house for the family on Grandma Aratani's property.

As fall ended, Yoshiko's asthma grew worse. A friend advised her to travel to Atami, a hot-springs resort two hours away from Tokyo. Accompanied by the youngest of Asae's three maids, Yoshiko took her friend's advice.

In November she sent a postcard from the resort to "Joji." "I trust that you are studying hard," she wrote. "I know that I must have worried you all, but I'm feeling much stronger and am eating well and taking walks." She also mentioned that she would be bringing gifts for George and his friends.

A month later, on December 20, her maid called the house in Tokyo. "Aratani-*san* and the son must come as soon as possible," she told Grandma Aratani. The maid said that Yoshiko was fine, but George was still worried. He knew that most Japanese people would avoid delivering bad news at all costs. Was the maid telling the truth?

On the train, George told his father, "This is serious. Maybe leaving Japan would be a good idea. Maybe you should take Mama home, where it is drier."

The maid was waiting for them at the train station. She was a teenager, even younger than George. "Thank you for coming," she said, smiling.

"Oh," George said to himself. "Mama's okay."

"I'm very sorry about my call last night," the maid added, and George's heart began to sink. "The truth is—Aratani-*san* passed away yesterday. She was having one of her attacks, and then her heart failed. I'm very sorry."

Setsuo didn't say much. Neither did George. They both remained silent during the taxi ride to the resort cottage where Yoshiko had been staying. Once they got there, George barely noticed the pungent smell of sulfur from the nearby hot springs.

Yoshiko's body was laid out on the *tatami* floor, her pale face drained of color. Setsuo approached the body first. Kneeling on the floor, he stroked her hand, and then he began to cry. George himself felt sobs rise from his chest. Mama had urged him to get married early. She had wanted grand-children. Now that possibility was gone forever.

The mortician was instructed to transport Yoshiko's body to Tokyo, where the funeral was held on December 22, 1935, in the Tokyo Tsukiji Nishi Hongwanji Temple. During the ceremony, musicians in court robes played the ancient Japanese *gagaku* (court music) songs. The blend of bamboo flutes, cymbals, and other percussion instruments resonated with sadness.

George's half brother and half sister also attended the funeral. Takao was now a manager at an Osaka factory that manufactured sails for ships, while Sadako was engaged to be married to a businessman. Another relative, Masuko, was among the mourners. She remembered fondly how her aunt Yoshiko had sewn beautiful clothing for her when she was a child—there would be no more new handmade outfits.

After the funeral the family gathered outside in the temple's cemetery. As was the tradition, a photographer perched up on a ladder asked the family to stand together before Yoshiko's headstone. This was too much for George. While everyone else solemnly looked at the camera, he could not bear to raise his face. Usually he could suppress his emotions and go along with rituals and conventions, but this time the pain overwhelmed him.

Throughout the next few days relatives continued to visit the Aratani house, but just one day after Christmas, studies resumed. Rather than withdrawing from his academic responsibilities and returning to America, George became even more determined to succeed in Japan—Yoshiko had wanted him to be accepted by a Japanese college. Although her death at age 46 cast a shadow on his experience in Tokyo, he pushed away all grief and depression. He would persevere in his studies to honor his mother's memory.

George refocused his attention from his mother's tragic death to the upcoming entrance exam in March. With the knowledge that he would be running his father's businesses one day, he was aiming for Keio's School of Economics. He knew, however, that his scores needed to be exceptionally high.

By the second week of April, all four students had learned that Nakamura-*sensei* had succeeded in his mission. George had been accepted by Keio, and his three friends had gotten into Meiji. The "four musketeers" were heading for college.

—•◆•—

While George studied for his exams, Setsuo Aratani made preparations to return to his life back in Guadalupe. His relatives in Tokyo, Osaka, and

Setsuo Aratani and Masuko Matsui were married on May 31, 1936, in a Shinto ceremony in Tokyo. (99.30.97)

Hiroshima all gave him the same advice: remarry immediately. As a leader in the Santa Maria Valley, Setsuo needed someone who could manage his home and entertain his friends.

As was customary among elite Japanese families, a prospective candidate for Setsuo's wife was sought from within the clan. And the front-runner turned out to be Masuko Matsui, the niece for whom Yoshiko had sewn so many outfits. Though born in Sapporo, Masuko had spent most of her years in Tokyo. She had majored in English literature at the exclusive Nihon Jyoshidai (Japan Women's College) and was prepared to teach school. She was intelligent, sophisticated, and accustomed to big-city life. Masuko was a tall woman with striking features: a well-defined nose, large eyes, and a wide forehead. Now, at the age of 27, she was to wed a man of 50 (while the age gap was substantial, it was not that unusual among Japanese immigrants).

Grandma Aratani asked George his opinion of the upcoming nuptials between his father and Masuko, whom he had known as *Nēsan*, or Big Sister. George chose his words carefully. He hadn't been keen about Setsuo remarrying. Nevertheless, he understood his father's position both within the extended family and the Guadalupe community. Even the late Yoshiko had understood about family duty: Hadn't she, after all, taken her relatives' advice and come to America without her children? "If it has to be somebody, it should be Masuko-*nēsan*," he answered.

Dressed in a beautiful kimono, Masuko Matsui married Setsuo Aratani in a simple Shinto ceremony on May 31, 1936. Two weeks later, Setsuo returned to Guadalupe on a ship sailing from Yokohama. He was alone. As a Japanese immigrant Setsuo was not eligible for American citizenship. He remained only a legal permanent resident, and as such he could not easily bring his new bride to the United States under the restrictive immigration laws of the 1930s.

So Masuko stayed behind in Tokyo until September. Finally able to obtain a sightseeing visa, she sailed aboard the *Taiyo Maru* accompanied by Albert Matsuno, the team manager of the Guadalupe YMBA baseball team. She arrived in San Francisco in October, and she was welcomed to America by her new husband. After a stay at the Aki Hotel on Post Street, they drove down to Guadalupe. Tokyo-bred Masuko was a bit shocked as she looked out at the expansive fields of Santa Maria Valley. "This is *inaka* [country]," she thought. And her new home.

—◆—

Setsuo had been busy in the months following his second marriage. With three fellow Issei from Hiroshima, he launched All Star Trading in August of 1936. The company was initially founded to import fish meal for fertilizer, as well as Kamotsuru Sake from Hiroshima. While many Santa Maria growers used chicken manure to fertilize the soil, Setsuo also utilized fish meal with very good results. Most of All Star Trading's prewar business, however, revolved around sake. With the end of Prohibition in December of 1933, sake began to freely enter California from Japan, and competition was fierce for the Issei market. In Saijo, Hiroshima, the manufacturers of Kamotsuru Sake had heard of Setsuo's business successes, and they agreed to let All Star Trading sell their product to stores and restaurants throughout Southern California. Later, Hilo-Masamune, a sake from Hawai'i, was also imported by All Star.

Compared with Setsuo's other enterprises, All Star Trading was never a large moneymaker. It would prove, however, to be an important launching pad for George Aratani's multinational corporations: Mikasa, Kenwood, and AMCO.

— ◆ —

The uniform now! It was a thrill to try it on for the
first time!—paid up my first semester's fees—
and I'm about set.
—Diary of Masato Inouye, 10 April 1936

Now officially a Keio student, George could don the standard university uniform, slacks and a dark jacket with a white Mandarin collar. Distinguishing the outfit as belonging to a Keio student was a round cap with the school's special insignia on the front; the brass buttons on the jacket also indicated that the wearer was a Keio man.

Japanese universities were divided into *senmonbu*, specialized departments: *yoka*, the preparatory division similar to junior college, and *honka*, the regular course of study. George, unfortunately, had not scored high enough on his entrance exam to enter the department of economics. Instead, he headed for the law department. Masato also planned to study law at Meiji, with aspirations of entering the foreign service. Jimmie and Bob were in the *yoka* section and would eventually enter the fields of diplomacy and international business.

Keio was divided into two campuses. All of the lower classmen attended classes on the outskirts of town, while the main buildings were in downtown Tokyo. The students within a department were divided into a *kurasu* (class) of about 50. Each group stayed together, taking classes in diverse subjects ranging from history to accounting, until graduation. There was only one other Nisei in George's class: Juro Shibayama, from Honolulu.

George began to understand that, while he looked like his classmates physically, he was still labeled "son of an emigrant." Wealthy people from Tokyo typically didn't migrate to California. Instead, adventurers from more agricultural regions—Hiroshima, Wakayama, Kumamoto, and Fukuoka—were more likely to take the risk for a better life.

One day an instructor entered the classroom with a message for George. "Report to Koizumi-*sensei* today at three o'clock."

George froze. Shinzo Koizumi was the president of Keio University. He was the *gakuchō*, the top man.

**George Aratani, a student at Keio University,
leaving the house of a friend in Tokyo, ca. 1937.** (99.30.22)

"Aratani, what did you do wrong? You are going to get it," his class-mates teased.

Entering the president's office, George was prepared for the worst. "Were you born in the United States?" asked Koizumi.

George nodded. "*Hai.*"

"Tell me a little about your background. What brought you to Keio University?" The administrator was quite pleasant, not threatening at all. George relaxed and explained his father's wishes.

"The manager of the Meiji judo team tells us that your father, Mr. Aratani, was very helpful to their team when they went to California."

George had heard the entire story from a friend in Los Angeles, but in the presence of the college president he feigned some ignorance. It had not been a pretty situation—in fact, it had been downright shameful.

In Little Tokyo the judo team had been invited to a dinner at a Japanese restaurant called Ichifuji, located on the second floor of a building on the northwest corner of First and San Pedro streets. The liquor flowed freely. About two o'clock in the morning, the team began to take their clothes off. The hosts tried to restrain the muscular, inebriated judoists. "Please don't do that," they pleaded.

"Hell, *shinpai nai* [no worry]," the judoists, flushed with alcohol, responded. And, stripped down to their underwear, they marched barefoot down the stairs and out onto the street.

The police were called, and 10 members spent the night in jail. The judo federation, seeking to keep the incident out of the media, called George's father in Guadalupe. Setsuo hurried to Los Angeles where he not only kept the incident out of the newspapers, but he also arranged another dinner for the Meiji team, this time under more restrained conditions.

"I wonder," Koizumi-*sensei* asked now, "if your father would be willing to sponsor the Keio judo team on their American tour."

George blinked. The president obviously knew nothing of the trouble the Meiji team had created. George agreed to cable his father, but in the back of his mind he planned to tell his father not to sponsor Keio University's judo team because he knew that the team members were heavy drinkers. Meiji, Keio—he figured they were all the same. His father was going to have trouble again. George suggested in his telegram that Setsuo make up some excuse and gracefully decline.

Within days, his father's reply came. "Send the Keio judo team right away!" Setsuo would do anything for sports.

Came out seventh best in my law class—learned thru
Tsutsui Sensei last nite—can it be a dream—
six A's, eight B's, C's.
—Diary of Masato Inouye, 1 April 1937

George was totally immersed in language study during the first years of his college curriculum, although he did find time to serve briefly as backup third baseman on Keio's baseball team until he reinjured his knee. While Masato kept a diary in English, George maintained one in Japanese. Even Grandma Aratani noticed his progress. "Joji, you've really picked up Japanese," she commented.

But learning the language was only one dimension of absorbing the Japanese culture. There was also socializing to be done.

"Okay, boys," the class president announced one day, "we are going to have our first class party. We'll hold it in the Shibuya area so it won't cost too much."

"What do we do?" George asked.

"We get drunk."

George, a lover of fish, curry rice, and *manjū* (red bean cake), asked, "Don't we have some food?"

"Food is secondary. We get together and get drunk."

George had not been a teetotaler in high school, but he had not been a heavy drinker, either. He and his friends had wanted to stay in good physical condition for sports. After George injured his knee in 1933, however, he had begun drinking a little. Still, nothing in Guadalupe had prepared him for his first class party in a Shibuya restaurant. Classmates who were usually very quiet and reticent were already singing boisterously around the long table, even before they started drinking sake.

During the day the Japanese are very serious, concluded George, but at night they change completely, as if they have two different personalities.

At one of the class parties, all attention turned to George. "Hey, Aratani-*san*, you're from America, right? How did your parents get along? We've heard about the discrimination over there," one classmate said.

George thought for a moment. Although his life in Guadalupe had been idyllic, he knew that circumstances had been tough for his parents and other Issei. They had to contend with the various American alien land laws as well as the hardships involved with adjusting to a new country and culture. "Yes, there's discrimination over there. The Issei really have to struggle." As he said those words, George began to appreciate what it meant to be the son of emigrants.

Among the individuals who helped George overcome culture shock and ease into the Japanese lifestyle was Paul Rusch, an Episcopal layman and the "father of football" in Japan. Rusch had established a ministry for Japanese young people at St. Paul University in Tokyo in the 1920s. His faculty residence became a student hangout for sake- and tea-drinking sessions, philosophical discussions, and music. Troubled students with cash-flow problems were taken in and fed.

An earthy, vibrant man, Rusch socialized with the Nisei and Japanese students off campus as well, and like George and Tad, he frequented dance halls. At a dance hall men purchased a strip of ten tickets for one yen (about thirty cents at the time), and they exchanged one ticket for a three-minute box step with a dance-hall girl. Popular establishments in Tokyo included the high-class Florida Dance Hall in Akasaka and the Japan-Korea Center in Ningyo-cho; those on a budget rode to Chanclame in Warabi in a *yentaku* taxi, which took passengers anywhere for one yen.

Masato Inouye stayed away from the dance halls, but he often met George, Jimmie, and Bob at their favorite Western eatery, the Olympic Restaurant. He also went to movies to strengthen his multilingual skills.

And of course, there was always *ginbura*. *Ginbura*, or "strolling around the Ginza," was one of George's favorite pastimes with his Japanese classmates. The Ginza, lined with Tokyo's finest department and specialty stores, coffee shops, and theaters, was the place to spot good-looking girls.

One day George and another Keio student engaged in an afternoon of *ginbura*. Seeing a pair of attractive young women—one of whom was exceptionally tall—George and his friend followed them down Nihonbashi. At one point the tall one turned back and smiled, a daring gesture for a Japanese girl.

Encouraged by the woman's boldness, George asked the two to have tea with him and his friend. They accepted the invitation, and as they sat in a quaint coffee shop, George struggled to impress the women with his Japanese.

Finally, the shorter one turned to George. "Are you *Amerika-umare* [American-born]?" she asked.

"I am," George admitted in Japanese.

"You speak English?" The face of the tall woman brightened immediately. "I'm from Seattle, Washington."

A nite on a board bed—followed by a pretty fierce day on maneuvers, all tired and will that bed feel good!
—Diary of Masato Inouye, 13 May 1937

George's experience in Japan during the thirties was, for the most part, carefree. By 1937 Japan was recovering from the worldwide depression. Industrial production had almost doubled since 1931. Wages were up and the number of strikes was down. Farmers saw the prices for their products

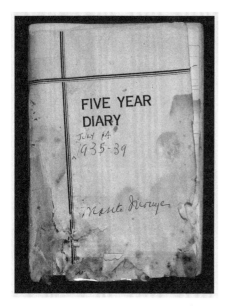
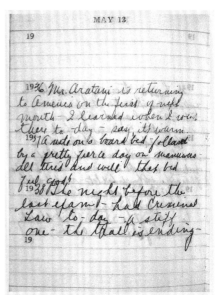

The five-year diary of Masato Inouye. Collection of Lt. Col. (Ret.) Masato Inouye (2.2001.1)

rise faster than inflation, and sumo champion Futabayama was racking up 69 consecutive victories.

Ominously, however, Japan's military machine had dramatically increased in size, accounting for a whopping 70 percent of the national budget. Across the East China Sea, Japan had already embarked on its military takeover of China in 1931. The Kwantung Army, which protected Japan's leasehold in part of Manchuria, had seized the city of Mukden, and by February 1932 Pu Yi, the last emperor of China, was a power in name only.

The four teenage Nisei—George, Masato, Bob, and Jimmie—were oblivious to Japan's military encroachment when they came to Tokyo in 1935. They knew little about Manchukuo, or Manchuria. Even the greater Japanese public did not seem to grasp the magnitude of the events in China, even after the official start of the Sino-Japanese War on July 7, 1937, when a company of Japanese soldiers tangled with a Chinese patrol southwest of Peking.

During his first year abroad, George rarely had time or even the ability to read a Japanese newspaper. However, he did consult an English-language periodical, the *Japan Times*, as well as issues of the *Los Angeles Times*. Even so, he and the other boys were more interested in reading the funnies and the sports section than the front page.

As time elapsed, however, the boys were exposed to Japan's rising militarism. After enrolling at Meiji, Masato was expected to participate in *kyōren* (military training), much like the ROTC, on a regular basis. Once a week students formed platoons, marched down to the parade ground, and conducted such exercises as water drills. They also trained for a week in the summer at a military camp at the foot of Mt. Fuji.

None of the college students were enamored of *kyōren* or military service, and most received a deferment until after graduation. George, as a Keio student, was also required to join in *kyōren* drills. Because George was tall, he was assigned to the coveted position of operating the light machine gun. All spent cartridges were collected because metal was a scarce commodity.

Initially George and the other young Guadalupeans were only engaging in drills with blanks and flares, but as the weeks and months passed, they saw more signs of the gritty reality of war. On September 15, 1937, Masato wrote in his diary: "The air-raid practices started to-night—hence couldn't study to-night."

Back at the Aratani household, Asae told George that no precious fuel would be burned for personal comforts—instead, he, like other students, would have to go to the neighborhood public bath. Supplies were short; George understood. This was just a little island, after all, with no natural resources to speak of.

News coverage of the events in China was carefully monitored by the Japanese government. As a result, when the military invasion of Nanking was reported in December 1937, there was no mention of the barbaric rape, pillage, and destruction committed by Japanese soldiers. Detailed accounts of these acts were later supplied by European and American missionaries who had created a Nanking safety zone for Chinese women and men.

Some Americans in Japan became bewildered observers from the sidelines. Paul Rusch, the former professor at St. Paul University, was now in Yamanashi prefecture under the guidance of the Brotherhood of St. Andrew. He was in the midst of an effort to raise funds in the U.S. for a Japanese rural community project, but the current political situation in Asia made that task increasingly difficult.

The Japan-America Student Association was founded to bridge the gap between both nations' youth. Masato was selected as a Meiji delegate to the fifth Japan-America Student Association conference in 1938, where approximately 45 students from American campuses met with representatives of Japanese universities. Later, a delegation even traveled to occupied

Manchuria. As they rode on the South Manchurian Railway toward the city of Mukden, they noted the beauty of the green fields lying alongside the tracks and were reminded of the expansive landscape of the United States. The countryside held "promise of a great possibilities in the future," the students wrote in their journals, unaware of all that had befallen the occupied region and its people.

Masato left Japan to pursue international studies at Yale University in April of 1939, arriving at the height of the cherry blossom season, while George continued with his law classes at Keio University. Then one day he received a troubling letter from his father—Setsuo had been diagnosed with "slight tuberculosis" by a doctor in Los Angeles, and he would be recuperating at a nearby sanatorium.

"Don't worry about me," Setsuo wrote. "I'm going to be okay."

But George was troubled. He had lost his mother only three years earlier: she had died unexpectedly even as she too protested that she would "be okay." Now his father, a chain smoker, had also developed respiratory problems.

The Maryknoll Sanatorium was located in Monrovia, about 15 miles from downtown Los Angeles at the base of the San Gabriel Mountains. Surrounded by an orange grove and lush green lawns, the sanatorium had been taken over by the Maryknoll Sisters in 1930. Dr. Edward Hayes, a prominent tuberculosis specialist, served as medical director. Hayes, himself a former tuberculosis patient, had wanted to acquire the hospital, but a Japanese immigrant and Catholic convert, Dr. Daishiro Luke Kuroiwa, beat him to it. Many other medical facilities served tubercular patients in picturesque Monrovia, but Maryknoll was distinguished by the presence of a Japanese nun named Sister Bernadette who provided nursing services and cooked Japanese meals once a week. The facility (which also treated Catholic clergy) grew to accommodate 50 beds.

Patients stayed in either a large ward that accommodated 12 people or in one of the small wooden cottages on the property. When Setsuo was admitted to the sanatorium in January of 1939, he began making arrangements to have his own cottage built on the grounds. The cottage would have two rooms—one for himself, and one for his wife, Masuko. Because exposure to fresh air was thought to be key to treating tuberculosis, the sanatorium's windows had screens but no glass. At night canvas tarps were rolled down over the screens to provide some insulation against the cold.

Europe and the United States had suffered through tuberculosis epidemics during their periods of industrialization in the eighteenth and nineteenth centuries, and Japan had experienced an outbreak in the early 1900s. In the 1930s and 1940s, the rate of recovery in America was still less than stellar: while one-third of patients recovered fully, one-third died and one-third remained chronically ill. Many of the deaths occurred from secondary infections rather than the disease itself.

Transplanted to Monrovia, Setsuo found himself suddenly torn from his numerous business and social activities in Guadalupe, but friends from Santa Maria Valley and Los Angeles did visit and update him on the latest happenings in the Japanese American community.

Setsuo was a difficult patient. He usually asked visitors for a cigarette, which of course was strictly banned by his physician, Dr. Tashiro. One visitor was Masato Inouye, now a graduate student at Yale, who reported to George that Setsuo "looked pretty good."

Some weeks later, another letter came from Butch Tamura, his father's business associate: "Your father is resting in a sanatorium. Best you come back and visit with him. Then you can go back."

After consulting with Grandma Aratani, in the summer of 1939 George purchased a one-way ticket on a ship to San Pedro. He hadn't seen California for three years, and he dreaded what he might discover upon his arrival two weeks later.

After renting a room at the Olympic Hotel in Little Tokyo, he was driven to the Monrovia sanatorium and taken to the Aratani cottage. It was the first time that George had spoken fluent Japanese to his father.

"My God," Setsuo exclaimed, "your Japanese is better than mine. If you speak and understand Japanese that well, you should not go back to Japan. Go to Stanford."

George could see that his father was lonesome. Sick and worried about the war between Japan and China, Setsuo wanted his son nearby. George looked at his father lying on the bed in the small cottage. "Fine, Papa. I'll ask Keio to send my transcripts to Stanford."

———◆———

As George made preparations to resettle in California, his father was getting stronger. By April of 1940 Setsuo had recuperated enough to be released from the sanatorium, and Masuko, who had been her husband's companion in the little cottage for more than a year, was elated.

Before he had a chance to return to Guadalupe, however, Setsuo was rushed to the Japanese Hospital in Los Angeles with a severe headache. Doctors detected a meningitis infection. The manager of Setsuo's All Star Trading company had heard that the fresh blood of koi could help ward off such an infection, and so he dutifully brought a washtub containing five koi to the hospital.

But Setsuo's condition continued to deteriorate, and the key managers of Guadalupe Produce—Naoichi Ikeda and Ben Kodama—finally convinced him to transfer his interest in the company to George. The document was signed on April 4, 1940, not long before Setsuo lapsed into a coma.

At 10 minutes before midnight on April 16, 1940, Setsuo Aratani died at age 54. Masuko, George, and more than 30 friends were at his side. The era of the Big Boss had come to an end; the future now rested on the shoulders of his American son. .

4

Taking Over the Farm

*There is future on the farm, because the world
has to eat. The kind of life they live in
the cities will depend on the kind of farmers
we have and what they produce.*
**—Reverend R. C. Isbell, speaker at Santa Maria
chapter of Future Farmers'
annual Father and Son dinner, 23 April 1940**

No time was wasted in spreading the news of Big Boss's death. Naoichi Ikeda sent a telegram to the *Santa Maria Daily Times,* and by the next morning, the front-page headline read: "Setsuo Aratani, Noted Leader of Japanese, Dies."

George was numb as the funeral arrangements were made and a blur of business associates and community members moved through the house on Peralta Street. There was talk of Buddhist priests coming from distant corners of California. The Los Angeles Flower Market reported that it was preparing a record number of floral arrangements. The telephone rang off the hook. Telegrams were delivered. Visitors, including men, often broke down and wept.

George bowed his head and thanked people for their thoughtfulness, but his heart was broken. Aside from Masuko-*nēsan,* he was truly alone in America. He couldn't allow himself to show any weakness; too many people were counting on him. "Take care of yourself. Be responsible. I can't

Setsuo Aratani's farm in Guadalupe, ca. 1930. Collection of Mary Tamura (2000.385.1)

**Setsuo Aratani's memorial service held on April 18, 1940,
at the Nishi Hongwanji Buddhist Temple in Los Angeles.** (43.1998.2)

always be around, so you have to watch yourself," Setsuo had taught his son in childhood. George held on to those words more tightly than ever now.

The funeral was held in the Veteran's Memorial auditorium in Guadalupe, the largest hall in the Santa Maria vicinity. Cars were parked solidly for blocks around as the services began on Sunday afternoon. "The stage of the large hall, on which a Buddhist altar had been set up, was literally buried in floral offerings," reported the *Santa Maria Daily Times*.

It had taken two semitrailer trucks to transport the more than 250 floral offerings sent in Setsuo's honor, including one from Viscount Hotta, head of the Royal Japanese Agricultural Society. Dr. Koizumi, Keio University's president, sent a telegram of condolence.

More than 3,000 mourners—Issei, Nisei, European American, Filipino, and Mexican—attended the service. From government officials to railroad executives, leaders from all over the state filled the auditorium to capacity. Nine Buddhist priests assisted the Reverend Issei Matsuura, who had returned to Guadalupe Buddhist Temple, while the Young Women's Buddhist Association choir, dressed in dark purple gowns, chanted the *nembutsu gatha* and sang "Lord Buddha Speaks to Me" in English.

"As an evidence of the affection held for the deceased, sobbing was audible throughout the large audience and grizzled men, as they went forward to pay their respects by offering incense at the altar, brushed tears from their cheeks," reported the *Times*.

Seven days later a memorial service was held. The Buddhist minister's wife, Shinobu, visited Masuko to offer her personal condolences a day later. "It was a splendid funeral," commented Shinobu, an elegant woman with delicate features.

Masuko bowed her head. "Thank you," she said, and then added, "I do not mean to sound reproachful, but rather than the great awards or the beautiful flowers, I still wish that my husband had lived even for a little while longer."

Shinobu blushed and apologized. Of course, she thought, all the trappings of a grand funeral could not make up for the loss of a leader, a father, and a husband.

A year after his death, Setsuo was honored by the country of his birth: in 1941 he was decorated posthumously by the Japanese government with a *kunshō* (national medal) both for his achievements in agriculture and for his efforts to further U.S.–Japan relations.

Today, more than 50 years after the death of Setsuo Aratani, reporters still write of him in local newspapers. As it was expressed in an editorial printed in the April 22, 1940, issue of the *Santa Maria Daily Times*: "Setsuo Aratani made a place in the valley that will not soon be filled. That the grief is sincere was fully demonstrated; that his loss will be felt in many quarters is certain."

Half of Setsuo's ashes were buried next to Yoshiko's plot in the cemetery in Guadalupe. The other half had to be taken to the Tsukiji Buddhist Temple in Tokyo, a task that was George's responsibility. On board the same ship to Japan was another Nisei, Tom Umeda. Umeda's father, a Little Tokyo barber, had tirelessly clipped hair in order to send his son to California Institute of Technology, where he had majored in aeronautical engineering.

Boeing, Lockheed, and Douglas all had refused to hire a Nisei, so Tom decided to go to Japan, where he hoped to put his skills to work. When they arrived in Yokohama, George shook Tom's hand. "Hope to see you again," he said, not knowing that would happen only after a war had torn Japan and the U.S. apart.

When George returned to Stanford University after his father's funeral in the spring of 1940, his plan was to stay in school for two years until graduation. He enjoyed the picturesque Stanford campus, and after so much personal turmoil it was a relief to go to classes on the principles of economics. Guadalupe would always be there, and so would the farm. He had been in touch with attorneys and accountants regarding his father's will, and he knew that the businesses were in the good hands of the Issei and Nisei managers. In two years, George figured, he could find his bearings and prepare for the future.

Stanford, known affectionately by its students as "The Farm," was located in Palo Alto, a posh, well-manicured community surrounded by rolling hills. The school's ties to Japan stretched back to its founding in 1891, and Japanese students were part of the inaugural class. Stanford's first president, David Starr Jordan, was an ichthyologist who had studied sea life around Japan. He had foreseen the potential of the Asian nation becoming a world powerhouse, and thus he cultivated relationships with both Japanese researchers and government officials. The university hired the nation's first Japanese professor of history, Yamato Ichihashi, whose expertise was Issei immigration patterns and Sino-Japanese relations. By 1940 Professor Ichihashi had become one of the country's most eminent Japanese.

Stanford had a Japanese Clubhouse, an ivy-covered cement-and-wooden structure on the north side of the campus. Like the Chinese Clubhouse, it was established after Encina Hall, a men's dormitory, had refused to house a Chinese student. Initially a refuge from campus bigotry, the Japanese Clubhouse became a congenial gathering place and residence for both Nisei and Japanese students.

George took advantage of the camaraderie of the Japanese Clubhouse and befriended young men from Japan. However, in less than a month disquieting news about the Guadalupe businesses reached him. Without the charismatic Setsuo at the agricultural empire's helm, the company was beginning to show signs of erosion.

One manager called George at his dormitory. Two others drove up to the university to make their case. Still others wrote letters. The management team was united on one point: George needed to quit school and come back to Guadalupe.

The Tamura family. From left to right: Yoshizumi "Butch," Uchitaro, Hiye, and Mutsuko Tamura, ca. 1930s. Gift of Kody Kodama (99.54.2)

"As much as you may feel education is important," they said, "being here is more important. Come back and learn the business as soon as possible."

Again George was forced to reassess and alter the path of his life. Thus far, most of his decisions had been dictated by his parents. Now both were gone, but their legacy was forever etched in his psyche. The oldest son was expected to carry on the family business. It wasn't a matter of whether George wanted to or not—it was his obligation.

———— ♦ ————

One of the Guadalupe Produce managers who had contacted George was Butch Tamura, the son who had dropped out of UCLA to help support his aging parents. Setsuo had later made Butch manager of both his accounting department and the company baseball team, and he remained one of the few Nisei executives involved with Setsuo Aratani's operation.

He also played an even more significant role by lending his name as co-partner of Central Produce, which leased land for the farming operation. Besides Butch Tamura, Setsuo had also handpicked as leaseholders other American young men of Japanese ancestry, including Miyokichi Matsuno, a Nisei from Hawai'i. After Setsuo's death, Butch and Miyokichi became the sole partners of the leasing company.

Setsuo—and later, George—trusted Butch and Miyokichi implicitly. No signed papers had established Setsuo's rightful ownership of the farming operation, yet everyone in the company had known of the arrangement and had respected it.

When Setsuo's new wife, Masuko, had come to California in 1936, Butch Tamura's mother and father, Uchitaro and Hiye, became her surrogate parents. Hiye taught book-smart Masuko how to prepare Japanese delicacies, while Uchitaro took care of any household repairs. The three of them—Uchitaro, Hiye, and Masuko—all lived together in the Aratani home on Peralta Street.

Because of the close personal ties between the Tamuras and the Aratanis, when Butch, an extremely taciturn man, told George, "Come back and learn the business," the words carried as much weight as if they had come from Setsuo himself. Without even completing his first academic quarter, George packed his bags and books. He was leaving "The Farm" in Palo Alto for the real thing in Guadalupe.

◆ ◆ ◆

> *Live for what is best in your country and help to*
> *make it better. You are living in the best country in the*
> *world; you owe no man anything except what*
> *you wish to owe him. Don't minimize any country, but for*
> *heaven's sake, don't minimize your own.*
> **—Reverend R. C. Isbell, speaker at Santa Maria chapter of**
> **Future Farmers' annual Father and Son dinner, 23 April 1940**

When George returned to Guadalupe, he found that much had changed. Some of his old friends, like his high-school buddy Tets Murata, had steady girlfriends. Tets was an assistant accountant at Guadalupe Produce working under Butch Tamura. Four years in Japan had also changed George. He was familiar with *ginbura*, the Japanese college system, and classical Chinese literature, but he knew nothing about celery and broccoli crops.

Even socializing with friends at old haunts reminded George how Japanese he had become. One night he was invited for a night on the town—dinner and dancing—with a group of young Santa Maria Valley men and women. As they sat at the round table full of greasy chow mein, crunchy almond duck, and bright-orange sweet-and-sour pork, George fielded the group's many questions about Japan. In some ways, he felt like an outsider here now. Not long ago he had sat awkwardly at a restaurant in Shibuya watching his Keio classmates drink sake like water; now he was at a Chinese restaurant observing his Nisei friends' social customs.

When the food arrived, half of the group ate with forks instead of chopsticks. They are rejecting their background, George thought to himself. They are getting away from being Japanese.

In Guadalupe George's world was different than that of his friends. Most of his management team were Issei, not Nisei, including Naoichi Ikeda, a Hiroshima native who had been Setsuo's classmate at Onomichi School of Commerce, and Reiji "Ben" Kodama, also from Hiroshima. Thanks to his four years in Japan, George understood these older men—and he was going to need that knowledge to keep the team working together.

Up until that point, George had known little about his father's business. From his visits to Guadalupe Produce and his summer work in the fields and packing shed, he was able to distinguish the different crops, which grew 365 days a year in Guadalupe's temperate climate: chili peppers, celery, broccoli, cauliflower, carrots, artichokes, lettuce. George needed to be able to do more than identify crops, however, and as the *sensei*, Ben Kodama was determined to instruct the young Aratani in every detail.

Ben was born in Hiroshima. Always sunburned, with a long face and strong jaw, he loved the solitude of nature. The younger generation considered him strict and even intimidating (although he was the person who gave George and Tets Murata jobs in the packing shed when they were in the eighth grade). Ben Kodama was now the general manager of the farm, the ideal person to teach George.

Waking up before 5 A.M., George pulled on a pair of jeans and laced up ankle-high boots. After eating breakfast prepared by either his stepmother or Hiye Tamura, he drove to the Kodamas' house, about a mile away, around 5:30.

"Let's go to Ranch 22," Ben told him.

As they drove along dirt roads and passed plowed fields, Ben kept up a running commentary in Japanese: "This is celery in the third week.

"The next thing that we need to do here is to irrigate.

"George, you see this broccoli? In two weeks, we will start harvesting."

George merely nodded, his hands gripping the steering wheel tightly.

He didn't tell Ben, but he felt tremendous pressure. After all, Ben had been involved in agriculture since immigrating to America at age 19; he had even managed a fruit orchard in the Sacramento region before coming to Santa Maria Valley in 1928.

George, on the other hand, had been in Tokyo immersed in books for years. And now he was responsible for an enormous farm operation with two packing sheds and 5,000 acres, not only in Guadalupe, but also in other locations within Santa Maria Valley, Lompoc Valley, and Santa Ynez. He couldn't admit, however, that he was overwhelmed. Later, in the quiet of the evening, he recorded everything Ben Kodama had taught him that day.

After his morning session with Ben, George would put on a tie and enter the Guadalupe Produce office, located at the end of a long, narrow building beside packing sheds owned by the Minami and Tomooka families.

This was the arena for business, where the salesmen made deals on rollers of vegetables, sake, and fertilizer. In charge of shipping and sales was the other Issei partner, Naoichi Ikeda. A man with round, dark eyes, he and Setsuo had been friends since the early 1900s. After graduating from college in Japan, Naoichi worked for a steamship company, and he later became a branch manager for the same company.

He decided to try his luck overseas in 1907. A year later he met his former classmate, Setsuo, in Gardena, where he began farming vegetables. In 1919 Naoichi was injured in an automobile accident. He eventually returned to Japan, where he married, but he and his new wife moved to Santa Maria Valley in the spring of 1929 to join in Setsuo's business endeavors. Naoichi initially served as the head of the sales division before taking charge of the entire Guadalupe Produce office.

Graying at the temples, he was the father of five boys, and he was known for his *niko-niko* (happy) disposition and his dependability. Naoichi had always represented Guadalupe Produce when Setsuo was away, and now he took his late boss's place on the State Department of Agriculture committee that monitored lettuce prices. Only a month after Setsuo's funeral, Naoichi had his hands full when valley vegetable shipments dropped dramatically due to seasonal declines.

As a result of Naoichi's duties away from the office, George usually sat alone at his father's former desk amidst piles of papers from the company's managers, bookkeepers, and accountant. His economics classes at Stanford

**One of Guadalupe Produce Company's
packing-crate labels.** (99.30.151A)

had not prepared him for the realities of a business that consisted of numerous partnerships.

In keeping with his team management philosophy, Setsuo had invested in numerous side businesses with other Issei and Nisei, as well as with European Americans. These ventures included a wholesale produce market in Los Angeles, a chili-dehydrating plant in Santa Maria, a hog farm in Guadalupe, a fertilizer and chemical plant, and finally, a small international trading company.

George, for the most part, did not get involved in the daily operations of these businesses, with the exception of the Guadalupe Hog Farm, co-owned with Butch Tamura. Setsuo had started the hog farm to make use of vegetable culls from the packing sheds, but George discovered that the hogs wouldn't gain weight unless they were also fed grain. Adding grain to their

Guadalupe Produce Company workers sort and pack tomatoes into crates, ca. 1930s. (99.30.135)

diet was the first change he made after his father's death, and he was uneasy until the hog operation finally began to pay for itself.

While Guadalupe Hog Farm was the least lucrative, the most profitable side enterprise was the Santa Maria Chili Dehydrating Company, managed by Chester Masunosuke Otoi. Leasing one thousand acres of land for his own farming operation, Chester had joined Setsuo in launching Santa Maria Chili Dehydrating Company, which had grown to encompass 2 drying plants and warehouses on 10 acres in Santa Maria.

Another moneymaker was the L.A. Vegetable Exchange, a corporation formed in 1933 to sell dry-pack vegetables wholesale to area grocery stores and restaurants. Encompassing five stalls in the wholesale terminal market on Central Avenue and Seventh Street in downtown Los Angeles, this particular enterprise involved a number of partners, including H. E. Kaesemeyer, who was Aratani's accountant, and many growers from the Imperial Valley.

All Star Trading, on the other hand, involved just three other partners, all originally from Hiroshima. Setsuo's widow, Masuko, had inherited his share of the company—and this was a very deliberate strategy because she was legally in America as an international trader. The daily operation of the company, which sold fish meal and sake from Hiroshima, was conducted by

Toshitaro Ishikawa, a very proper Issei recruited from San Francisco. Originally from the Japanese island of Shikoku, Toshitaro had come to the U.S. to help his parents, owners of a Japanese confectionery store that produced and sold red bean cake. When his father was struck down with pleurisy, Toshitaro worked two jobs to pay off the hospital bills: during the day he was employed by Sumitomo Bank; in the evening he toiled at a Japanese trading company specializing in the importing and exporting of seafood. He was working for another trading company, Hokubei Boeki, when Setsuo tapped him to operate the fledgling All Star Trading in 1936.

In the beginning, the company worked with another of Setsuo's enterprises, Guadalupe Fertilizer and Chemical Company, in importing fish meal from Japan. Soon All Star Trading also began distributing and selling Kamotsuru Sake, and Toshitaro opened a small sales office in Little Tokyo to service the local eateries and drinking establishments.

All Star Trading, not a large moneymaker, was the least of George's concerns in 1940—little did he know how important the company and Toshitaro Ishikawa would prove to be to his future.

———— •◆• ————

We Extend Our Best Wishes To The Success of
The Santa Barbara County Fair . . . Do Your Part . . .
Visit the Fair Every Day.
—Ad for Guadalupe Produce Company,
Santa Maria Daily Times, 23 July 1940

On the day after Memorial Day in 1940, a group of men from Santa Maria met with District Attorney Percy Heckendorf in Santa Barbara. They were key members of the American Legion's Americanization Committee in Santa Maria. Concerned about subversive "fifth-column activities," these Santa Maria residents offered their investigative services.

In response, the district attorney said that "he was already laying plans for a thorough combing of the county against any spy or subversive activities," the *Santa Maria Daily Times* reported. Details were not provided, but the article denied any rumors of arrests. Though the small, four-inch article was buried at the bottom of the inside pages, it was a foreshadowing of things to come.

Meanwhile, most of the Issei and Nisei farmers in the valley were preparing for a more pleasant event—the annual Santa Barbara County

Fair. For five days in July, farmers displayed their vegetables, livestock, and swine; ranchers showed their horses; children ate cotton candy and enjoyed carnival rides; and high-school students in Future Farmers of America and 4-H Clubs competed for prizes.

The fair opened with a street parade, complete with Shetland ponies, an Abraham Lincoln look-alike, tepees created by the Red Men and Pocahontas lodges of Santa Barbara County, and even a Filipino float, described in the newspaper as "a highly decorative affair in keeping with the love of that race for color and harmony."

The weeklong festivities culminated with a Japanese Day program. Guadalupe Produce did its part to promote attendance by placing two prominent advertisements in the *Santa Maria Daily Times*—one supported the fair in general, and another encouraged the community to come to the event sponsored by the Japanese Association of Santa Maria Valley. The ad clearly signaled the changing of the guard: at the bottom, under "Guadalupe Produce Co.," in small capital letters it read, "GEORGE ARATANI."

Despite the American Legion's suspicions about "subversive activities," the *Santa Maria Daily Times* reported that the Japanese Day program drew large crowds. "Hundreds flocked into the main tent last night for a program staged by the Japanese colony," reported the newspaper. The Los Angeles–based Japanese dance troupe, Kansuma, drew appreciative applause not only from a large audience of Issei and Nisei, but from just as many non-Japanese.

The fair was an effective promotional vehicle for the Japanese community as well as Guadalupe Produce, which won the sweepstakes prize in the "Commercial Packing of Produce" category. The company took 16 first places and 4 seconds in the packaging of asparagus, cherry rhubarb, onions, Utah cherries, cucumbers, California chili peppers, cauliflower, cabbage, potatoes, carrots, broccoli, and sugar beets.

It was a pleasant victory for George, but it would be one of the Japanese shippers' last triumphs in the valley for a long time to come.

Surrounded at work by *majime*, or serious-minded, married Issei men, George had no social life to speak of. For 60 cents, a young man could take a date to see such films as *Alias the Deacon* or *Danger on Wheels*. Unlike an older theater in town which showed only silent pictures, the Royal Theater, financed by Issei Chuhei "Charles" Ishii, was a modern facility, complete with air-conditioning and a "cry room" for mothers with irritable babies.

Older Nisei men such as Butch Tamura opted for membership in Guadalupe's recently chartered Rotary Club. While the club sponsored a wide variety of lectures and fund-raisers, Nisei involvement was heaviest during golf tournaments at the Santa Maria Country Club.

Certain Guadalupean mothers even became involved in community events sponsored by the *Santa Maria Daily Times*. Butch Tamura's wife Mary entered their 20-month-old son, Allen, in the newspaper's annual "Popular Baby Election." Under the headline "Another Trio of Young Politicians Out for Your Votes" appeared a picture of two little girls and little Allen Tamura in a striped shirt and overalls. In spite of the stiff competition, Allen, one of the few Japanese American contestants, came in fourth, no doubt because of Guadalupe Produce employees' votes for their favorite toddler.

*A fine of $1000 or imprisonment for six months,
or both, is the penalty for any alien who fails to register and
submit to fingerprinting, or for the failure of a
guardian to register an alien minor under 14 years of age.*
—Santa Maria Daily Times, 21 August 1940

As summer drew to a close in 1940, two federal registration plans were announced in the *Santa Maria Daily Times*: one was the registration of aliens; the other, registration of young men, 18 to 35, by the Selective Service. Under the provisions of the Alien Registration Act of 1940, those without U.S. citizenship—which included all Issei—were instructed to report to their local post office by December 26.

Acting on a presidential directive, the FBI was already collecting information on aliens whose backgrounds and activities were deemed suspicious. This list was filed with the Justice Department, which was also overseeing the registration and fingerprinting of aliens in December.

The first alien to register in Santa Maria was Mexican. Filipinos were also required to register, in spite of the special colonial relationship between the U.S. and the Philippines. Santa Maria Postmaster Reid E. Shamhart had ordered one thousand registration forms. "We are having no trouble registering applicants," Shamhart told the newspaper. "All seem able to answer the questions satisfactorily. However, I would like to make it very clear that it is absolutely compulsory for all aliens to register at some time before December 26. Failure to do so will make the penalty doubly severe." Despite this warning, a week later only 41 individuals out of the estimated 1,500 aliens had responded to his call.

Nationwide hostility toward foreigners—and specifically the Japanese—was intensifying. The Issei growers in Santa Maria Valley all felt it, and in November of 1940 the principals of the Aratani, Minami, and Tomooka farms met with attorney Leo T. McMahon. As a result of the meeting, Butch Tamura and Miyokichi Matsuno, co-owners of Central Produce Company (which until now had handled the leasing of Aratani farmlands), created a new California corporation. Vegetable Farms, Inc., was formally incorporated on November 8, 1940. All assets and liabilities were transferred from Central Produce, a partnership with a net worth of $74,703.43, to the new corporation.

The packing-and-shipping end of the business, Guadalupe Produce, was incorporated at the same time. The three principals of the Guadalupe partnership—George T. Aratani, Ben Kodama, and Naoichi Ikeda—agreed to transfer all of the business's assets to the corporation in exchange for 1,428 shares of stock.

Although neither Ben nor Naoichi had made any capital investments when they became partners in Guadalupe Produce, both had made substantial gains from accumulated profits. Setsuo, on the other hand, had withdrawn or spent his profits "so his investment was practically nothing," reported his accountant H. E. Kaesemeyer. Apparently the man who had always said "all right" to philanthropic projects and needy friends had freely spent a great deal of his Guadalupe Produce fortune.

Incorporation meant that the principals' personal accounts and properties were protected from corporate lawsuits and debts. For George, however, it also meant that he had to purchase a total of $43,625.18 worth of shares from the other two partners in order to equalize their interests in the new corporation. After the numbers were calculated, each stockholder owned 476 shares.

Four months after the agreement was signed, Naoichi Ikeda, the official president of Guadalupe Produce, was contemplating other options. The Supreme Court had recently ruled that the Japanese Hospital of Los Angeles could purchase property, even though most of its stockholders were Japanese. Now Naoichi wondered, "Why not farmlands?"

But their lawyer explained that the Japanese Hospital case was different: under a treaty between the United States and Japan, Issei could purchase or lease California property for "commercial non-farming purposes." Agricultural lands, on the other hand, could never be purchased by foreign-born Japanese—treaty or no treaty. "Such ownership or attempted ownership is, in fact, a criminal violation of the California Alien Land Law," McMahon wrote.

Of course, the situation was altogether different for U.S.–born George. On August 25, 1941, he purchased his first piece of commercial property: 40 acres in Lompoc, south of Santa Maria, near Guadalupe Produce's Lompoc packing shed. It was a purchase that would provide a key to George's future.

———◦◆◦———

While the Issei had to contend with alien registration and discriminatory land laws, young Nisei men faced their own struggles: the requirement that they register for the draft. All men between the ages of 21 and 35 had to register on October 17. The newspaper specifically noted that Filipinos were also required to register, and young Nisei men already knew that they were among those required to fill out a yellow draft registration card at precinct polling places.

The war in Europe had continued to heat up. Throughout the summer and fall the Germans bombed cities in Great Britain as British bombers attempted to cut off possible avenues for invasion. In ordering the nation-wide registration, President Franklin D. Roosevelt declared, "A few weeks have seen great nations fall. We cannot remain indifferent to the philosophy of force now rampant in the world. The terrible fate of nations whose weakness invited attack is too well known to us all."

Northern Santa Barbara County, including Santa Maria, was ready to do its part. The draft board even planned a free dance in the Veteran's Memorial building, complete with "patriotic boutonnieres" of red, white, and blue, and 50 dozen donuts.

On Wednesday, October 17, the mood was different. Lines had already formed before 7 A.M. outside the registration sites in Santa Maria.

The Nisei response to compulsory military training was mixed. Masato Inouye, George's high-school classmate who had studied at Meiji University in Tokyo, was pursuing graduate studies in international relations at Yale in 1940. He decided to enlist so that he could complete his military service early and then move on. However, when he arrived at the Los Angeles induction station for his medical exam, military doctors found signs of tuberculosis on his chest X-ray. He was sent to the Maryknoll Sanatorium in Monrovia, the same hospital where he had once visited Setsuo Aratani.

On the other hand, many young men wanted to avoid conscription. It was a tense time, with events culminating during the last week of October, when blue capsules containing individual registrants' draft numbers would be poured into a large glass bowl in Washington, D.C. One by one the capsules would be drawn, opened, and the numbers announced to the nation.

According to a preliminary quota, Santa Maria had to supply 73 men. The Issei managers of Guadalupe Produce nervously surveyed their young Nisei co-workers, including George and the assistant bookkeeper, Tets Murata.

Married men were classified 2A, a deferred status. One day, the usually quiet Ben Kodama approached Tets, whose draft number was 3436. "You better get married," he urged.

Tets had been dating a former Santa Maria Union High School classmate, Haruko Kuratani, for four years. That autumn in 1940, the two were married in the Aratani living room in a simple ceremony. There were no bridesmaids in pink taffeta with bouquets of white roses and lilies, but beside the couple, tall and smiling, was Tets's longtime friend, George.

————◆◆◆————

As the war in Europe and the Pacific intensified in 1941, so did anti-Japanese sentiments. In the *San Francisco Examiner*, its Harvard-educated publisher William Randolph Hearst wrote that Secretary of the Navy Knox "should come out to California and see the myriad of little Japs peacefully raising fruits and flowers and vegetables on California farms and basking with Oriental satisfaction in the California sunshine, and saying hopefully and wishfully, 'Some day, I come with Japanese Army and take all this. Yes sir, thank you.'"

In contrast, Santa Maria Valley, especially Guadalupe, seemed to largely be a protected paradise, at least on the surface. Unlike the Hearst-owned *Examiner*, the *Santa Maria Daily Times* never used the word "Jap" in its headlines to describe either the conflict in the Pacific or the Japanese in the valley, perhaps because of the group's sheer economic dominance.

George, Big Boss's sole heir, had thus far detected little or no prejudice—his focus was entirely on the business. It had been a full year since he first began his training with Ben Kodama, and now he was busy driving from ranch to ranch and monitoring the progress of the packing sheds in both Guadalupe and Lompoc. Occasionally he would drive three hours to downtown Los Angeles to check on the wholesale produce enterprise and then return home the same day.

There were tax forms to file, salaries and bonuses to pay, inventory to record. Bank statements came in from Security-First National Bank in Guadalupe, as well as Sumitomo Bank in Los Angeles. Renters of property originally purchased by Setsuo sent in checks monthly. Numbers constantly floated in George's mind—sometimes he even dreamed about balance sheets with columns for accounts receivable and accounts payable.

But the business was more than numbers. George recalled how his father had taken him on that walk through the fields when he was 13. "Try to surround yourself with good people, and you can accomplish a lot more than you can do alone," Setsuo had said. "Kodama-*san*, Ikeda-*san*, Matsuno-*san*—Papa takes good care of all of them. You will have to take good care."

Sometimes, however, a raise in pay required the involvement of unions. As an example of the growing strength of the Mexican Field Labor Union, Roland Clark, the group's secretary, successfully negotiated an hourly wage increase for beet toppers and harvesters from 35 to 40 cents in August of 1941. When most of the employees in Guadalupe Produce's Lompoc packing shed joined the union, it was Clark who made sure that they all received the union-negotiated wages.

Despite intensifying tension outside the valley, in 1941 Guadalupe Produce again participated in the annual Santa Barbara County Fair, and like the previous year, the company placed an ad in the *Santa Maria Daily Times* publicizing the Japanese Day festivities organized by the Japanese Association of Santa Maria. The local jeweler, H. Y. Katayama, offered a free drawing for an RCA Victor console radio, while Charles Ishii's El Amigo advertised a Maytag washer as a prize.

During the final event of the evening, Wataru Sutow entertained the crowd with magic tricks, while Kaname Kai, a local Japanese dance group, performed on the vaudeville stage in the main tent. Hundreds of community members attended the Japan Day event, almost oblivious to the anti-Japanese sentiment that was engulfing the rest of the West Coast.

Through the fall and winter of 1941, George and the other Guadalupeans continued with the familiar patterns of their daily lives. Guadalupe Produce employees and their wives geared up for another wedding—this time a ranch foreman was marrying a girl from Fresno. The wedding was set for Sunday, December 7, 1941.

Ken and Mutsuko Kitasako, close friends of the Aratanis, were not celebrating that morning. Their eldest child, Edwin Tetsuo, had pneumonia, and Mutsuko was pregnant with their third child. They were leaving for the hospital in Santa Maria when the phone rang. It was Harold Shimizu, a friend who had built a successful Chevrolet car dealership and garage business during the depths of the Depression.

"Ken," Harold blurted out, "Pearl Harbor is being bombed."

"Come on, Harold," said Ken, glancing at his wife, Muts. "What are you trying to do, pull my leg?"

"No, no. Turn on the radio."

Back on Peralta street, where George and Masuko lived alongside the Ikedas and Tamuras, the Aratani house was buzzing with the news. George was incredulous.

There was no time to waste. He called together Ben Kodama and next-door neighbors Naoichi Ikeda and Butch Tamura. Then he called attorney Leo McMahon.

I need to protect the business, thought George. There's no way the government will touch the Nisei—we're American citizens, after all. But Ben and Naoichi were both Japanese nationals, so corporate assets of Guadalupe Produce needed to be transferred to Vegetable Farms, wholly owned by American citizens Butch Tamura and Miyokichi Matsuno.

A couple of blocks away, Komano Ishikawa looked at her husband, Toshitaro, the earnest Issei who managed All Star Trading for the Aratanis. "Should we go to the wedding?" she asked.

They went, but it was hard to concentrate on the nuptials. The guests around the tables at Guadalupe's Kikusui Tei restaurant had only one thing on their minds: war with Japan.

Tets Murata sat with his wife Haruko, his wife's sister, and her fiancé, Howard Suenaga. They shared their apprehensions, their fears about the future, and worries about the war. While the four were all Nisei, American citizens, who knew what might be in store for them? Suddenly, it was decided—Howard, a physician, would marry Haruko's sister that night.

They didn't waste any time: after the reception the four of them took turns driving the 400 miles to Reno, Nevada. After the couple exchanged vows in front of a justice of the peace in the middle of the night, the group returned to Guadalupe. Groggy and with bloodshot eyes, Tets went in to work the next morning. The office was eerily quiet. Ben Kodama wasn't there, and neither was Naoichi Ikeda.

The FBI had taken them away shortly after they had returned home from the wedding reception.

5

Let Us Not Be Witch Hunters

Let us not be witch hunters and at the same time,
let us not be too trustful.
—**"We Have a Ticklish Task Here," editorial in**
Santa Maria Daily Times, 10 December 1941

The arrests of the Issei occurred in waves. On the night of December 7, 1941, 736 Japanese nationals across the United States and Hawaiʻi were seized. In New York the Japanese were taken to Ellis Island, the place where multitudes of predominantly European immigrants had once entered the country. In Southern California authorities arrested several hundred people on Terminal Island, a tight-knit Japanese American community of fishermen and cannery workers in San Pedro Bay.

Some Issei attempted suicide. In one case in New York, a 50-year-old man unsuccessfully tried to take his life with a pocketknife and a large needle. In other incidents Issei accidentally set fire to their homes while burning materials that might be construed as suspicious.

Late that night in Santa Maria Valley, 14 men were picked up and taken to Los Angeles. Although their identities were not immediately revealed in the newspaper, the Japanese American community knew they included the most prominent valley Issei, among them Guadalupe Produce's Naoichi Ikeda and Reiji "Ben" Kodama.

Japanese Americans being forcibly removed from Guadalupe in
March 1942 and taken on buses to the Tulare Fairgrounds near Fresno.
Gift of Grace Shinoda Nakamura (97.324.1)

Pictured before their arrest in December 1941 are H. Yaemon Minami of Minami Farms (seated, second from left) and Naoichi Ikeda (seated, second from right). Also pictured are Setsuo Aratani of Guadalupe Produce (seated, far right) and Masuko Aratani, a principal of All Star Trading (standing). (99.30.152)

As the days passed, the names of those arrested appeared in the paper. There was no doubt that if Setsuo Aratani had been alive, his name would have headed that list.

The response in the valley was largely divided along generational, social, and political lines. Harry Miyake, leader of the local chapter of the Japanese American Citizens League, immediately issued a statement to the newspaper denouncing the bombing: "The outrageous attack on Pearl Harbor by the Japanese government was totally unjustified and we the American citizens of Japanese ancestry, without any reservations whatsoever, declare ourselves prepared and willing to take up arms against any and all enemies in the defense of our country, the United States of America."

The day before the attack on Pearl Harbor, leaders of the Japanese Public Service Association of Santa Maria had pledged to "follow the American way." Before his arrest, local businessman Chuhei "Charles" Ishii had told the press, "Japanese people living here for between 35 and 40 years and raising their children as American citizens naturally don't want to be known as foreigners here. We are also foreigners in Japan."

In the fields of Vegetable Farms, rumors were rampant. George heard stories that all the Issei would be picked up and shipped back to Japan. The majority of his management team, including those in the packing shed and fields, were first-generation immigrants. Their deportation would threaten the whole agricultural operation.

Even the U.S.–born Butch Tamura had been picked up by the FBI on the evening of December 7; he was released the next day. Naoichi Ikeda and Ben Kodama, however, were on their way to the Santa Barbara Jail with armed escorts from the Immigration and Naturalization Service. The three Nisei managers—24-year-old George, Butch Tamura, and Miyokichi Matsuno—conferred in the hushed quiet of the packing-shed office. "What are we going to do?" George asked the two older, more experienced Japanese Americans.

At least second-generation Japanese Americans would be protected, they thought. "There's no way they are going to do that to American citizens. We've got to promote some Nisei," they finally decided.

However, within a few days, an FBI agent showed up at Guadalupe Produce Company.

"I'm looking for George Tetsuo Aratani," the agent said.

"He's an American citizen," an office worker explained.

"Never mind. We want George Tetsuo Aratani. Where is he?"

"He's out in the fields, but he'll be back."

It was late in the afternoon when George returned to the packing shed. "The FBI is looking for you," the office workers told him.

George was incredulous. He directed an office worker to call the FBI, whose agents were making their base in the Santa Maria Inn, a landmark hotel near the high school.

As George waited in the office for the agent, his mind whirled. Are they going to take me? he wondered. Maybe it was a mistake—none of the other Nisei were being questioned. They must be looking for my father, George decided. The only difference between our Japanese names is an "S" and a "T." Surely that is the source of the mix-up.

When the FBI agent arrived, George was direct. "There must be some mistake," he said.

"Is your name George Tetsuo Aratani?"

"Yes."

"Then there's no mistake."

"You must want my father, Setsuo Aratani."

"No, no, he's dead."

"But I'm an American citizen," George protested.

"Where were you born?"

"In the Los Angeles area."

"You got your birth certificate?"

"Sure, I have it at home."

"We're going to check with Washington. We'll be back tomorrow. Make sure you're here."

That night, in the house on Peralta street, Masuko helped her stepson find his records. She was worried. There were only the two of them in America. What would she do if they took George away?

The next day the FBI agent came back to the office, this time equipped with records from Washington about George's activities.

"We would like to verify some information," the agent said. "Are you a member of the Guadalupe Buddhist Church, Japanese Association, Guadalupe Agricultural Association?"

"Yes, yes," George replied.

"Well, how about that. Did you participate in this meeting for the Japanese consul general?"

George shook his head. "No, I was not there."

The session continued, and finally the agent excused himself. "We have to do some more checking," he said, and he left in a black sedan.

What more did they need to know? thought George. And what about Naoichi and Ben? He needed to get in touch with them. But how?

---

*Much as we would like to have things different,
it is incumbent upon us, for our safety and the safety of our
nation, to be careful before we are generous.*
—Editorial, *Santa Maria Daily Times*, 10 December 1941

That week—and for weeks after—Guadalupe was in turmoil. New Year's Day was almost an afterthought; who wanted to celebrate openly with the pounding of *mochi* (rice cake) in times like these?

Despite the chaos, stoicism prevailed. George warned Issei families not to believe rumors, but he also told them to be prepared. "Put all your things that you need together," he told them. "We will take care of everything else—the house, furniture, car—until the war is over." Guadalupe Produce Company had plenty of trucks, cars, and personnel. They would be caretakers of the Issei personal effects and property—if it came to that.

Like darkness descending at night, the once jovial, close-knit environment of Guadalupe and Santa Maria Valley changed suddenly and dramatically. No longer were Japanese Americans welcomed in the local Rotary Club. European American children canceled plans to play with Nisei classmates after school. Multiethnic sports teams lost their unity.

The same *Santa Maria Daily Times* that had celebrated the accomplishments of leader Setsuo Aratani now cast suspicion over all Japanese Americans in the valley. In an editorial titled "We Have a Ticklish Task" in the December 10, 1941, issue, the newspaper espoused "caution" in assessing the community's loyalty. "It is not our fault," it stated, "if the race to which they belong has, by the action of the war and military arms of their original homeland, demonstrated that to trust it is to be deceived."

Ignoring the fact that it was patently unfair to brand the Japanese— once viewed as friends—as traitors, the editorial stated, "to continue to accept them all in the same unquestioning manner in which they have been accepted in the past" would be unwise.

The newspaper editorial also assumed that each arrested individual would be fairly tried by an American court of law, pointing out that the same right would not be accorded them in Japan. At their trials, they would have the opportunity "to prove their innocence of any seditious act," the writer claimed, forgetting that in America it is supposedly the accuser who must prove guilt.

"Their innocence . . . would in large measure reestablish the trust between the rest of us and those of Japanese ancestry, by demonstrating that Japanese in America are superior to their representatives at home who stab you in the back while embracing you as a brother," the editorial concluded.

A military proclamation ordered curfews for citizens of Japanese ancestry, who were not allowed to go more than five miles from their homes and who had to be indoors before dark. The curfew and movement restriction prevented Butch Tamura from being present at the birth of his second son, Raymond Shuji; his wife Mary delivered their baby at a hospital in Santa Maria, just 10 miles away.

Blackouts, signaled by the sharp blasts of a siren, were also instituted throughout Santa Maria Valley. Once the air raid alarm sounded, residents were expected to extinguish all forms of light, even cigarettes.

On December 16, 1941, the *Santa Maria Daily Times* published "What to Do in an Air Raid," a full-page announcement provided by the U.S. Office of Civilian Defense. "Whether or not a black-out is ordered, don't show more light than is necessary," the announcement instructed. "If planes come over, put out or cover all lights at once—don't wait for the black-out order. The light that can't be seen will never guide a Jap. Remember a candle light may be seen for miles from the air."

In Guadalupe, where a number of Japanese American businesses lined the main drag, Tad Yamada hung a sign reading "We are American citizens" outside his father's butcher shop and grocery store. Tad, who had recently returned from his studies at Meiji University in Tokyo, didn't want any bombs thrown through the window.

Tad's fears were not unwarranted. On December 30, 1941, someone "decided to take the Japanese war into his own hands and fired a shot into the M. Tachihara residence on North Blosser road," the *Santa Maria Daily Times* reported. Hearing a knock late at night, 18-year-old Ben Tachihara cracked the door open. A hand pushed through a hole in the screen door, and Ben saw the glint of a revolver. He slammed the door shut just as he heard the pop of the gun. The bullet was later found lodged in the edge of the door. The assailant was never apprehended.

Tension also deepened between the Filipino workers and the Japanese, many of whom owned farms in the valley. By the end of December Japanese air squadrons were bombing the Fortress of Corregidor, which protected Manila Bay. Reflecting the general mood of the times, Filipinos viewed Japanese Americans as an extension of the foreign enemy. When a fire destroyed the local Filipino hall during the holidays, fingers pointed to the Japanese. In the state's other agricultural centers such as Stockton, incidents of violence erupted between the two minority groups.

—◆—

The Japanese were not the only ones being targeted. The FBI also picked up German and Italian immigrants, although in smaller numbers. By December 9, 1,291 Japanese were being held nationwide, in comparison to 865 Germans and 147 Italians. United States Attorney General Frank Biddle also announced that naturalization applications filed during the past two years by German and Italian immigrants would be held up for the duration of the war. However, the government didn't need to shelve applications from Japanese immigrants—they had never been given the option of naturalization.

United Press International circulated reports that Japanese spies in America were part of a fifth-column espionage network that "paved the way for Japan's surprise blow at Pearl Harbor." Evidence of these alleged spies' activities included big arrows cut in sugar cane fields on Hawaiian plantations which pointed to military objectives, "innocent-looking" newspaper ads containing supposedly coded messages, and Issei vegetable dealers with knowledge of Navy port movements.

According to these United Press reports, "Many of the Japanese residents are American citizens with the right to vote. Partly for this reason, Japanese of American nationality infiltrated into the police department and obtained jobs as road supervisors, sanitary inspectors or minor government officials." The report, which was published in the *Santa Maria Daily Times,* also speculated that "many went to work in the post office and telephone service—ideal spots for spies."

Such reports from unnamed sources stoked embers of racial hatred and wartime paranoia. Soon, shortwave radios and cameras belonging to Japanese, Italians, and Germans were being confiscated.

"If the radio belongs to my son and he's an American citizen, what am I to do?" an Issei reportedly asked the Santa Maria Police Department.

"Bring 'er in," the officer replied.

George had in his possession Setsuo's prized 16mm movie camera, a still camera, black-and-white portraits, and canisters of footage documenting acres of Guadalupe fields and happier times—picnics in the dunes, the Aratani baseball tour in Japan, George at Keio University. Being a Nisei, he did not feel compelled to hand over the cameras and film reels. These memories belonged to the family.

The day after the bombing of Pearl Harbor, the Treasury Department froze all bank accounts belonging to Japanese aliens. This order was relaxed a week later to allow aliens to withdraw money from American banks for household and personal use, but no more than $100 a month. Farmers and shippers delivering valuable food products were given more leeway, depending on the bank.

Those who had funds deposited with Japanese financial institutions such as Sumitomo Bank and Yokohama Specie Bank found themselves in dire straits. On Monday, December 8, they discovered that the doors to their banks had closed indefinitely. Under the mandate of the Trading with the Enemy Act, the U.S. government confiscated and liquidated the banks' assets; the monies were eventually placed under the Alien Property Custodian, a federal agency that assumed control of foreign assets in time of war.

George had his personal and company accounts with Security-First National Bank in Guadalupe. His father, however, with his ties to Japanese corporations, had purchased yen deposits and established loans with Sumitomo Bank on East First Street in Little Tokyo.

Amidst the confusion, these accounts were the last thing on George's mind.

Much more pressing was the status of Guadalupe Produce, two of whose three partners were considered enemy aliens. While Naoichi and Ben were still incarcerated in Santa Barbara, the corporation held an emergency meeting with attorney Leo McMahon on December 14 in the county jail. Naoichi, the president of the corporation, presided, while George took notes as secretary.

McMahon had prepared a legal document. "RESOLVED," it stated, "that George T. Aratani, the Secretary-Treasurer of Guadalupe Produce Company, a corporation, be and he hereby is appointed General Manager of the corporation (effective as of December 7th, 1941), with full power and authority to act for the corporation in all situations and in every transaction."

One by one, the three men signed the document. First Naoichi Ikeda, graying at the temples, with dark bags under his eyes. Then Ben Kodama, George's *sensei* who had explained to him the details of the business. And finally, George. In a matter of minutes, the transfer of power was complete.

However, the future of Guadalupe Produce was still vulnerable. The three partners, especially George, realized this. Therefore, immediately after being elevated to general manager, George sold the assets of the company to Vegetable Farms, the operation owned by his two Nisei co-workers, Butch Tamura and Miyokichi Matsuno. This transfer would protect the business, George thought. Surely this solution would help them survive the war.

— ◆ —

While George was immersed in the minutiae of legal paperwork, a ranch hand came to the office. "George, take a look at the chili pepper crop," he said. They drove out to one of the ranches, where George saw acres of bright red chili pepper and paprika plants brightening the cloudy winter day. The peppers were ready to be picked and dried, but there was a problem. He could not renew his processing license for the dehydrating plant.

His partner in the dehydration enterprise, Chester Masunosuke Otoi, had been one of the 14 Issei taken from their homes in Santa Maria on December 7. He, along with Ben Kodama, Yaemon Minami, and Toyokichi Tomooka, had been sent to an alien detention camp in Fort Sill, Oklahoma. Still others had been sent to remote centers in Texas, Montana, New Mexico, and North Dakota.

Apparently partner Otoi's Japanese citizenship was the roadblock to renewing the processing license. With tons of chili peppers about to go to waste, George sent telegrams to the state Agricultural Department in Sacramento in which he appealed for a renewal of his license. He even traveled to L.A. for a hearing, but without success. After consulting with H. E. Kaesemeyer, to whom Chester had given his power of attorney, George decided that the only way to save the crop was to purchase Otoi's share of the company. Kaesemeyer agreed that it was the best plan of action.

Unfortunately, Kaesemeyer did not inform Chester Otoi until some months later. On April 26, 1942, he sent a telegram to the Fort Sill Alien Detention Camp. "Sold your share in dryer to George Aratani as of January first for $17,525.90."

In Fort Sill, Chester Otoi read the telegram in disbelief and dismay. Why would Setsuo's son do this to him? he wondered. Why was he not consulted beforehand? He spoke to Naoichi Ikeda, the former president of Guadalupe Produce, and Jitsutaro Tokuyama, a Lompoc packing-shed manager, also jailed in the camp. "George-*san* is most likely protecting you," they told him. "Don't worry."

Chester nodded. But inside something didn't sit well. He had helped to build up that dehydrating plant. Could he trust Setsuo's son? Chafing at his sense of powerlessness in the camp and overwhelmed by the sudden upheaval of his life, he resolved that what he had built was not going to be so easily taken away from him.

In February another wave of arrests hit Santa Maria Valley. The FBI, for the most part, was very precise as a result of information gathered in the months before the bombing of Pearl Harbor: they only targeted homes of Japanese aliens. Businessmen, community leaders (such as Guadalupe's Buddhist minister), and middle managers of ranches and packing sheds were among those arrested. Anyone in a leadership position, even as a Japanese-language schoolteacher, was considered a threat.

The manager of All Star Trading, Toshitaro Ishikawa, who had just turned 41, always went to the post office to pick up the mail before going to work. But on one particular morning, Toshitaro sensed that something was wrong. Instead of reporting to Guadalupe Produce, he came straight home from the post office. His only child, eight-year-old Hiromu Stanley, had already left for school; his wife Komano greeted him at the door.

"What's wrong?" she asked.

"The town is very *okashii* [strange]. There's all these black cars and these FBI-looking guys wearing black suits," he said. "We may be taken away next."

Soon, a black car pulled up in front of their house. A tall European American man in a black suit came to the door. "Is Mr. Ishikawa here?"

"Yes, come in." Komano was calm, although her hands trembled.

"You probably know," the FBI agent said to Toshitaro, "but we need you to come with us."

Toshitaro turned to his wife. "Please pack my suitcase."

"He's going someplace cold, so pack something warm for him," the agent added.

Komano nodded. She went into the bedroom and took out a warm wool sweater, jacket, underwear, shirts, socks, and several pairs of pants. In the bathroom she wrapped up a bar of soap and then looked at his razor. I shouldn't pack that, she thought to herself.

When she brought the suitcase into the living room, the agent looked over the contents. "You didn't include a razor," he said.

"I did not think—" Komano said haltingly.

"Put it in."

Returning from the bathroom with the razor, Komano heard the agent ask her husband, "Do you have any money?"

Toshitaro reached for his billfold.

"Where you are going, you won't need money. Leave it with your wife."

The agent's instruction was kind and helpful, thought Komano, who showed little emotion. *Shikataganai*, she and others had said—it cannot be helped.

The agent noticed her restrained demeanor. "Japanese women are strong," he said. "They don't even cry. It's much easier for us."

Who would benefit from my crying? thought Komano in response. Inside I'm full of tears, but I don't want to show that face.

She did, however, appreciate the agent's words. He must have been a family man himself, for when he left with Toshitaro he said to her, "When your son comes home from school, tell him that we are going to ask his father some questions, but that in time he will be back."

Komano nodded and silently watched as her husband was led to the black car and driven away.

The FBI came back to search the house after Stanley returned from school. Komano figured that the agents were counting on a child's natural honesty—even if she were hiding something, they could count on an eight-year-old to tell them.

They checked everything, from the toilet bowl tank and cover to the icebox. Opening a closet, the agents pointed to a wrapped box. "What's this?" they asked.

"My Boy's Day dolls," Stanley replied.

After the FBI had completed their intensive search of the Ishikawa house, Komano went into the garage, where boxes of toys had been dumped out onto the dirt. On top of the pile was a Japanese toy sword, a *katana*. They must have known that it was just a toy.

Through the bay window in his house on Guadalupe Boulevard, Ken Kitasako, the Nisei general manager of Santa Maria Produce, saw town policemen and FBI agents go up and down his street. They were picking up Japanese and taking them to the American Legion Hall, which was being used as an assembly point.

Ken's wife Muts was worried as she looked out the bay window. She was ready to deliver their third child at any time. "Eventually they will come for you, after they make their rounds and pick up the first group," she told him.

"No," Ken said, "I don't think so. I'm a citizen. They can't pick up citizens."

Without their husbands, certain Issei women now turned to the Nisei managers of the farms and packing sheds for help. One woman called Ken after her husband, a crate-machine operator at the Santa Maria packing shed, was taken into custody. "I have these three small kids," she said. "I don't know what to do."

"Just sit tight," Ken said. "There's nothing you can do yet. Some of us are left here, so we'll try to organize whatever we can. We'll see to it that you're all right."

Zentaro Yamada, Setsuo's co-partner in All Star Trading, was among the 250 Issei in Guadalupe to be arrested in February. A man in his eighties, he was already packed and ready to go, as he had been ever since the first wave of Issei arrests.

"Shoot, what the heck," thought the Hiroshima native. "They must think I'm a loyal American or something. They don't even pick me up." He was beginning to feel isolated from his fellow Issei, many of whom had already been arrested. Then, on February 18, 1942, Zentaro got his wish.

Relatives learned that Yamada and others had been taken to the Civilian Conservation Corps camp in Tujunga Canyon within the Santa Monica Mountains of Southern California. That weekend Zentaro Yamada's daughter Kikuye, along with three other Nisei young people, drove south in search of their fathers.

They found them in a compound surrounded by a cyclone fence. The camp had guard towers manned by military police, and six soldiers patrolled the premises carrying machine guns.

The four young people parked and walked over to the cyclone fence. They hoped to ask the Issei prisoners huddled outside in topcoats for news about their fathers. Then Kikuye Yamada saw her father, Zentaro, and she called out to him. He hurried over, and they talked briefly through the fence until the guards spotted them.

The guards yelled at Zentaro and ordered Kikuye to stand several yards away from the fence. During this disturbance, one of Kikuye Yamada's friends slipped inside the compound and found his father, who told his son that the prisoners were being shipped out to a Justice Department internment camp in Bismarck, South Dakota.

"Don't worry," he said. When we get there, we will let you know."

<hr/>

In February and March of 1942, the worst fears of the young Nisei were realized. On February 19, 1942, President Roosevelt signed Executive Order 9066. All people of Japanese ancestry, including citizens, were to be evacuated from the western region. Like their fathers, the Nisei would also be uprooted from their homes and sent to concentration camps. Four days after the signing of the executive order, the shelling of an oil refinery at Goleta, north of Santa Barbara, by a Japanese submarine, was prominently reported by the press, further whipping up the public's paranoia.

While George had initially told worried Issei that the company would be the caretakers of their property, now the Nisei businessmen needed caretakers themselves. Earlier in the year Ken Kitasako, the Santa Maria Produce general manager, had received a phone call from Santa Barbara attorney Leo McMahon. "Ken, get yourself over to the Kashiwagi Hotel. We have to meet," said McMahon. He had also called the managers of Vegetable Farms and Minami Farms.

At that initial meeting in the Kashiwagi Hotel were four men: McMahon; Ken Kitasako, representing Tomooka's Santa Maria Produce; Bob Hiramatsu, representing Minami's General Farms; and Butch Tamura, representing Aratani's Vegetable Farms. "It may reach a point where you won't be able to farm," McMahon told them. "We have to set up some kind of machinery here to run the farms for you."

Ken looked at the other two Nisei, Bob and Butch. "Yeah. That's true. We've got to do something. We have to."

McMahon then presented his plan. A trust would be set up with one of the European American businesses in the county acting as trustee. The owners of Puritan Ice Company—Theodore Paul Dalzell, Leon R. Phillips, and P. R. F. Marshall, all based in Santa Barbara—would take over the operation of the three farms and packing sheds. They were the logical choice because they furnished ice to the packing sheds and were fairly familiar with the three managers' ways of operating.

Puritan Ice Company had a long history with Guadalupe Produce. Shortly after establishing the ice company in 1921, the owners had created shed accommodations for then-newcomer Setsuo Aratani. While other growers had pulled out of the valley after crop failures, Setsuo had stayed, and he'd flourished. Soon other farmers set up sheds to accommodate lettuce production: Chester Masunosuke Otoi, Yaemon Minami, and Toyokichi Tomooka, as well as European American interests.

Providing a vital source of ice for the shipping of produce, the Puritan Ice Company was located next to the packing sheds of Minami Farms, Guadalupe Produce, Santa Maria Produce, and C. M. Otoy. It also had a plant in Santa Barbara designed to ice cars in transit, as well as an ice plant and cold-storage facility in Atascadero.

Acting as trustees for the three Japanese agricultural giants was a good deal for the then principals of Puritan Ice. The company relied on the success of the Guadalupe growers' packing business. Under the current circumstances, they couldn't miss: with the United States involved in a war, the price of all vegetable produce was going to go up.

Therefore, in April 1942 the directors, officers, and shareholders of Vegetable Farms, Santa Maria Produce, and General Farms entered into a trust agreement with the three Santa Barbara men. Through the creation of an independent company called California Vegetable Growers, the trustees would operate the growing, packing, and shipping operations of the three farmers while the managers were in confinement. Then, when the war was over, the trust would be dissolved and the individual companies would revert to their original management. In theory, this seemed like a reasonable plan—and it was the only option available to the growers.

In their haste to preserve their businesses, details of the trust—such as the distribution of profits—were not clear to the Nisei managers. What was important at that moment was that California Vegetable Growers would operate the farms during their absence. The Nisei managers would work out the details later.

Meanwhile, George was consumed with making arrangements for his other businesses as well as his personal property. He couldn't find an operator for the hog farm, so he and partner Butch Tamura sold it at a loss of $13,500. The situation with Guadalupe Fertilizer and Chemical Company was even more disastrous. While he was able to sell off his supplies of potash and chemicals such as dusting sulfur, the large mixer and other equipment, worth more than $20,000, had to be abandoned.

In addition, he and seven other partners of the Los Angeles Vegetable Exchange had to unload their inventory, leasehold, and goodwill for a mere $8,000, a loss of $165,800. California Vegetable was interested in assuming control of the dehydrating plant, but in deference to Chester Otoi, still being held at Fort Sill Alien Detention Camp in Oklahoma, George knew that he couldn't sell. His father's old partner was still smarting from the abrupt transfer of his interest in the plant to George.

And then there was the Aratanis' personal properties and real estate. Through purchases made over the past two years, George owned not only his Peralta home and the neighboring houses occupied by Naoichi Ikeda and Ben Kodama, but also a strip of land along the main boulevard, the site of the Nokai (Japanese Agricultural Association) building, a garage, and the offices of the Southern Pacific Railroad.

Because most of the buildings' tenants were being sent to concentration camps, a caretaker needed to be found, so these properties were also placed under a trust held by California Vegetable Growers. Rather than leaving their furniture and personal belongings in government storage, George and Masuko opted to store their possessions in one of their bedrooms.

Neighbors and friends also brought over their belongings, from household goods to Japanese paintings to golf clubs. Everything was properly labeled and locked away in a shed near the garage.

Komano Ishikawa, the All Star Trading Company manager's wife, was weighed down with responsibilities. Following her husband's arrest she focused on taking care of their son Stanley, who had lymphatic problems. After Toshitaro was taken away, eggs began to appear on their doorstep. Komano soon discovered that the benefactor was the mother of the neighbor boy whom Toshitaro routinely had driven to school along with Stanley.

When it came time to leave her Guadalupe house, people came by every day. They coveted the new icebox and stove that the Ishikawas had just bought for $500—and they offered Komano just $100 for them. Surveying her new appliances, the sewing machine, and the bedroom and living room furniture, Komano decided simply to give everything to her neighbors; she felt better about giving it all away rather than sell her things for a small fraction of their value.

Just before the day they were to evacuate, another Nisei woman stopped by the Ishikawa house. "Who is going to take care of your belongings?" she asked.

"My neighbor has been so nice, so I'm going to give her everything except for one box of important items."

The woman was aghast. The neighbor's husband was a blue-collar worker, not one of the elite of the valley. "If you give your things to such a person, you are going to get them stolen," she said.

"If they get stolen, fine. These people were nice to me, and that made me happy," Komano said. "Who are you going to give your things to?"

"To a judge in town," the woman said proudly.

Years later, Komano Ishikawa felt vindicated by her decision: the judge had appropriated all the belongings left with him, while Komano's neighbor had beautifully maintained the Ishikawas' property.

———◆◆———

During the last week in April, all the evacuees met either at the Guadalupe Buddhist Church or on Mary Street in Santa Maria. Such gatherings in the past had often been on the occasion of funerals for friends or neighbors. The crowd this time marked the death of a community and the demise of a country life rich with baseball, summer picnics, and vegetable fields. Now each of their lives was compressed into a single suitcase or duffel bag and tagged with a number.

From Guadalupe and Santa Maria, they were taken north on buses to an assembly point in Arroyo Grande. Their bags—mountains of the past and present—were then piled onto trucks and later unloaded at Tulare Fairgrounds, west of Sequoia National Park and south of Fresno.

Two young Nisei men were left behind to move items into storage space designated by the War Relocation Authority (WRA). As the two worked, the streets of Guadalupe seemed particularly quiet. Abandoned was the Yamada grocery store, which once sold seaweed, dried fish, and soy sauce, as well as fresh ground beef. Closed was the Kodama Boarding House, once filled with young Japanese laborers. Gone were more than 1,000 people, some of whom had ties to the land dating back to the turn of the century. After loading the final box, the two men departed for Tulare Fairgrounds.

A wind blew through the empty streets. The fog grew thick. There were now no Japanese Americans left in the town of Guadalupe.

6

Losing Guadalupe in Barracks 57-10-B

*To be frank, I have learned a great deal
about my business and personal affairs after the
outbreak of war.*

**—George Aratani, in a letter to attorney
Leo McMahon, 18 October 1944**

Before April of 1942, George had never traveled to Tulare, California. The closest he had ever been to the town was Fresno, the Central Valley's rich agricultural hub off Highway 99. He knew that it was hot and that it was located at the base of the Sierra Nevadas. And he had heard of the fairgrounds where, as at Santa Barbara County's annual event, the choicest cows, vegetables, and baked goods were displayed every spring.

The Tulare he arrived in, however, was quite different. As he got off the bus, all he could see were hundreds of people, all of Japanese descent, walking past armed sentries. Some were friends, neighbors, and Guadalupe Produce employees. Most were strangers. Other than the crying of babies and the whining of children, the crowd of 5,000 was eerily quiet.

**George Aratani with stepmother Masuko Aratani and Guadalupe
friends who shared their barracks, Uchitaro and Hiye Tamura (seated),
at the concentration camp at Gila River, ca. 1943.** (99.30.47)

George and Masuko were led to a racetrack, and then they were sent to makeshift barracks constructed from cement, wood, and tar paper. Less fortunate people were assigned to horse stalls; the stalls had been rinsed out, but they were permeated with a lingering stench.

Six to eight people were assigned to each room. George learned that his two-person family would now extend to include Uchitaro and Hiye, the elderly parents of Butch Tamura, as well as Komano Ishikawa and her ailing eight-year-old son, Stanley.

The camp had literally been thrown together with no thought for privacy needs or human dignity. The toilets were in an open room with no dividers. And the food—bland mush stretched by flour and water, in contrast to the fresh vegetables always available in Guadalupe—was served in a mess hall. Bitterness rose into George's throat, but it was never given voice. Instead, as he rested on his hay mattress, his mind created a wall of protection. Concentrate on the family business, George told himself as he pulled out a pen and paper. Somehow, dwelling on tangible tasks had always helped George survive the losses in his life.

Over the next five years George would labor over details affecting the farming operation and personal assets. Literally millions of dollars were at stake, representing the livelihood of hundreds of Issei and Nisei. Both his parents were dead, and he had a widowed stepmother to care for. These were indeed heavy responsibilities for Big Boss's son, then just 25 years old.

———— ◆ ————

Masuko, meanwhile, was struggling to deal with the dry heat of Tulare, where temperatures in the summertime sometimes hit 110 degrees. Keeping the door to the barracks open, she spoke softly to Hiye Tamura, who was like her second mother, and to Komano Ishikawa. Would there be no relief from this misery?

In 1942 a total of 16 temporary detention centers were established for Japanese Americans in California, Washington, Oregon, and Arizona. In comparison to the other centers, Tulare was midsized, with most of its internees from the coastal region of Southern California, including Los Angeles County.

George lived in two worlds. One was within the confines of barbed wire, while the other—within his mind—was Guadalupe Produce back home. On May 5 George received a letter from the farm trustees, California Lettuce Growers (also known as California Vegetable Growers), inquiring about his seller's permit number and a recent purchase of Guadalupe Fertilizer and Chemical Company by a plant in Los Angeles.

George sat amidst the army cots and suitcases in the bare barracks. The seller's permit number? The past three weeks had been a nightmare. Papers had been hastily thrown into boxes before they left. Valuables were stored in a safe in the middle room of the Peralta home. He had no idea where the permit number could be.

Occasionally the outside world managed to penetrate Tulare, as it did when Joe Kanter of California Lettuce Growers visited that first summer. It was difficult to do business, he told George, because of anti-Japanese sentiment—people don't want to deal with California Lettuce Growers because of our ties with you, he reported. And there were other managerial concerns. Paul Danielson, the company's assistant secretary-treasurer, wrote letters about "the trouble getting labor."

"The plan now is to use some high school boys which we hope to gather around the nearby towns. In checking elsewhere, the situation is acute everywhere, so this area is no exception," he wrote to George on June 3, 1942. Apparently, employees for the dehydrating plant were also difficult to come by. And the market for automobiles was at a longtime low: with gasoline and tires rationed, who would want to purchase Guadalupe Produce's fleet of cars?

George weighed these concerns as best he could. Confined as he was in the heat of Tulare, it was difficult to discern what was true or false.

—— ◆ ——

When he wasn't working on letters regarding his business concerns, George socialized with old friends like Yoichi Nakase, and he met new ones. Yoichi, who was known as "Sunshine" in high school because of his warm demeanor, took an interest in the camp's youth. After taking charge of organizing activities for them, he got a new nickname: "Mayor."

Among George's new acquaintances was Shig Kawai, a jovial, down-to-earth young man about his same age. Shig was from Pasadena, California, and his older brother Nobu, a tall, handsome man, was well known among the Santa Maria Valley members of the Japanese American Citizens League (JACL).

George himself had been a member of the JACL, and although not an active participant, he felt that the group had played an important role in easing the negative effects of the evacuation. He was aware, however, that others—especially those based in Los Angeles and San Francisco—had a very different viewpoint. Some critics accused the group of kowtowing to governmental authorities and even serving as informants for the FBI.

Such tensions drove a deeper wedge between the Nisei who were raised in Japan and those who wanted to firmly identify themselves only as Americans. George, who had experienced Japan as a young adult, somehow stayed in the middle. Besides, he had never felt very connected to politics—the community, in his mind, always came before divisions of class and philosophy. And right now his community, although it was temporarily relocated, remained Guadalupe.

Everywhere George turned, he ran into employees of Guadalupe Produce. When he was picking up his mail, he encountered some of the packing-shed workers from Hawai'i. They were older Nisei who had once lived in the Kodama Boarding House.

"We got mail from home," they told George, ripping open envelopes postmarked Hawai'i.

"What, are your folks in camp, too?" George asked.

The former workers shook their heads. "They don't have camps over there."

George was surprised. The December 7 bombing had occurred in Hawai'i, after all. Why put us into camp and not them? It didn't make sense.

In fact, some Issei and Nisei had been incarcerated in Hawai'i, but only a small minority (less than one percent). The government, for political and economic reasons, decided to use alternative surveillance methods to keep tabs on Japanese Americans in Hawai'i rather than resort to wholesale removal of them, for they were too valuable a labor force on the Islands.

The inconsistent treatment of Japanese Americans mystified George. For the first time, he began to suspect that the real reasons behind the forced "evacuation" had little to do with national security.

In July of 1942 news from the administration spread within the Tulare Assembly Center: the military had reclassified all Nisei males as 4-C, enemy aliens. Those who had joined the Army before the war would be released from service.

George barely reacted to this change of status. The government had locked them up in these camps, after all. At least we won't have to go to war, he thought.

Nonetheless, some Guadalupeans were still directly assisting the war effort as interpreters and teachers at the Military Intelligence School in Minnesota. George's friend Tad Yamada, who had been educated at Meiji University in Tokyo, was an early recruit. Even before the West Coast "evacuation," in January of 1942 Tad had volunteered to teach at the Fourth Army Military Intelligence School, which at the time was located in an empty aircraft hangar in the corner of the Presidio in San Francisco.

When all other Japanese Americans had been evacuated from the West Coast, Tad and other Nisei instructors and students at the MIS were allowed to stay in San Francisco's Japanese Town and commute to the Presidio. At the time the government had few Japanese-speaking workers to decode, translate, and interpret the many messages that they were intercepting.

By the summer of 1942, the language school had been moved to Camp Savage, Minnesota, and there was a need for more bilingual teachers to train recruits. George, with his education at Keio University, was a prime candidate to be an instructor, but he couldn't leave his stepmother and the business in all its unsettled state. Besides, they were soon forced to pack up their meager belongings once again. The Tulare prisoners would all be moved—to where, George did not know.

⋅—◆—⋅

Five hundred prisoners at a time were put on trains in late August of 1942. The compartments' shades were kept lowered. Some believed that they were traveling north towards Colorado, but when the train finally stopped, they found themselves in the middle of a desert surrounded by purplish-red buttes and saguaro cactus shaped like tall men. A nearby water tower read "Casa Grande."

It was in the town of Casa Grande that evacuees were herded into buses and taken to a place called Rivers, located approximately 40 miles southeast of Phoenix, Arizona, on a Pima Indian reservation. The Indian community members were unaware of the new guests who would be inhabiting their land.

According to the *Gila News-Courier*, the camp newspaper, the town was named after the first Pima killed in action during World War I, a soldier named Jim Rivers. With the addition of more than 10,000 Japanese Americans, in a matter of weeks Rivers became the fourth-largest city in Arizona. Chandler, the site of Poston concentration camp, grew to be the third largest.

The Gila River camp was divided into two sections, Canal and Butte. Most of the Santa Marians were sent to Butte, or Camp II, tucked away in the Casa Grande Valley. Construction of the camp was still incomplete: open trenches revealed pipes, some of which were broken and leaking. The red-roofed, white-walled barracks were furnished only with Army folding cots.

The day after their arrival, the Santa Marians looked out at the horizon beyond their new home and noticed a brown dust cloud approaching. It was a desert sandstorm. They rushed to close the windows and doors, but to no avail. Dust entered the barracks through flimsy wooden floorboards. Enveloped in dust, George and Masuko felt as if they had been shoved into hell.

As they had done in Tulare, the Aratanis tried to make the best of their situation. At least they were able to continue to share their new living quarters with friends: the elderly Tamuras and the Ishikawas, including Toshitaro Ishikawa, who had been allowed to rejoin Komano and little Stanley after his internment in Bismarck, North Dakota.

While the accommodations at the Gila River camp were a slight improvement over those at Tulare, the climate was not. Under the extremely dusty conditions, both at Tulare and then in Arizona, many of the internees contracted valley fever, which Komano Ishikawa described as *tochi no byōki*, a "disease of the land." In medical terms valley fever is known as coccidioidomycosis; it is a disease caused by fungus spores that attack the lungs, lymph nodes, skin, and bones. Soon George himself would sense a tightness in his lungs. In time valley fever, reminiscent of the asthma of his childhood, would also come.

— ◆ —

In Gila River George was becoming increasingly frustrated about the difficulty in getting an accurate picture of the situation in Guadalupe. Certain representatives of California Lettuce Growers kept insisting that the current business climate was difficult due to anti-Japanese sentiment. Seeking answers from another source, George wrote to some former employees, Swiss Italians and Portuguese, who continued to work in the packing shed. They wrote back in brief, handwritten notes: "No problems that we can see."

George received some solace from a European American woman named Ethel Allen, a single mother of a frail boy who suffered from bronchitis. An employee of California Lettuce Growers, she had moved to the Guadalupe office to oversee the personal trusts of several Japanese Americans, including the Aratanis. George, who exchanged weekly letters with Ethel concerning details about his property, described her as a "woman of high ability." Both George and Ethel shared a common aptitude for efficiency and attention to details.

Ethel faithfully responded to George's countless requests for everything from sending to Rivers a can of *shōyu* (soy sauce) and his typewriter to locating a precious trunk of Masuko's kimono. As a low-ranking office worker, however, she was not in a position to inform George on what was really going on with the business.

Within months of the Guadalupeans' arrival in Arizona, attorney Leo McMahon visited the Gila River camp. Arriving on September 12, 1942, he called a meeting of the principals of the Big Three—Ken Kitasako (Tomooka farms), Butch Tamura and Miyokichi Matsuno (Aratani farms), and Bob Hiramatsu (Minami farms). The Nisei men sat and listened to McMahon as he explained recent difficulties with the three farms. "We're getting to a point where we can't operate very well with a trust," he informed them. As an alternative, he informed them, the trustees were willing to negotiate for the purchase of the corporations' assets.

Later, the four men talked amongst themselves. "There's something going on," one of them said. "They must be hiding something."

But the managers were at a disadvantage: they couldn't go to the farms and investigate for themselves, so how could they prove anything? The Issei founders of two of the Big Three, Yaemon Minami and Toyokichi Tomooka, were in Justice Department camps in Santa Fe, New Mexico, and Missoula, Montana. It would be impossible to find an alternate manager for their properties.

The four felt they had no other option—they had to sell their businesses to the trustees. George also reluctantly agreed, deferring to the decision of the older Nisei.

A lease arrangement was devised which ultimately benefited California Lettuce Growers at the expense of the three properous farm operations begun and run by Japanese Americans. What was at stake were thriving million-dollar businesses, flush with money and a wartime demand for fresh vegetables. At the time of the transaction, George's Vegetable Farms boasted $114,125.48 in cash assets, with current accounts receivable totaling

$38,246.96. However, according to the lease agreement, Vegetable Farms would only be paid $20,000 initially.

"Why, that will barely cover the income taxes we have to pay," George said. "We'll hardly have anything left." What would he say to all the employees, the ones he saw daily in the mess hall?

Butch nodded. They were being cheated out of their hard-earned money, but if they didn't accept the deal, their land would just go fallow and customers would be lost forever. This way, at least, they hoped to recover some money from the trustees in the future.

Realizing that his family's once-mighty agricultural empire had been reduced to a mere pittance, George was happy that his father was not alive to witness the death of Guadalupe Produce. Papa would be destroyed, thought George. It was difficult to imagine that all of Setsuo's dreams and hard work had come down to this travesty.

To add insult to injury, within a week of that September meeting a member of California Lettuce Growers sent George a letter regarding details of the farm: "Maybe you will be in competetion [sic] to the Guadalupe area soon. If you do too good at it maybe you will show us all up over here."

<hr />

It gives me a feeling of satisfaction and relief if you close this matter because being here in camp, I am helpless.
—George Aratani, in a letter written in Rivers to attorney
Leo McMahon, 26 December 1942

With the loss of the farm, the members of Guadalupe Produce considered taking advantage of work-furlough programs in demilitarized zones, programs available initially only to Nisei who had never lived or studied in Japan. Butch and Mary Tamura planned to use the opportunity to move their family to Mary's hometown of Salt Lake City, Utah. Also considering the same move was Hawai'i-born Miyokichi Matsuno, the other partner of Vegetable Farms.

George, however, needed to stay put in order to continue to sort out business matters. The loss of Guadalupe Produce was only the beginning of a larger battle against two governmental agencies, the Superintendent of Banks and the Alien Property Custodian.

Setsuo, like other successful Japanese businessmen, had had bank accounts with both American and Japanese financial institutions. He had made a series of yen deposits in the 1930s in the Sumitomo Bank as a means of sending money to relatives in Japan, to George while he studied at Keio, and as collateral for business loans. Many Issei businessmen in the United States purchased yen certificates during the period in order to take advantage of the favorable conversion rate of four yen to one dollar.

Before Setsuo's death, the certificates had all been transferred to George. In total, George had more than 706,000 yen deposited at Sumitomo's Los Angeles branch. At the prewar exchange rate, this was equivalent to $176,525, a small fortune in the 1940s. George also had loans, or promissory notes, with Sumitomo Bank. With interest the debt was about $65,000—a large sum, yet less than half of his total deposits.

The start of America's war with Japan changed everything. After December 7, 1941, the Superintendent of Banks assumed control of Sumitomo Bank, and all of George's accounts were frozen. And suddenly the Superintendent of Banks not only sought to liquidate George's assets, but the agency also attempted to force him to repay the $65,000 in loans.

Although other evacuees also had accounts with such Japanese financial institutions as Sumitomo and Yokohama Specie Bank, George's was not a routine case. So while other depositors merely filed claims with the camp evacuee property office, George needed outside legal help.

He once again turned to Leo McMahon, the same attorney who was now being sued by the other growers because of his role in the sale of the farm operations. George himself could not cut off his relationship with the Santa Barbara-based attorney—he would soon be entering a legal conflict with the government which would plague him for decades.

At first, both McMahon and George's accountant Kaesemeyer seemed optimistic that he could settle the lawsuit by paying $25,000. The $170,000 in yen deposits would subsequently be returned to George, to be exchanged at the end of the war or when trade resumed between the two countries. As time went on, however, it became clear that the U.S. government was out to get George Tetsuo Aratani.

For the most part George was not active in camp politics, but he certainly was not oblivious to the tension between certain factions. A further aggravation to the internees was the winter cold spell of 1942. By December, most of the barracks still did not have any type of heating.

In the nearby Canal Camp, relations between the Issei and Nisei generations had become increasingly bitter. A Nisei internee who had been accused of favoring American-born residents in the disbursing of clothing allowances had been beaten with ironwood clubs. An Issei had been apprehended, convicted, and sentenced to jail. When he returned to camp a month later, the assailant was heralded as a hero.

Acting camp director R. B. Cozzens attempted to downplay the significance of the assault-and-battery case. The *Gila News-Courier* described him as "positive that the people in the entire Gila Project are not in favor of mob or gang rule."

News of the beating in Canal Camp particularly distressed George, because he was assisting his roommate and Issei colleague, Toshitaro Ishikawa, who was in charge of Butte's Clothing Allowance Office.

One day a man barreled into the office, obviously angry. "When are we getting our clothing allowance? You guys aren't doing your jobs." The allowance came in the form of checks or scrip, not actual clothing; payments ranged from two dollars to $3.50 a month. The man swore at the frightened female typists who bent their heads over their paperwork. The only sound in the office was the click-click of the manual typewriters.

"Look," replied Toshitaro, as serious as ever, "no one is playing around. As you can see, everyone is *isshōkenmei* [working hard]. Please wait a little longer and you will receive your allowance. *Sumimasen.* I'm sorry."

Both Ishikawa and George had decided to work in the clothing allowance department because of their ability to deal with numbers, and they also hoped to help the more impoverished people in camp. "I have found many families that are in dire need of clothing and we're trying not to miss anybody that are [*sic*] entitled to it," George wrote.

But after hearing about the beating of the Canal clothing allowance director, George also commented, "As a matter of precaution, I thought of getting myself a steel helmet to protect myself before I do any walking around this camp at night."

The incident at the Canal Camp exposed the ideological clash between a group of mostly Issei and Kibei (those who were born in the U.S. but raised in Japan) and members of the JACL, who were predominantly Nisei. The Issei and Kibei objectors felt betrayed by the American system, while others thought that alignment with groups such as the JACL would eventually prove their loyalty.

The JACL, after all, had been created in the 1930s by Nisei seeking to affirm their identities as Americans. No Issei (or noncitizens) could officially become members, but that hadn't stopped Japanese leaders like Setsuo from donating money to the organization or hosting receptions. George himself had been a passive member of the Santa Maria chapter of the JACL, and he felt that the group had aided both immigrants and citizens during their tumultuous removals from their homes. Although he didn't know JACL president Saburo Kido personally, George considered him a good man who was working for the benefit of the Japanese American community.

Gila River, unlike the other camps, formed its own JACL chapter under the guidance of leaders from Pasadena and Santa Maria Valley. The creation of such a chapter—the Gila River JACL—could not have been possible in camps like Manzanar, where strong feelings about the organization completely polarized the community. (There was a group called the Manzanar Citizens Federation, which involved some leaders of the JACL.) Emotions in Manzanar ran high: after the beating of a JACL leader and the arrest of a Kibei labor organizer, violence broke out in the camp on December 6, 1942. When it had ended, the guards had shot at least 11 men, 2 of whom died.

While Gila River also had its share of JACL detractors, feelings were not as strong for several reasons. First of all, the Gila River JACL leadership did not uniformly support national policy, and in fact challenged it at times. They were a more liberal group on the whole: the Pasadena contingent had been affiliated with labor unions on the West Coast and had supported Larry Tajiri, the editor of the JACL house organ, *Pacific Citizen*.

Also mitigating the conflict between pro-Japan and pro-American forces in Gila River were the Santa Maria Valley JACL leaders. They had worked side by side with the Issei in the farmlands, and they opted for compromise rather than antagonizing those born in Japan. "We must not forget that the JACL is also working for the safety of our fathers and mothers," said one older Nisei from Santa Maria.

Others were not convinced of the group's intentions. In anticipation of an upcoming mass meeting, a former member of the Santa Maria JACL chapter said, "If the JACL is like what they were in the past, it's no use in joining. They never did tell us what was going on. I realize the Nisei need a voice, but I want to put my trust in an organization which I am sure about."

———•◆•———

Meanwhile, as older Nisei debated issues of patriotism and constitutional rights, members of George's Nisei generation were more concerned about the social scene.

Young people met their future mates at Saturday-night dances, such as the holiday Winter Hop, as well as at outdoor screenings of such films as Abbott and Costello's *Pardon My Sarong* and *Pride of the Yankees*, starring Gary Cooper.

George attended dances with his bachelor buddies, but his heart was actually in another Arizona camp. Months earlier, before the war, he had met a young Gardena woman in Little Tokyo. She was Sakaye Inouye, a pretty, fair-skinned Nisei known for singing at weddings and in talent contests. Now she was interned at Poston.

The eldest daughter of Eijiro and Katsuko Inouye, in addition to being popular among the boys, she was also extremely hardworking. With her sister Victoria, who was 12 years younger, Sakaye had helped her parents operate a poultry farm in Gardena. Vickie, a tomboy in pigtails, would perch in a large tree beside the farmhouse. As customers drove in, she jumped down and filled their orders.

Sakaye's job was to deliver cartons of eggs to various restaurants and grocery stores in the family's Model A Ford. Although the Inouyes had at times struggled financially, Sakaye had once saved up to buy her little sister a new pair of high-tops.

Their father, Eijiro Inouye, was an intuitive, quiet person who had a great love for botany and *shodō* (Japanese calligraphy). In contrast, his wife Katsuko was an outgoing person with a booming laugh who liked to entertain friends. However meager the family's earnings during the Depression, Katsuko would leave food on the doorstep for down-on-their-luck travelers. Similarly, her daughter Sakaye was known for always extending a helping hand. When a friend asked Sakaye to drive her to Los Angeles one evening to meet a family friend in town from Guadalupe, she readily agreed.

They drove to the Olympic Hotel, an impressive brick building on San Pedro Street, where they found a young man with thick, jet-black hair and heavy eyebrows waiting for them. Strong and muscular, he had a sharp grin.

"This is George Aratani," her friend said.

As George and the young woman chatted, Sakaye watched, duly impressed. Here was a young man with good manners and a lot of responsibilities, apparently.

For his part, George was smitten. Since taking over the farm, he had not allowed himself to pay much attention to the opposite sex. But he liked Sakaye: she was attractive and friendly yet had little pretense. And she was wholesome, much like the people of Guadalupe. He got Sakaye's phone number from her friend, and he began calling her regularly. Then, the bombing of Pearl Harbor and the chaos of the "evacuation" suddenly disrupted this emerging romance.

During the early months of 1942, Sakaye's family, grandparents, and uncles abandoned their businesses and moved into a demilitarized zone in central California. Within nine months, however, they discovered that they would still be forced to relocate to a concentration camp in Poston, Arizona, near the California border.

How could he get to know Sakaye? George wondered. She was so far away, and they were separated by barbed wire and the bureaucracy of the War Relocation Authority. In Guadalupe he could hop in his Chevrolet and drive down to Gardena; now he could only rely on letters and friends to further his cause.

As 1943 began, Gila River was again filled with contention. Rumors about Japanese Americans being drafted had circulated through the camps for months, and on January 28, 1943, the War Department made this news official. No longer were Nisei males automatically considered enemy aliens and classified 4-C; instead, those from 18 to 38 years of age were now required to register for military service. In addition, volunteers were being recruited for an all-Nisei combat team of approximately 5,000 men from Hawai'i and the mainland—the 442nd Regimental Combat Team.

Within a week of the War Department's announcement, the U.S. government disseminated a loyalty questionnaire to all internees 17 and older. Serious debate swirled around two specific questions. Number 27 asked: "Are you willing to serve in the armed forces of the United States in combat duty?" And Number 28: "Will you swear unqualified allegiance to the United States of America and faithfully defend the United States from any or all attack by foreign or domestic forces, and foreswear any form of allegiance or obedience to the Japanese emperor, to any other foreign government, power or organization?"

"What are you going to do with this crazy questionnaire?" friends asked George.

"I'm saying 'yes' and 'yes.'" George was pragmatic, but it *was* a crazy document. Titled "Application for Leave Clearance," the questionnaire was confusing. In the first place, who said that the Nisei had any allegiance to the emperor? Most of them can't even speak or read Japanese, thought George. And what about the Issei? Because by law they couldn't become naturalized American citizens, would they then become people without a country if they renounced Japan?

Despite any reservations he had about the questionnaire, George nonetheless answered the two most controversial questions in the affirmative. So many senseless events had already transpired—what was one more? Besides, he knew about Japan, and he didn't belong there. Japan was going to lose the war, anyway. George was sure of it. The country had no natural resources. How could they defeat a nation like America?

The formation of the 442nd Regimental Combat Team, along with the ill-conceived loyalty questionnaire, divided internees in all the camps. A week after the announcement about Nisei military service, Saburo Kido, the president of the national JACL, was beaten with clubs by fellow internees in his barracks in Poston. It was well known that the JACL as a group had supported the reinstatement of Japanese Americans by the Selective Service. "Somewhere on the field of battle, in a baptism of blood, we and our comrades must prove to all who question that we are ready and willing to die for the one country we know and pledge allegiance to," Mike Masaoka, a prominent JACL leader, argued at the JACL national conference in Salt Lake City, Utah, in November 1942.

The Gila River JACL chapter faced much apathy as it set about organizing a membership drive within camp. In response to criticism that the leadership was a closed group, they had already made a concerted effort to widen their circle. The Santa Maria JACL contingent turned to two steady, well-liked figures: Ken Kitasako and George Aratani.

On February 4, in barracks 58-1-D, George attended his first and last board meeting. Eleven men were in attendance, the largest such gathering to date. As George looked around the room, he saw that most of the others were family men in their thirties or even forties. At 26, George was by far the youngest. What the hell am I doing here? he thought.

The meeting was succinct, lasting about an hour. After such general housekeeping topics as *Pacific Citizen* subscriptions and the JACL membership drive, discussion turned to more pressing subjects: namely, the military registration of Nisei and the 442nd Regimental Combat Unit.

"There's a lot of questions about this all-Nisei combat unit," one board member said.

"Yeah, shouldn't the Nisei boys be mixed in with the rest of the Americans? Why separate them?" someone asked.

"We should sponsor a mass meeting with the administration and Army officials," one leader from Santa Maria said.

They all nodded in agreement.

George stayed quiet for most of the discussion, aside from nominating Santa Maria Valley's Ken Utsunomiya as program chairman for the informational meeting. Because military registration was set to begin on February 10, the JACL board decided to hold the meeting the day before.

On February 9, 600 people filled Mess Hall 52 to capacity; an overflow crowd of more than 400 stood outside in the cold, listening to the meeting via public-address speakers. Was it true that all Nisei would be subject to the draft? they wondered. Many listened cynically as army officials encouraged the Nisei men to voluntarily enlist in the 442nd and join the Hawaiian Nisei, who were already training in Wisconsin as the 100th Battalion. Critics objected: Why should we volunteer and sacrifice our lives for a government that throws us in here? This JACL, they're the ones that got us into this mess.

Others hoped that this would be an opportunity for the Nisei to indeed exhibit their patriotism to those who would question it. These people believed that the JACL and its national leaders were right. Reactionary groups like the Native Sons of the Golden West didn't want the Nisei to fight for the United States; in fact, the same group was attempting to strip the Nisei of their citizenship. Going to Europe and defeating the Nazis and Fascists would be one sure way to prove them wrong.

After the meeting, many of the other JACL board members later went through the camp to explain military registration to the Issei, but George continued to maintain a low profile. He knew that he wasn't a charismatic speaker, and he didn't like philosophical debates. The political arena simply was not for him.

Nor was George the star athlete, "one of the most dangerous and renowned Japanese sluggers in his hey-day," as the *Gila News-Courier* had heralded, and he wasn't making concrete plans to leave camp for college or work. He was stuck in camp, still on the sidelines of the internal political debate and on the fringe of Gila River's social scene. He was more concerned with his displaced community, Guadalupe.

That community was struggling to deal with military registration. The second son of a Guadalupean widow, for instance, told his mother that he was going to volunteer as a means to help preserve his father's memory and gravesite. "When I go to war, the people back home will surely be moved to take care of the grave," he said. The widow, moved by the passionate words of her son, agreed with his decision even though it had social consequences for her. When the son left to fight in Europe, the mother had to endure critical glances and cold shoulders from the other internees. How could she allow her son to fight when the government had treated them so unfairly?

During this period, an Issei former Guadalupe Produce employee and his wife came to see George. Their faces were pale and drawn as they explained that they were at odds with their son about military registration. "You have to help us, Joji-*san*," the father said. "You have to help us explain to our son that he has no obligation to go to war. He can't understand our broken English."

George listened quietly. He understood the parents' perspective—why *should* an American citizen be forced to fight for his country when that country didn't respect his rights? *Gimu* (duty) was one of the most important principles in Japanese culture. But do you still have a duty to a nation that has branded you an enemy alien?

George agreed to talk to the entire family the next day, even though he had little idea what he would say. That night he suffered from a bad case of insomnia. He sat up and listened to the soft breathing of Stanley, the Ishikawas' boy, asleep on the other side of the barracks, with only a blanket dividing their spaces. There were principles at stake here, but also lives. How could he make this right? As the former de facto head of Guadalupe Produce, he expected that other Issei parents would also seek consultations with him. What he said tomorrow would have wider implications beyond one family. He needed to come up with an answer.

George met with the Issei parents and their son in their barracks. The boy was so young, a mere teenager with scant hair on his upper lip. First the father addressed his son. "It's okay that this happened to me," he said in Japanese, referring to the forced "evacuation," "but not you. You're a citizen. To be in this camp means that you've lost your rights. You should just forget about registering."

The son stood up abruptly and picked up a bunch of letters tied together with twine. "Look at this, Pop. These are all from my high-school buddies. They're in training camp. So they're in one kind of camp, and I'm in another. Why should they risk their lives and not me?"

"You don't understand, son." The father continued to talk about *gimu*. The teenager's face grew tight with frustration.

Finally, George intervened. "You're right, *Ojisan*," he said to the father. "But your son's right, too. If the Nisei don't register or accept the call to duty, I'm sure they are going to be picked up by the United States military police. That means that you all might have to go to Japan, and what will happen to your children there? They have a Japanese face, but they cannot speak the language. So what's their future going to be?"

The parents listened silently; this was not the advice they'd hoped to hear. Their son's face softened. He knew that George's argument would convince his parents to let him go. "I'll be all right," he told them. "Don't worry."

In May of 1943 nearly 106 Gila River internees, including 5 Issei, volunteered for military service and reported for medical examinations in Phoenix. Within weeks, more than 30 of them—some wearing suits and at least one donning a wide-brimmed straw hat—were inducted into the armed forces in Salt Lake City.

Not all Nisei chose to support military registration or take the loyalty oath. In a camp in Heart Mountain, Wyoming, a group called the Fair Play Committee resisted the draft in a formal way. Their members would go to war only if the government completely restored the constitutional rights of all Japanese Americans and released them from the camps. Eventually 63 Fair Play members were tried and convicted of resisting the draft, and they were sent to prison. A total of 267 from all the camps refused to serve.

Many more individuals answered "no" to the two loyalty questions. From Gila River, more than 2,000 men, women, and children were transferred to Tule Lake concentration camp, which became a segregation center for those labeled "disloyals." In addition, 77 Gilans took the even more drastic step of applying for repatriation; in 1943 they were sent to Japan on the *Gripsholm*, a prisoner-of-war exchange ship.

<hr />

We just went through the worst wind storm we ever had and which virtually covered the whole camp with dust. Yesterday and today are the busy days for housewives.
—George Aratani, in a letter dated 26 January 1943

Valley fever struck George down in mid-February, and camp doctors ordered him to rest in bed for at least a month. "I certainly pick a nice time to get it when everybody is busy with the military registration and applying to leave camp," he wrote in a letter on February 20, 1943. Other Guadalupeans also came down with valley fever: there were a reported 30 cases of coccidioidomycosis treated in the Gila River Hospital that year.

Dr. George Baba, one of the Gila River camp physicians, found that the barracks were too poorly constructed to provide adequate housing. "Every time any wind came up, the dust would come up through the cracks and they'd inhale it and come down with cocci. . . . They'd come down with what sounded like the flu, and some would get better, but some wouldn't."

At Gila cocci manifested itself in a variety of ways, including meningitis, arthritis, and pneumonia. Some patients developed a skin condition called erythema nodosum. Sputum and blood samples were sent to a doctor at Stanford University who was an authority on coccidioidomycosis.

"I think we got to be fairly expert on cocci, too, but there was nothing you could do except make the diagnosis," reported Dr. Baba. Indeed, the treatment of valley fever was the same as that for tuberculosis: simple bed rest.

Barracks 57-10 was becoming a hospital ward: not only was George's case quite severe, but Toshitaro Ishikawa also came down with the sickness shortly after George fell ill. Komano Ishikawa became a nursemaid not only for her son, but for her husband as well.

It was four full months before George was back on his feet—and this would not be the last appearance of his valley fever, either. As one assault after another tested his stamina in Gila River, George would have to continue to find the strength to fight other battles as well.

———— ◆ ————

Too many people have been telling what had
happened to their homes because they were not occupied and
had many of their things stolen.
Altho [sic] I know my houses are in good hands, it still
worries me a bit. Perhaps, I worry too
much about it and should leave the whole matter with you.
—George Aratani, in a letter to Ethel Allen, 20 February 1943

Santa Maria Valley residents' true feelings about their former Japanese neighbors were difficult to assess. During those seemingly idyllic early days, it had appeared as if the valley was indeed a harmonious global village. Setsuo Aratani had played alongside European American golfers at the Santa Maria Country Club. Filipino guitarists and Mexican dancers had once performed with Japanese singers on a makeshift wooden stage at Guadalupe Produce picnics.

However, when the Japanese were sent to concentration camps, ugly reactions emerged, especially from newcomers to the valley who had come to escape the poverty of the Depression. Many of these recent arrivals had

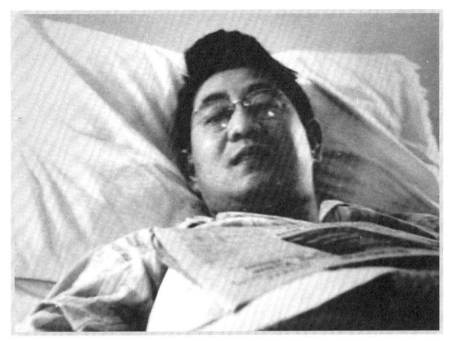

George Aratani, recovering from valley fever at Gila River, February 1943. (99.30.21)

been part of the exodus from the Dust Bowl states in the Midwest. A Nisei mechanic spoke in an interview about the situation in Dorothy Swaine Thomas's book *The Salvage*:

> A lot of these people later agitated the most about the evacuation because they were jealous of the Japanese since they had nothing themselves. I suppose a lot of the old time *Hakujin* [European American] residents were jealous too but they never said too much against us and the Japanese managed to keep on friendly terms with them. Their real feelings came out after the war started and I know a lot of these *Hakujin* wanted to get us out of the valley. They were just two-faced about it.

Internees heard disturbing reports from outside camp which substantiated these charges. In one instance, a grower sponsored a large barbecue and invited the whole community. "Did the Japs ever do this for you?" he asked, conveniently forgetting the legacy of Setsuo Aratani, who lay buried nearby in the Guadalupe cemetery.

All the interned Guadalupeans were very concerned about their property, which they'd left stored in their residences and businesses. After the Tulare internees were transferred to more permanent concentration camps, news of vandalism back home spread. Early in 1943 a resident reported that a fish market had been broken into in Guadalupe. The Evacuee Property Division of the War Relocation Authority later investigated and determined that the market had indeed been ransacked; according to reports from deputies in Guadalupe, clothing, furniture, and household goods were pulled from their now-splintered crates and vandalized.

George's house on Peralta Street was also vulnerable to attack. Someone had in fact attempted to pry open the house's screen door, but one of his trustees, Kenneth Dalzell, spotted the damage during a routine check of the property, and it was quickly fixed.

Ethel had found tenants for George's properties, including his home on Peralta Street. "I am mindful of the fact you will not wish just everybody and anybody as tenants," she wrote. "So will have to be choosy. Lots of people want houses, but mostly they are not the people you would want there."

Ironically, when Ethel and her son were homeless and staying in a hotel in Guadalupe, George wrote from camp to offer assistance. "Your favors in spite of your present predicament is [sic] appreciated and I hope I can help you in finding a residence. Let me know if I can do [something] to help you. If there is a vacancy in Guadalupe and the owner here, I will be glad to contact him for you."

Even as they dealt with the various pressures and hardships of camp life, Masuko and the other women around her concentrated on a much more pleasant task: finding a wife for George. He was 26, after all. And many of his peers were getting married in camp. Masato Inouye, one of the original "four musketeers" who traveled to Japan, wed a Nisei woman from Sierra Madre, a quaint town near Pasadena. The ceremony took place in Chapel 40 before 200 guests, and the reception followed in Mess Hall 39.

George was certainly considered a "good catch"—not only had he been a leader in his community, but he was also a handsome man. Any female would be glad to be George Aratani's girl. For the older women who knew him, though, she had to be just the right one.

One day an Issei woman, a family friend of the Aratanis, stopped by to see Masuko. "Do you know of this Inouye girl, Sakaye?" the woman asked.

Masuko shook her head.

"You met her, Masuko-san, when you visited me after our house burnt down."

**Sakaye (Inouye) Aratani at camp
in Poston, Arizona, in 1943.** (43.1998.8)

Masuko struggled to remember. Before the war, this woman and her elderly husband had operated a chicken farm in Gardena. After their home was destroyed in a fire, the childless couple struggled to make ends meet.

"Sakaye was the one who was helping us with the farm, remember?"

Masuko pictured the young woman who had been collecting eggs; she remembered the girl's big eyes and wavy hair. "Yes, I remember," she finally said. "Pretty girl."

Her delighted friend then described how Sakaye had been a godsend during a traumatic time. "She's coming to Gila from Poston for some dental work. I think she knows George. You should tell him that she's staying with us for a week."

After her friend left, Masuko smiled. Although nothing was explicitly stated, they were all on the same wavelength.

Later Masuko happened to mention Sakaye's name to Ken Kitasako's wife, Muts. "Sakaye Inouye? I know her," Muts exclaimed. "I was her

Sunday School teacher when I lived in L.A. She's such a nice girl."

Masuko was curious. She had received strong endorsements from two friends—maybe this Sakaye Inouye was the one.

Sakaye did come to Gila River, not just once, but twice. Receiving special clearance to leave camp, she rode a train to Phoenix; after staying one night at the YWCA there, she took a taxi to Rivers. Sakaye was impressed with the camp's appearance. The white walls and red roofs of the barracks were a lot brighter than the bleak tar-paper walls and roofs of Poston.

During her first visit to George's barracks, she was surprised to see him lying in bed during the day. He seemed listless, nothing like the energetic man she had met back in Los Angeles. Worried about his health, she promised to send him a miracle cure. "When I get back to Poston, I'll send you a package," she said.

Sure enough, within weeks a box—perforated with air holes— arrived at Rivers, Barracks 57-10-B.

Upon opening the package, George, Masuko, and the Ishikawas stared at the contents: live turtles, which Sakaye apparently had gotten a friend to catch from the Colorado River. They all had heard of the fresh-turtle-blood cure, but it was not a job for novices. The turtle's neck had to be stretched out and then sliced with a sharp knife so that drops of blood could be collected in a small cup; the blood had to be quickly ingested before it coagulated. This seemed a task for an expert, so the turtles were taken to a cook in the mess hall. Their blood was extracted, and the meat and shell were placed in a vat for turtle soup.

George drank the blood enthusiastically. He figured this is what one did in the name of romance.

———◆———

While George was confined to his bed, his close friends were undergoing a stringent security clearance in order to leave camp. They were leaving to work: listings of job opportunities throughout the Midwest in cities like Chicago and Detroit were published daily in the camp newspaper. A total of 16,655 people were interned in Rivers; more than 4,000 went on indefinite leave to engage in farm work, while 3,786 relocated to unrestricted areas of the U.S.

George's longtime friend Tets Murata and five other men left camp for three months of seasonal agricultural work in Montana. On their way back to Gila River camp, the men had to transfer from one bus to another, but the second driver refused to let them board.

"You Japs have to wait in line. You can get on if there's room," the bus driver said brusquely. The bus, half empty, then departed, leaving Tets and his friends behind. They had to spend the night in town before catching a train to Salt Lake City.

The usually easygoing Tets Murata was livid. His work away from camp had been a War Relocation Authority–sponsored program. When he got to Utah, he went straight to the WRA office and explained what had happened. "This is a heck of a way to treat us." His voice shook as he spoke. "You want us as labor to harvest the crops, and then you ignore us."

Tets and his family eventually left Rivers in 1943 to join his sister, who had moved to Detroit as part of a WRA resettlement program. There, he worked odd jobs in a lumberyard and on a farm.

Even Ken Kitasako, who had been so involved with the camp co-op and the Student Relocation Council, left to work at a defense plant in Chicago. Like many other husbands and fathers, he went alone, leaving his wife and children temporarily in camp—there were too many unknowns in the outside world.

Friends advised Toshitaro Ishikawa to do the same when he decided to resettle. A former Guadalupe Produce employee told Toshitaro, "It's dangerous out there. You should go first, establish yourself, and then call your family."

But his child was still frail, and Toshitaro explained, "I'll feel *anshin* [better] if my son is with me." Without making any concrete plans, Toshitaro, his wife Komano, and son Stanley left behind the barbed wire of Gila River. They traveled by train and stayed in different hostels until they eventually landed in New York, where they lived in the attic of a businessman's house in Scarsdale. Attitudes toward Japanese were less extreme in New York, they discovered. People were used to Japanese, many of whom worked for large corporations such as Mitsui and Mitsubishi. Komano Ishikawa found that there, "all Japanese were *rippana* [respectable]."

As George's body became stronger, his financial problems seemed to grow worse. As he continued to battle against the government, on the advice of his Santa Barbara attorney Leo McMahon he retained a downtown Los Angeles law firm, Mathes and Sheppard.

McMahon wrote to George on March 5, 1943:

> The Sumitomo Bank matter is going to have to be handled very astutely. The reason is that there is a new Superintendent of Banks—Warren's administration is anti-Japanese and there is considerable feeling in California at this time unfortunately engendered against loyal Japanese Americans—you desire to keep the time deposit certificates, and a disposition of the matter must be presented to Court and a hearing must be held.

George did not know how seriously to take the Sumitomo matter. In addition to dealing with his personal real-estate investments, he was busy trying to get the proper forms from the Federal Reserve Bank of San Francisco so that he could assume the All Star Trading inventory. More than three hundred cartons of Hilo-Masamune brand sake, made in Hawai'i, were being stored in downtown Los Angeles, and George wanted to sell the rice wine as soon as possible.

When George was advised by McMahon to dissolve Guadalupe Produce in order to protect his interests, he and Ben Kodama—who had been released from a Midwestern detention camp to Gila River—received passes to travel. They set off for another camp administered by the Justice Department for a four-day conference with Naoichi Ikeda and Jitsutaro Tokuyama, who had been in charge of Guadalupe Produce's Lompoc division.

The camp, a two-and-a-half mile drive from Santa Fe, New Mexico, was in the foothills of the Sangre de Cristo Mountains. It was much cooler there than in Rivers, Arizona, and the air was thinner due to the high altitude. Renovated barracks stood on one side of the camp, next to prefabricated Quonset huts. Santa Fe definitely looked nicer than Butte camp, thought George.

But there was a strange feel to the place. There were only men, mostly Issei—no women, teenagers, or children. George recognized many faces, among them Yaemon Minami, newspaper publishers, and other stalwart leaders of the Japanese American community. He knew that this would have been the home of his father as well.

On June 30, 1943, Naoichi, Ben, and George gathered in a simple room at Santa Fe internment camp. "I need to dissolve the company," George said, telling them about the Sumitomo lawsuit. "The government's coming after me."

Naoichi nodded. At two o'clock in the afternoon, the three signed the papers to liquidate the corporation.

From New Mexico George and Ben traveled to Denver, where they met with Butch Tamura and Miyokichi Matsuno. The men discussed their futures, and both Butch and Miyokichi were in agreement: they wanted full payment on the promissory notes issued to them by California Lettuce Growers. By now Butch and Mary Tamura and their three sons had moved to Mary's hometown of Salt Lake City, one area where Japanese Americans were free to settle from camp.

Upon his return to Gila River, George sent letters and a copy of the document dissolving Guadalupe Produce Company to Leo McMahon. But the action had not been taken early enough. McMahon explained that the legal firm of Mathes and Sheppard had been meeting with the Superintendent of Banks, who insisted that $60,000 in outstanding loans be paid in cash. Meanwhile, the government would continue to retain George's yen deposits.

"While negotiations were pending and without notice or warning, the Superintendent of Banks, through its attorney, who is a young political appointee by the name of Saroyan, filed suit against you and Mr. Ikeda and attached all property of yours in California, including your bank accounts and everything," McMahon wrote.

Stating that he regretted "this development over which we had no control," McMahon attempted to appease George. "We are not concerned about the ultimate outcome of the matter," he continued. "Incidentally, if you find that you need money for living expenses, etc., I believe I can arrange to personally advance it to you."

Two days later another letter came to Barracks 57-10-B. Dated September 29, 1943, it was written by A. E. Skinner, manager of Security-First National Bank, who reported that a writ of attachment had been placed on George's personal account of $7,944.72.

A week later Ethel Allen informed him that a check written in payment of his income taxes had been refused by the bank because of the attachment. Fortunately, she had forwarded a cashier's check to the IRS from his trust account.

Although he had more to lose than did many other Japanese Americans, George was not alone in his financial woes. Numerous other Guadalupeans faced penalties or foreclosures for failing to pay their property taxes. Being locked up at Gila River did not release the internees from financial obligations, even though they were cut off from their funds.

As he received these notices of attached properties and accounts, George felt sick to his stomach. He had always prided himself on balancing his accounts and keeping tabs on all financial details. His ultimate plan was to compensate the executives and top managers of Guadalupe Produce if and when sufficient funds were received from California Lettuce Growers. But for now he had to go to friends in camp to borrow money.

"I must say it was a complete surprise to me," he admitted to Leo McMahon in a letter on October 11, 1943. "It seems rather strange that Sumitomo Bank should make attachment on my property without any notice or warning whatsoever to either me or the associated law firm. However, it was done and we must check this action before the situation gets worse."

In December of 1943 the situation did get worse. A summons arrived at camp ordering George to appear in the Superior Court of Los Angeles. It was indeed a ridiculous demand: the courts were requiring that George be present in a military zone where individuals of Japanese descent were prohibited.

George immediately sent a telegram to Leo McMahon. Legally he could not appear in his own defense, but as his representing counsel McMahon could. McMahon, in Washington, D.C., at the time, replied immediately with his own Western Union telegram. "Of course I will represent you. Airmail summons and complaint to my Santa Barbara office. And don't worry about suit. Your friend. Leo T. McMahon."

Selective Service was reinstituted for the Nisei in January 1944. Draft boards began to reclassify all 4-Cs of military age as 1-A. "Nisei Draft Opens," announced the *Gila News-Courier* in its January 22, 1944, issue.

Masuko Aratani was increasingly worried about the possibility of George being inducted into the Army. George was worried, too. With that prospect looming, he made arrangements to ensure that all of Masuko's papers were in good order. "I may be called at any time," he wrote to Ethel Allen back in Guadalupe. "My number hasn't come up yet but when it does I'm quite sure the army will use me in limited service because of my trick knee which pops in and out when I pivot on my heel." On March 10, 1944, George wrote to California Lettuce Growers' Paul Danielson that the "442 Infantry—all Japanese American—will be going across soon, it seems to join the 100 Battalion, also all Nisei now fighting on the Italian front. Perhaps one of these days I'll find myself over there too."

Within his circle of friends and colleagues, George was among the last to leave Rivers. He had considered resuming his college education, and he had even visited schools in Iowa during a trip he took to Iowa City to have his knee examined by an orthopedic surgeon.

One option seemed always to be available: the Military Intelligence Service in Minnesota. Recruiters, including George's old friend from Japan, Paul Rusch, came to Gila River on a regular basis, looking not only for students but also for civilian teachers. Who would be more appropriate for the job than a bright young man with a Keio education?

Then valley fever hit George again in 1944. The disease was persistent, and he was fed up. He wrote Danielson in March of 1944:

Although now I'm out of bed and manage to walk around this desert city, I still feel the effects of the fever and knowing that it can cause me more trouble, I'm not taking any chances. I haven't been to work for some time now and by all appearances, I won't be able to do any work for quite some time to come.

The doctors have been telling me to go some place where the climate is different and not so dry as they believe it is the only cure for their sickness. I'm thinking about this seriously now.

In fact, he had been thinking about the lush state of Minnesota and its many lakes. He definitely felt that the time had come to move on with his life: the farm operation was now under the trustees' option to buy, and the Sumitomo Bank matter was in the hands of the attorneys. Before he could leave, however, he still had two important matters to take care of.

Sakaye was visiting Gila River again. This time she stayed with Ken and Muts Kitasako, and George made sure to see her every day. Traveling by bicycle, he sometimes rode over with books for her. She also came to the Aratanis' barracks for dinner instead of going to the mess hall.

George felt comfortable with Sakaye, who seemed to epitomize femininity and kindness. He could trust her. From the beginning he made it clear that his intentions were serious; there were no secrets between them. He told Sakaye about his family, his half brother and half sister back in Japan. And he also outlined his business woes. "Our family is no longer as comfortable as before," he said. He didn't want Sakaye to have any illusions about his financial situation.

Sakaye, for the most part, simply listened. She was a private person, but she was drawn to George's straightforward style. He wasn't a smooth talker who paid her easy compliments about her looks. His words had weight, a sincerity that she appreciated. She was falling in love.

It was difficult to find any privacy in camp—especially during the daytime—so the two often strolled hand in hand at night. Sometimes, they even sang together during their walks. "You are my sunshine," began George, and Sakaye chimed in. Later, with the outline of the desert buttes in the distance, they would kiss for the first time.

One evening, during one of their walks George stopped in front of a ditch being prepared for pipe to be laid in. He jumped down and then reached out for Sakaye. "Come on," he said.

Sitting together at the bottom of the ditch, George and Sakaye felt truly alone. The stars seemed brighter and bigger than Sakaye remembered them being back in Gardena, and she could sense what was going to happen next.

George turned to her. "I love you," he said. "And I want to marry you."

Their courtship had been a brief one conducted in unusual circumstances and marred by their forced separation. Yet somehow, the two knew that they were meant to be together.

"I don't want to get married in camp," George continued. "I want to wait until I'm settled in Minnesota."

On her way home to Poston, Sakaye felt like she was walking on air. She had told George that she needed to get her parents' permission to get married, but she also knew that her father would not say no. In Phoenix she stopped at a department store to buy an overcoat—she would need something warm for Minnesota.

Because gossip spread in the camps like wildfire, Sakaye kept the proposal a secret. Rather than having to answer people's questions about the ceremony, their plans, and even future children, it felt good to keep the engagement under wraps.

But back in their barracks in Poston, 11-year-old Vickie Inouye began to suspect that something had changed during her sister's recent trip to Gila. She watched as Sakaye and her mother crocheted a colorful bedspread. In the center was the letter "A." "'A,'" thought Vickie. "We are Inouyes. We have nothing to do with the letter 'A.'"

Within weeks a man came for dinner at the Inouyes' barracks. He was from Gila River, and his name was George Aratani. After dinner he spoke privately with Vickie and Sakaye's father, and then he was shown the magnificent crocheted bedspread. The letter's significance finally dawned on

Vickie: "George Aratani is taking my sister away from me!"

George's other task before he left Gila River was to speak with Chester Otoi, who had recently been released from Santa Fe internment camp. Otoi had been moved by the government from one detention center to another, and he was weary and impatient.

Late one April night in 1944, in Barracks 52-3-C, George explained why he had bought out Otoi's share of the dehydrating plant. "It was the only way to continue its operation; otherwise, the license would have been revoked," he told Chester.

George also revealed details about the Sumitomo suit and its impact on his accounts. "I'm not making money on these deals," he said, referring to the sale of Vegetable Farms and the leasing of the dehydrating plant. "In a few days, I'll be leaving to teach Japanese at Camp Savage."

Chester listened intently. He too had plans for the future—he was even considering returning to farming in Santa Maria Valley after the war was over. He wanted more answers, but George had little time to meet with him—he was on his way to a new life.

He had already retrieved his car from storage in Guadalupe. (A WRA administrative staff person on vacation in California had driven the car back to camp for him.) George and some friends would be making the drive together to Camp Savage, 25 miles southwest of Minneapolis.

On May 1, 1944, after two long years in camp, George loaded the car with his suitcases and his typewriter. Masuko, along with the elderly Tamuras, saw him off. There were no hugs or tears, because they all knew that they would be reunited some day.

As he and his friends drove up the highway, headed towards Minnesota, George felt liberated and optimistic. Once free of camp, he would also be free of the valley fever, he thought. And soon he would start his life as a married man. Like a desert snake shedding old skin, George shook off his worries about the Sumitomo lawsuit, his attached properties, and his financial problems. His eyes were on the future: he would gather a team, a team that would challenge centuries of an established industry's practices and confront decades of discrimination against Japanese Americans.

7

Lines of
Communication

*Never before in history did one Army know
so much concerning its enemy prior to
actual engagement as did the American Army
during most of the Pacific campaign.*
—MISLS Album, 1946

In 1940 only 51 Japanese Americans lived in Minnesota. By June of 1942 that number had quadrupled with the official opening of the Military Intelligence Service Language School (MISLS) bordering the tiny town of Savage, southwest of Minneapolis.

The goal of the top-secret school was simple, but the attainment of that goal was not. Captain Kai E. Rasmussen, the school's commandant (who was later elevated to colonel), along with Lieutenant Colonel (later Brigadier General) John Weckerling, identified the need for linguists in order to break Japanese military codes and extract information from prisoners of war. Rasmussen, a native of Denmark and graduate of West Point, had learned Japanese during the four years he spent with the U.S. Embassy in Tokyo, but he realized that he was one of only a few such soldiers in America.

When the school's headquarters was first established in an airplane hangar at San Francisco's Presidio in November of 1941, resources were minimal. Fruit boxes and crates served as chairs; borrowed books became

George Aratani working overtime on his correspondence at the Military Intelligence Service Language School (MISLS) in Fort Snelling, Minnesota, ca. 1945. (99.30.53)

part of the curriculum. A handful of Nisei, including Tad Yamada, became the first instructors. By mid-May of 1942, 45 students were celebrating their graduation in a restaurant in San Francisco's Chinatown. Within months, 35 of them shipped out to the Pacific, while 10 stayed on as instructors who would make the move to Minnesota.

Rasmussen's decision to move the language school to America's northern hinterlands has been attributed to the region's social climate. Minnesota "not only had room physically but also had room in the people's hearts," according to that state's newspapers. There was some reason to believe that Minnesota's heart was not quite so spacious, however: in November of 1943 the Regents of the University of Minnesota passed a resolution prohibiting the admission of Japanese American students during the course of the war.

Some former MISers claim that Rasmussen, a Northern European immigrant, felt connected to the people of Minnesota, many of whom were of Scandinavian heritage. And logistically, Camp Savage, as it was called—which encompassed 123 acres—was capable of quickly accommodating the physical needs of the school. Formerly used by the Civilian Conservation Corps, it had more recently housed indigent men; hence, a flower bed spelled out the ironic message, "Homeless Men's Camp." Rasmussen reportedly had the flower bed removed before the first Camp Savage class began with 15 instructors and 200 students, a majority recruited from concentration camps.

At the time, the exact role that MIS played in the war effort was classified information. Perplexed residents of St. Paul watched as the population of Japanese Americans rose from 10 families to dozens. When neighbors complained to the FBI that one of these families was entertaining Japanese soldiers, it turned out that the visitors were relatives and other Nisei soldiers assigned to the Military Intelligence Service. Rasmussen intervened and advised the family to put a service flag decal in their window to show that they had a relative serving in the U.S. Army.

Although most students and instructors found their time in Minnesota peaceful and harmonious, it was no utopia. Some native Minnesotans believed the Camp Savage language school to be a Japanese prisoner-of-war camp. Moreover, the commissioning of Nisei officers—especially in the school's early years—was uncommon. The highest-ranking officer at the school was the legendary John Aiso, a former attorney for the British Tobacco Company who had studied at Chuo University in Tokyo and worked for a brief time in Manchuria. A cum laude Brown graduate with a doctorate in jurisprudence from Harvard, Aiso was appointed academic director and subsequently elevated to the rank of major.

Many of the men at the MISLS, both students and teachers, were like George Aratani—Nisei in their mid-twenties, fluent in Japanese language, well educated, bicultural, who had spent some time in Japan. Although the government did perform intensive security checks on them, no questions of loyalty needed to be asked of MISers. These men were used to the grays of biculturalism, and each struggled internally with the contradictions of the war and their simultaneous love for America, the homeland that had imprisoned them, and Japan, the enemy country where they had once played baseball and strolled the Ginza.

———◆◆◆———

When George arrived in Camp Savage in 1944, the fourth class was in full swing. Savage was flat and spread out, with a few large trees shading the campus buildings. Lining a rectangular space were wooden barracks filled with uniformed students and officers, as well as civilian instructors dressed in suits and ties. Newly constructed buildings—classrooms, a theater, and a gym—had replaced the barns that had served as a makeshift campus the first year.

George was assigned quarters in a bachelor's barracks called "Camp Seven," down the road from Camp Savage, which had previously gained a reputation for its Saturday-night parties. One account in the book *Yankee Samurai* recalls that the bachelors would cover windows with newspaper, spread blankets on the floor, and break out forbidden whiskey, together with salami, cheese, potato chips, pickles, and canned goodies. "Singing, dancing and general carousing went on into the wee hours."

George, who was preparing for his upcoming marriage and still struggling with the paperwork involved with the Sumitomo lawsuit, was amused by such antics, but he stayed focused on his responsibilities. In the bachelor's barracks he was reunited with his old friend from Guadalupe, Tad Yamada, and he met such new friends as Paul Tekawa of San Francisco (who served as the school's technical director) and Hiroshi William Kasuga, known as Bill.

A thin man who wore metal-framed glasses, Bill had tried to join the all-Nisei 442nd Regimental Combat Unit from a concentration camp in Poston, Arizona, but he was rejected because of his slight build. He then contacted an old friend, Captain Rasmussen, who considered Bill a strong candidate for MIS instructor.

After his rejection by the armed services, Bill worried about being accepted. "How can I be an instructor?" he asked, after completing an examination in both Japanese and English.

"You know Japanese well enough. You can be a civilian instructor," Rasmussen said. "Military personnel have to be transferred every three years. We need civilian instructors to give the school some continuity."

"Heck, if I don't have to go to war, I'd rather be civilian," said Bill.

In spite of his outward enthusiasm, however, Bill felt somewhat conflicted. He was technically a Kibei-Nisei, a person who was born in the U.S. but raised in Japan. He knew that back in Japan he would be viewed as a *kokuzoku*, a traitor, for teaching Americans how to break Japanese military codes, yet he intentionally aligned himself with the American side of the conflict. He still had a sister in Japan, however, and while he couldn't help worrying about her safety, he had chosen his country—he felt he had to be loyal to America.

I'm gradually getting used to my work but I still
find it necessary to burn the mid-night oil. One thing that
I'm really happy over is that my
Valley Fever has practically left me—for good, I hope.
—George Aratani, in a letter to Ethel Allen, 28 May 1944

When George first arrived, some of his superiors eyed him with suspicion. "A Keio student," they thought. "Rich boy. Probably plays around quite a bit. We may have trouble with this one."

But George surprised them. Preparing for his classes as vigorously as he had studied for Nakamura-*sensei*'s tutorials back in Tokyo, George was exceedingly conscientious. He shared a desk in a long room where all the instructors sat, bent over their papers and surrounded by stacks of Japanese dictionaries and textbooks. One hundred instructors, crammed together in that faculty room, were constantly bumping elbows with one another.

Classes lasted seven hours a day, from 8 A.M. to 4:30 P.M., with an hour-and-a-half lunch break; at night there were two additional hours of study. Exams were held on Saturday mornings. The academic term was extended from a more typical six months to nine months. Rather than dividing students by abilities, the administration had established collegiate divisions, identified alphabetically.

Most of the students were of Japanese ancestry, but there were groups of European Americans as well. Many of the latter rose through the military ranks and became officers, fueling speculation that they were placed in the language school specifically to monitor the Nisei men's patriotism.

By the time George joined the MISLS teaching staff, the curriculum had fully evolved. The subjects taught included reading, writing, and speaking Japanese; translation, interpretation, and interrogation; captured-document analysis; Japanese geography and map reading; radio monitoring; and the social, political, economic, and cultural background of Japan.

Because military intelligence was the purpose of the training program, special attention was paid to *heigo* (Japanese military terms), as well as the different forms of Japanese writing: *kaisho*, the printed version of kanji (Chinese characters); *gyōsho*, hand-written Japanese; and *sōsho*, a shorthand rendering of *kanji* which was extremely difficult to read. All of these subjects were taught to aid the students in later decoding and reading intercepted messages out of the South Pacific jungles.

One report published in the *MISLS Album*, a publication of the Military Intelligence Service Language School, showed the results of their work:

> A captured map of the enemy infantry regiment was brought in by the Infantry boys on the 23rd of March. The map was brought into this section at 1700 the same day. Here was the primary opportunity to utilize the knowledge we acquired from the many months of study at MISLS. The language team worked feverishly to decode the vital message contained on the map. The initial interrogation was only the beginning of a multitude of "hot info" we were able to get.

With this goal—obtaining information—in mind, the instructors labored to sharpen the skills of their student soldiers. "My work is getting heavy again and is keeping me up late," George wrote to attorney Leo McMahon in July 24, 1944.

The academic session ended in August with a parade and commencement, which took place on a grassy plot next to a wooded square. The students were in full uniform—tan shirts and pants with service caps over their crew cuts. "Last four or five days were spent correcting exam papers and I found out that correcting and grading couple hundred papers is no cinch—and the terrific humid weather we're having didn't make things any easier," George wrote Butch Tamura and Miyokichi Matsuno, who were now completely resettled in Salt Lake City. "Now that one crisis is over, we're in the second one, namely, entrance examination for the new arrivals."

Around the same time, the instructors were informed that the entire school would be moving 25 miles nearer St. Paul to Fort Snelling, a much larger facility. "While here at Savage," the letter continued, "we instructors had a tough teaching schedule, but when we start in again at Snelling, what we had so far would seem like a picnic, no doubt. We'll be dragging our butts on the ground, that's a cinch. What I don't like about this place is the summer heat. I thought the humid heat in Tokyo was the worst of its kind, but this beats all. No fooling."

Since the start of the war, I have done the best I
humanly can to safeguard the interests of my business
associates and myself. It was very difficult
because of the anti-Japanese feeling and also because of
the legality phase, this condition will
exist for a long time yet so we must be on guard.
—George Aratani to Chester Otoi, 14 September 1944

Although George was focused on teaching, other matters, remnants from his life at Gila River, tugged at his attention. One was the Sumitomo bank lawsuit, the other the money owed to Chester Otoi for his half of the dehydration plant in Santa Maria. And of course there was his fiancée, Sakaye, back in the Poston camp.

After being shuttled from camp to camp, Chester Otoi had finally been reunited with his wife, Kimiko, in Gila River. By the end of September the camp had experienced an exodus of internees, most of them able-bodied Nisei men. Left behind were a number of older Issei men and women, as well a significant population of children under 18. The resulting physical segregation further widened the cultural and social gap between Issei and adult Nisei. Moreover, in comparison to the other 9 camps in the western region, Gila River was more isolated, both its physical location and in terms of the psychological distance it imposed. Although news from California did trickle into camp, the internees had little knowledge of the level of hostility directed towards Japanese on the West Coast.

With time on his hands and surrounded by elderly Issei, Chester thought about the sale of his stake in the dehydrating business, and the more he thought, the angrier he became. On September 5, 1944, he sent a letter to George at Camp Savage. The lengthy letter, in English and type-written, attempted "to put all of [his] cards upon the table without hiding."

Sent via registered mail, the letter was blistering. Invoking the name and reputation of George's father, Setsuo, to whom Otoi referred as a "brother," he accused George of "trying to grab my interest during my absence . . . instead of extending your possible effort on protecting and preserving your partner's interest which should be done to any persons and especially, during his suffering away from his home and bitter internment life."

Referring to a letter of gratitude written to Chester by Setsuo a month prior to his death, Otoi maintained, "You should give me at least some consideration in offering your purchase value on my share more than the net book value. I wish to end in a clean record with you as I did [with] your father."

The attacks on his integrity and the reference to his father pushed George's buttons. He quickly sent off a reply dated September 14, 1944, which addressed each of Otoi's issues. "Last of all, I want you to know that I've learned a good lesson from my now deceased father and that is, honesty. His spirit lives with me and if you think that I have committed dishonesty and as you wrote 'trying to grab my interest during my absence' was my intention, then you are gravely mistaken."

For George, business ethics had always been of foremost concern. He had given Otoi a note for half the worth of the chili pepper dehydrator, payable in annual installments starting in 1943. That outstanding debt nagged at George, but he still had to resolve the Sumitomo lawsuit before he could get access to any large amount of cash.

Otoi, on the other hand, had his own future to worry about. "We Japanese people are today on the road of unspeakable struggle and crying and worrying on the matter of how to protect and preserve their assets and properties," he responded to George on September 29, 1944. "They worked hard for many years of bitterness."

The only way Japanese Americans had been able to succeed before the war was through cooperation between the first and second generations, wrote Otoi. And now it was completely up to the Nisei to blaze the trail out of the camps toward a stable future. "I wish you will do not only your share but to lead others since you are one of [our] leading and outstanding citizens," Otoi challenged.

During this exchange of emotional letters between Gila River and Camp Savage, George also received bad news about the Sumitomo Bank lawsuit from Leo McMahon.

"The attorney for the Superintendent of Banks is putting up a terrific fight on this matter," wrote McMahon on September 23, 1944. The attachments on George's assets in that bank remained in place, and the trial in which George would have to defend himself against the government's charges was set for January 15, 1945. George still hoped that they could wait to resolve the matter until the war ended, but McMahon was adamant about the gravity of the suit. "You have been sued by the Superintendent of Banks as Conservator of the Sumitomo Bank demanding that you pay in cash now some $65,000.00," reiterated McMahon on October 11, 1944.

The Santa Barbara attorney warned that unless the suit was challenged, George could stand to lose his Lompoc land, his own interest in the dehydrator, his interest in Guadalupe Produce Company, as well as "any monies owing to you." The time deposits, worth approximately $130,000, would be sold "for little or nothing," leaving George with no reserves.

George was at a crossroads. Creditors and the government were pressing upon him, demanding money. His work at MISLS was taxing and time-consuming. He felt as if he had aged a decade since leaving Guadalupe two-and-a-half years ago.

"If you remember, at the time of my father's death, I was a student at college not knowing the first thing about business or the Sumitomo matter which is before me now," he admitted to McMahon on October 18, 1944. George felt inadequately prepared to make hard decisions on the serious financial matters before him. "Most of the business and also the banking matters were handled by my father's business associates and I had little knowledge of such affairs of which some were my personal things. It is embarrassing but there is nothing I can do about it now."

One thing was now definitely clear to him, however. "I must oppose the suit being brought before the court in January of 1945 by the Superintendent of Banks," he announced to McMahon.

In spite of the confusion regarding his money matters and his meager annual salary of $2,000, George also resolved to take another dramatic step in his life. "It's about time I got married," he wrote to McMahon in the same letter, "and therefore, in all probability, I will next month."

Back in Poston, Sakaye Inouye got her bags ready. She asked a seamstress in camp to sew her a white suit and matching pillbox hat; Sakaye told her exactly what she wanted, but she did not reveal what the outfit was for. The

Minneapolis wedding reception of George and Sakaye Aratani on November 23, 1944. From left to right: Michael "Shig" Yasutake, Kanaru and Yoshio Nagano, Sakaye Aratani, George Aratani, Masuko Aratani, and Reverend Francis Hayashi. (99.30.148)

whole engagement and wedding ceremony, in fact, were planned in secrecy. Many of the internees had heard of the Aratani family, and Sakaye didn't see the need to further feed the rumor mill. A day before she was to leave for Minnesota, she passed out 30 little handmade scrolls that read: "Mr. and Mrs. E. Inouye announce the engagement of their daughter Sakaye to Mr. George T. Aratani."

Her girlfriends were thrilled, while male suitors were disappointed. Also mourning the future nuptials was Sakaye's younger sister, Vickie, even as their mother tried to comfort her. Sakaye's father, meanwhile, took a break from tending a spectacular Japanese garden—complete with waterfall and bridge—within the confines of the concentration camp. Standing in front of his eldest daughter, with camp soil under his fingernails, he said little, but Sakaye could interpret the silence. Take care, my daughter, he was saying. Have a safe trip. I wish we could be there.

Masuko Aratani, delighted at the impending marriage, traveled from Gila River to Poston, where together she and her future daughter-in-law boarded a train heading north to Minnesota. Upon their arrival at a Minneapolis hotel, Sakaye and Masuko discovered that most of the wedding plans were already in place. With the help of Tad Yamada and Paul Tekawa, George had arranged for everything, including a luncheon, the church, and the minister.

The wedding was very simple. Because there were no Buddhist temples in the area, they were married in a Christian church, with a Nisei Methodist minister presiding over the ceremony. The MIS technical director, Paul Tekawa, an affable man with a broad face and heavy eyebrows, served as best man. No one from Sakaye's family was able to leave camp to attend the wedding. In fact, she knew only two of the guests: academic director John Aiso, who had been friendly with Sakaye's family before the war, and another MISer, Shig Yasutake. The only woman she knew was her mother-in-law.

Nevertheless, the ceremony and reception were blissful. The wedding took place on Thanksgiving Day, Thursday, November 23, 1944. Lobster was served for dinner, with a white wedding cake for dessert. George wrote that he was "the luckiest guy on earth."

<hr />

Work resumed the next Monday, so George and Sakaye undertook the difficult task of finding an appropriate apartment in town. Wartime housing was difficult to secure. Finally, responding to a newspaper advertisement, Sakaye found a two-bedroom downstairs duplex. It was dilapidated but completely furnished. The landlady had never seen Japanese Americans before, but fortunately she took a liking to the fresh-faced Sakaye.

Masuko, meanwhile, prepared to return to Gila River. The elderly Tamuras, Uchitaro and Hiye, had become her surrogate parents, and she wanted to be with them in camp. Before she left she purchased a fur coat for Sakaye to make sure that her daughter-in-law would stay warm during the cold winter months.

In preparation for her and George's first Christmas together, Sakaye bought a small tree that she placed on a table and decorated with miniature balls purchased at a grocery store. On Christmas Eve, however, Sakaye was overcome with intense abdominal pain, and George had to rush her to the local hospital. Diagnosed with acute appendicitis, she spent Christmas in a hospital bed.

Financial setbacks continued for the young couple. A few weeks into the new year, George's car broke down in the freezing cold of winter. In addition, the expense of living in town was greater than living in camp. With the bills piling up, George was obliged to ask for extra funds from attorney Leo McMahon. McMahon, who was awaiting payment of his legal fees, was reluctant to wire any money from George's trust fund.

Then, near the end of 1944 the Supreme Court ruled that the West Coast was no longer off-limits to Nisei. The War Relocation Authority was opening up offices in Seattle, San Francisco, and Los Angeles. Already George was longing to get back to California. But what about his commitment to the war effort at the language school?

Even after Masuko's departure the newlyweds did not find much time to be alone, because their extra bedroom was always open to friends who could not find a place to live. And almost every weekend, a group of single instructors—Bill Kasuga, Paul Tekawa, and Jimmy Kawata—came by for a home-cooked meal. By eating only chicken and fish during the week, married couples could save their rationed "meat points" in order to serve pot roast on the weekends.

Many of the married MIS instructors entertained the bachelors in their homes, which were more comfortable than the bachelors' accommodations; at Fort Snelling, located between the fertile banks of the Mississippi and Minnesota rivers, the housing for bachelors—six men living in each tar-paper hut—was less than comfortable.

In addition to hosting parties at his and Sakaye's apartment, George also spent some time with his friends on the local golf course at Fort Snelling. He had asked Ethel Allen to forward his golf clubs to him, including a new set of Bobby Jones irons, and he taught a group of 10 friends the finer points of the game. Now George was glad that Setsuo had insisted on his learning the game years ago.

Sakaye didn't seem to mind George's excursions. She was looking forward to a long-delayed honeymoon with her husband in the spring of 1945: the instructors and their soldier-students had learned that the school was closing for a week then.

Before the break, the bachelors came over for an evening at the Aratanis.

"What are you going to do next week?" Bill Kasuga asked George as they played cards after dinner.

"We're going on our honeymoon."

Sakaye looked at her guests with a smile of anticipation. "We're renting a cabin near a lake just a short distance from here," she said. If she was expecting expressions of joy, she was disappointed. The three men—Bill,

**Bachelors Jimmy Kawata (standing) and Paul Tekawa (kneeling)
join newlyweds George and Sakaye Aratani on
their honeymoon at lakefront cabins in Minnesota in 1944.** (99.30.51)

Paul Tekawa, and Jimmy Kawata—looked a bit crestfallen.

"Why don't you come with us?" she said, feeling sorry for them.

"Sure," George agreed. "Let's all go."

So George and Sakaye spent their honeymoon with the three bachelors. They rented three cabins near a lake, where the men fished. In photos Sakaye, the young smiling bride, is surrounded by four Nisei men holding fishing rods. She was well aware even in her early twenties that when she married George Aratani, their home and life would never be just theirs.

---

*With the battle conditions out in the Pacific as it is [sic],
we who are here at Fort Snelling are kept quite busy with
little time for relaxation.*
—George Aratani to Leo McMahon, 26 April 1945

Back in Salt Lake City, Butch Tamura worked days at a friend's dry cleaning business and at night took correspondence courses to learn the techniques of spot removal. His wife, Mary Tamura, was sticking two stars on her living room window.

"What's that for, Mom?" asked Allen, the oldest of her three sons, pointing to the stars.

"They're for your uncles at war," Mary answered. "One star for each of my brothers."

By the spring of 1945 the conflict in Europe was at its height. The 442nd/100th Regimental Combat Team and other all-Nisei military units had suffered thousands of casualties in skirmishes in Italy and France.

The weapons of the MIS graduates, on the other hand, were not hand grenades, bombs, or guns, but their minds and tongues. At times their lives were also at risk.

Santa Maria–born Tsuneo "Cappy" Harada, for example, was one of the MIS linguists. First assigned to Indooroopilly, New Guinea, Cappy studied muddy diaries and documents by the faint light of a gasoline lantern. At times he would have to scrape away a bit of blood, dirt, or stuck-on flesh to see the shape of a *kanji.*

After America's invasion of New Guinea, Cappy was sent with the Sixth Infantry Division to the Philippines aboard a U.S. aircraft carrier. A bomb from a kamikaze pilot hit the ship, killing and wounding many on board. Cappy and another MISer, Spady Koyama, suffered injuries. In fact, during the course of the conflict in the Pacific, Harada was wounded three times. Cappy knew that if he were ever captured he would be especially vulnerable to harsh treatment, because he was using his own heritage to defeat Japan.

The gravity of the war effort also weighed upon George. Although Leo McMahon wrote often about the Sumitomo lawsuit and the upcoming trial, George was now more concerned with his work at Fort Snelling. He led the committee in charge of purchasing war bonds, which raised amounts far in excess of their assigned quota. After the defeat of Germany in the spring of 1945, the Allies turned their attention to the Pacific theater. Linguists were needed more urgently than ever.

Even when his attorney requested that George obtain a special week-long leave in order to provide a deposition at the trial, Colonel Rasmussen interceded with a letter to McMahon: "To have Mr. Aratani away during this time would work an extreme hardship on the teaching staff and to that degree would make more difficult the prosecution of the war against Japan with our maximum effort."

George was apologetic that he could not adhere to his attorney's legal plans. "But as you will agree my work with the army comes first," George concluded in a letter on August 4, 1945.

Weeks prior to the exchange of letters between George and McMahon over the deposition, someone else in the Aratani family was also encountering legal problems. In Gila River, Masuko Aratani returned to her barracks, 57-10-B, after lunch in the mess hall. She found that she had received an official-looking letter.

"What is it?" asked Hiye Tamura in Japanese.

"I don't know," Masuko replied. Her knees felt a little weak. She sat on her bed, now covered with one of her bedspreads sent from storage in Guadalupe. "Something from the government."

Because she had studied English at one of the top women's universities in Japan, Masuko's English reading comprehension and writing were excellent. She quickly scanned the correspondence. It was signed by Herman R. Landon, chief of the Exclusion and Expulsion Section and district director of the Immigration and Naturalization Service in El Paso. Masuko's large eyes widened.

"It's a warrant for my arrest," she told Hiye. "I'm being deported."

Masuko Aratani had originally entered the United States nine years earlier on a sight-seeing visa. After marrying Setsuo, her status was changed to wife of an international trader. Because Setsuo was a major partner in All Star Trading, which imported fish meal and sake from Hiroshima, he was eligible for a special merchant immigration status under the Immigration Act of 1917. After his death, Masuko had been made president of All Star Trading, and so she also officially became an international trader. But that was all before the outbreak of war. Obviously, now there was no bilateral trade treaty with Japan.

The concentration camps, ironically, had forced Masuko into America's interior. Now the government wanted her and people like her out of the country. She quickly wrote a brief note to George and sent the notice to him in Minneapolis.

"What the heck goes?" George said to himself as he examined the warrant for his stepmother's arrest. He went straight to the office of John Aiso.

Even before the war, John Aiso was famous among Japanese Americans for his oratory skills. Every Nisei knew the story of how this Hollywood High School valedictorian and champion speaker had been prevented from representing his school in a national speech contest because of his Japanese ancestry. He had shown the administrators how shortsighted they were: he

Colonel Kai Rasmussen, head of the Military Intelligence Service Language School, recognizing the service of George Aratani as an MISLS language instructor, ca. 1946. (99.30.163)

not only graduated from Brown University with honors, but he also got his law degree from Harvard. In a matter of years he had become one of the more distinguished graduates of Hollywood High.

Now Major Aiso listened carefully to George. "Well," he finally said. "This is serious, because there's no treaty between Japan and the United States. Now your mother is in this country illegally."

"What can I do?" George asked. Ever since the evacuation, Masuko's health had been poor. She constantly worried about what was happening to her relatives back in Japan and if she would ever see them again.

"Listen, George, you're helping the war effort, so let's take this to Colonel Rasmussen," John advised. But Kai Rasmussen was known as a severe taskmaster who ran a tight ship. There was no telling how he would respond to George's request.

Rasmussen looked over the INS letter. "Oh, bullshit," he said. "What the hell. Don't worry about it. I'm gonna pick up the phone and call the War Department, all right? I'll squash this stuff."

Within a week George was called back to Rasmussen's office. "I got a reply," he said. "I was told that 'Mr. Aratani's stepmother will be okay as long as Mr. Aratani is involved in this military intelligence language school.'"

George expressed his gratitude and left the office. Once outside, the thought hit him: "Now, even if I wanted to, I can't leave the MIS."

◆ ◆ ◆

Masuko was relieved to hear that she could remain in America, although she did miss her family, especially her mother, long widowed, who lived with relatives in Hiroshima. As she walked through the Gila River camp, she was impressed by how much had changed there. Now practically every barracks had a garden outside its doors. Curtains hung over the cracked windowpanes. There was even a tofu factory in camp, and *shōyu* had become readily available thanks to shipments from the *Gripsholm*, a prisoner-of-war exchange ship. The camp had come to feel like home.

Even within her own barracks, she now had some familiar belongings around her, which had been sent from the Peralta house. She had laid a rug down on the wooden floor, and she had her own dishes for special Japanese meals. Ethel Allen had sent a package of photographs, so she could look at the black-and-white prints of Setsuo wearing his characteristic felt hat and warm smile.

She and Mary Tamura had traveled to California in April to check on the house in Guadalupe. It still looked quite neat and tidy. Surprisingly, Masuko hadn't felt like a stranger in the new Guadalupe, now predominantly populated with Mexican Americans and newcomers from such places as Oklahoma. *Atarimae* (of course), she was not expecting it to be exactly the same.

It had been 10 years since Masuko had walked down the gangway of the *Taiyo Maru* and onto the soil of San Francisco. She had been 27 years old then. She had never borne any children herself, but her stepson and friends made her feel as if she had a place here in America. She and George did not share their feelings with each other; they didn't have to. Both had suffered in their lives, and that connection, along with their shared love of Setsuo, tied them together.

Unfortunately, before the war ended, even more losses would come.

◆ ◆ ◆

The Ishikawas were passing Times Square when they felt some sort of electricity in the air. Crowds pressed into the streets and cheered. Something was going on.

When they reached home—an attic apartment in Scarsdale—they discovered that the war had suddenly ended. And they discovered the heavy cost of that victory: new types of bombs had been dropped on Hiroshima and Nagasaki. "You'd better not go out," their landlord warned, "for your safety's sake."

Upstairs in the privacy of their temporary sanctuary, Toshitaro and Komano Ishikawa bent their heads and began to weep. While others were celebrating in the streets, they were overcome by shame and grief. Their beloved Japan had lost the war.

In Minnesota, headlines of "PEACE" in block letters and "Tokyo Says: Japan Surrenders" were splashed across the front pages of newspapers like the *Minneapolis Star Journal-Tribune* and the *St. Paul Dispatch-Pioneer Press*. George stayed in the apartment with Sakaye, because classes had been canceled for the day. The students were forbidden to enter town "lest incidents occur."

As George read the newspaper accounts and listened to the radio, he couldn't help but think about the people he knew in Japan. What had happened to Grandma Aratani, the jovial woman who loved to play the Japanese card game of *hanafuda*? His old classmates? His former professors?

Down in Gila River concentration camp, Hiye Tamura spoke softly to Masuko. "I'm sure your mother and sister are all right," she said.

Masuko straightened out her bedspread. She couldn't eat dinner, but she couldn't sit still either. What was this bomb the Americans had dropped on her former home?

<hr />

Over time, news about family and friends trickled in. In most cases it came orally, by unofficial word of mouth. Most of the communications were via Nisei GIs in Japan who agreed to check on relatives in the war-torn cities of Hiroshima, Tokyo, and Nagasaki, as well as the island of Okinawa.

With friends from the MIS school now stationed in Japan, George had a line of communication. Grandma Aratani, he learned, was alive. So was his half sister, Sadako. His former mentor at Keio University, Koizumi-*sensei*, one of the most handsome men in Tokyo, had been badly burned in a fire caused by an incendiary bomb, half of his beautiful face ruined.

Two brothers of Bob Ishii, one of the "four musketeers" who had gone to school in Japan with George, had been forced to join the Japanese forces and had died in combat, while Bob's father, once a successful Guadalupe entrepreneur, was now penniless and homeless in China.

Letters finally made their way to the U.S. from Japan. George's half brother, Takao, a Japanese army officer, had been killed at sea, somewhere between Japan and the Philippines.

And finally, news came about Masuko's family. Her mother survived the atomic blast, but the bodies of Masuko's older sister Yoshie and her two daughters were never recovered from the charred rubble.

The entire city of Hiroshima was filled with grieving survivors. There was no formal funeral for Yoshie and her children, but a tombstone for them was placed at the family gravesite in the mountains of Hiroshima.

The past three years had been arduous for every soldier and civilian on the front lines. While the media on both shores had attempted to portray the enemy as barbaric and subhuman, George and the others knew better. The victims in Japan, like the men, women, and children in other countries, had experienced joy, sorrow, and fear in their lives. Politics and military machinations aside, the Issei especially felt a natural affinity towards Japan. However, there was no question that the U.S. was their families' new home.

With the end of the war, the Issei and Nisei attempted to sort out conflicting feelings. How could they function in this land that had thrown them off their farms and out of their houses? How could they rebuild, or would they even be able to rebuild? For some, the bitterness burned so intensely that they vowed never to trust the government again. Others renounced all connections to things Japanese: if they had been imprisoned because of their Japanese heritage, then they would attempt to obliterate any distinguishing signs of their ethnic culture.

George, on the other hand, blocked any feelings of hostility or pain. This was not the time for emotion, he thought. It was time to think and to act.

8

Gathering the
Home Team

Guadalupe is not the same place we left it.
—Butch Tamura, in a letter to
George Aratani, 29 December 1945

For many of the evacuees, the end of the war did not automatically mean returning home. Masuko Aratani, for instance, remained in the concentration camp barracks until late fall of 1945. "Home" had little meaning to her anymore. "Home" was not defeated Japan, but neither was a Spanish-style home near fields replete with bright red chili peppers and crisp heads of lettuce. Now that the war was over, where was home?

For the former Guadalupeans, their homes had either been taken over or ransacked, or sometimes literally moved: without George's knowledge, a building on his property had been hauled to another location. "This will give you a good idea how much I am informed on things around Guadalupe," George wrote to a Nisei friend from Fort Snelling.

During the three years of the Pacific war, the Santa Maria Valley that George once knew had changed dramatically. The Santa Maria Chamber of Commerce, to which Setsuo Aratani and Chuhei "Charles" Ishii had once belonged before the war, sent a petition in 1943 to congressional representatives asking that Japanese American evacuees not be allowed to return to their farmlands.

Newlyweds Sakaye and George Aratani stand in front of their first home, an apartment in Minneapolis, Minnesota, ca. 1946. (99.30.50)

Not everyone was in agreement. A local minister, the Reverend Aaron Allen Heist of the First Methodist Church, challenged the resolution in a bulletin issued to his church members: "We deplore the conditions that took them out of our communities and we look for as speedy a restoration as possible of their full rights as American citizens."

Yet Lieutenant General John L. DeWitt, head of the Western Defense Command, cast suspicion on the Japanese of Santa Barbara County, who, he claimed in January of 1944, had purposely set out to undermine national security. "Throughout the Santa Maria Valley in that county, including the cities of Santa Maria and Guadalupe, every utility, airfield, bridge, telephone and powerline or other facility of importance was flanked by Japanese. They even surrounded the oil fields in this area," he stated. DeWitt maintained that after the bombing of Pearl Harbor and before the evacuation, every ship leaving a West Coast port was attacked by enemy submarine; however, he claimed that after the removal of Japanese Americans from the West Coast, attacks were reduced and suspicious radio signals virtually eliminated.

Harry Miyake, the Hawai'i-born spokesman of the Santa Maria Japanese American Citizens League (JACL) and chairman of the Butte Community Council, did not allow these comments to go unchallenged. In a retort published in the *Gila News-Courier*, he explained that the Japanese residents had preceded the utilities, airfields, and bridges. In fact, they were the pioneers who had established much of that infrastructure. "The farm project was there when those so-called oil fields were discovered," Miyake pointed out.

As if walking in a thick fog, the former Santa Maria Valley farmers and ranch owners cautiously took their first steps toward the future. The Tomookas at first stayed close to the Gila River concentration camp and started a farm near Phoenix. The Minamis, another of the Valley's former Big Three, farmed onions, sugar beets, tomatoes, and lettuce near Trinidad, Colorado, before moving their agricultural operation to New Mexico.

One of the Minamis, Yataro, spent a week in Guadalupe and Santa Maria searching for land to lease, to no avail. Issei Matsuura, the Buddhist minister, and his wife, Shinobu, applied for a permit to return to Guadalupe, but they were initially refused permission on the grounds that racial prejudice was still strong in the area. Matsuura reapplied, stating, "As a minister, I am bound to return. I can endure the hostile winds of prejudice." Eventually the couple were given the okay to come back, whereupon they opened up the temple and hall to create a makeshift hostel for returnees.

Butch and Mary Tamura traveled from their wartime home in Salt Lake City to assess their options back in California. What they found was a Guadalupe that felt "foreign, with the people so different," Butch wrote to George on December 29, 1945. The town was filled with so-called "Okies" who seemed, at first glance, to be *kato*, or coarse and rough.

The Tamuras drove to Peralta Street to check on George's properties. The grounds around the Spanish-style house were overgrown: "The front yard and garden seem [to have suffered] very much lack of care," wrote Butch. "Mary went inside just to see, and found the place unoccupied and smelly. It would be worthwhile to have that place cleaned and aired and also have the garden taken care of . . . otherwise deterioration will set in." On the other hand, George's other house two doors down looked neat and tidy. "Aguilar's brother wants to buy it if you wish to sell," Butch informed him.

Guadalupe Boulevard, the main drag, was no longer bustling with Issei and Hawaiian-born bachelors. The former Chevrolet dealer in Guadalupe was having trouble getting his business back. The former president of the Santa Maria JACL had taken over what had been the Tsujiuchi Fish Market, which vandals had damaged during the war.

The minister's wife, Shinobu Matsuura, was struggling to prepare meals for close to a hundred people living at the temple and youth hall. Some shopkeepers on Guadalupe Boulevard refused to do business with the Japanese, and they turned their backs on the hostel workers seeking to buy food. One night someone even shot a gun into a room where the Japanese Americans slept.

George had already heard such stories. Through the efforts of dependable Ethel Allen, he made arrangements for friends to move into his houses on Peralta Street. "Many of the people who have been forced to leave the relocation centers are having a difficult time resettling due to lack of living quarters," George wrote to Leo McMahon on November 3, 1945. "I have been informed that many of them are living under bridges and in tents, conditions which are much worse than in the centers. Thus I am helping some of them the best way I know."

There was even more hostility in nearby Santa Maria and San Luis Obispo, the community north of Guadalupe. Santa Maria officials didn't want anything to do with the return of Japanese Americans, and they went so far as to refuse a meeting with the War Relocation Authority (WRA). Reactionary groups attempted to plant seeds of hatred at the same high school that had recognized George and Masato Inouye as outstanding students: youths in the Future Farmers of America (FFA) were told, "We may not be able to keep them out of California, but you boys can keep them out of the FFA." Pins depicting a coiled snake with a Japanese face, along with a pledge not to "talk to, patronize, associate, or fraternize with any Japanese," were distributed among the FFA members. To the students' credit, all but one had discarded the pins by the end of the week.

The San Luis Obispo County sheriff's department was widely known in official circles as the source of "the greatest conglomeration of Nippomaniacs." One afternoon two officials from the War Relocation Authority visited with a sheriff's deputy who emotionally declared, "I have done business with the Japs for years. And they are all disloyal. They all have a double citizenship. You can't trust any of them!"

Facing such hostile attitudes, many Japanese Americans looked towards resettling in urban areas such as Los Angeles. Even there, finding shelter was still a challenge. "The city is really congested and the housing is critical," Butch wrote. "The hostels and living quarters given to the evacuees are somewhat like the camps but the conditions make it worse than camp because they have to pay for everything on their limited reserves."

News trickled in about other former employees of Guadalupe Produce. The Lompoc ranch manager and one of the principals of Vegetable Farms were running residential hotels in Little Tokyo. Ben Kodama, the Issei general manager of Guadalupe Produce, had started a wholesale packing business with his son in Denver. Naoichi Ikeda, who had served as company president after Setsuo died, had relocated first to San Jose and then to Palo Alto, where he started a chicken farm. "Mr. Ikeda seemed quite aged," commented Butch.

Before the war, more than 40 percent of Japanese Americans were involved in agriculture. Now, because only 25 percent of farmers actually owned land, most would either have to turn to other occupations in the cities, or start from the bottom again as migrant farm workers.

Ken Kitasako, the former general manager of Santa Maria Produce who had married Butch's sister, also moved back to his hometown of Palo Alto. For two years the Stanford-educated man worked at his father's former profession: gardening.

George, meanwhile, remained with the Military Intelligence Service Language School in Fort Snelling. In November of 1945 Masuko had moved into their second bedroom after leaving Gila River concentration camp. "As there is no one in Japan to look after her, I want to keep her here, and also . . . she is not too healthy," explained George in a letter to Ethel Allen.

Peace in the Pacific hadn't slowed the demand for Japanese linguists; in fact, the need for their services became even greater. General Douglas MacArthur's Supreme Commander of Allied Powers (SCAP) operation needed bilingual men and women to enforce America's occupational policies, which meant altering the school's curriculum to meet these new goals. Instead of translating handbooks on military tactics, soldiers were required to learn conversational Japanese and take courses on "civil affairs terms" and Japanese government and administration.

Those trained at the language school also served as translators and interrogators at the war crimes trials in Tokyo. Other MIS graduates gathered statistics for the Atomic Bomb Survey or screened letters and newspapers for the U.S. Civil Affairs branch. During this peak period of activity, Fort Snelling accommodated 160 instructors and 3,000 students. "Here at Fort Snelling things are still buzzing and keeps [*sic*] me on the go right along," George wrote to a Guadalupean friend in November of 1945.

George, however, knew that he would not remain at the school as a civilian instructor forever. He knew he needed to be making plans for the future, but the question was what those plans would be.

Restarting a farming operation seemed a difficult task, judging from the experiences other former Guadalupe ranchers were having. Ironically, the enterprising Chester Otoi, who had been so angry about his earlier losses, was one of the first to reestablish himself in California with a wholesale produce market, the C. M. Otoy Company in Fresno. But none of the former Big Three felt that they would be able to achieve the same level of success in agriculture that they had before the war.

On top of everything else, George's financial and legal outlook remained dim. Even after the war ended, the attorneys for the Superintendent of Banks were unrelenting in their demands for payment of the $60,000 in outstanding loans. George's property and his personal bank account were still attached, a situation that would continue until the middle of 1947.

And though he filed a claim to recover his Sumitomo yen deposits, he had no idea when that money might be made available.

Meanwhile, the Minnesota winters remained brutally cold—George didn't know if he could tolerate another year of scraping a layer of ice from his windshield or trudging through the streets, knee-deep in gray snow. "The weather dropped to five below today," he wrote to Ethel Allen that winter. "I wish I hadn't come way up here."

On December 23 he wrote to Ethel again, saying that he and Sakaye would no doubt be having a "white Christmas but to a native Californian like myself, I'll take a sunny Christmas. . . . The winter up here is much colder this year than last, and it seems in the other states around here many people are dying from cold."

In spite of George's winter blues, he still had much to look forward to: Sakaye was pregnant. Their first child was due in January.

I'm finally a "papa" and it's grand to be one.
—George Aratani, in a letter to H. E. Kaesemeyer, 24 January 1946

Shortly after they were married, George and Sakaye talked about starting a family. "You have one sister; I have no brother or sister. So let's start with half a dozen," George said.

Sakaye readily agreed. Her family was small, but her childhood home had always been filled with people, including her two uncles, grandparents, customers, and friends. She loved the hubbub of people—having six children would be wonderful.

Their first baby came on January 22, 1946, in Minneapolis. Husbands were not generally allowed to stay with their wives during delivery in those days, and Sakaye didn't want George to see her in pain. After a long labor, she delivered a seven-pound girl, Donna Naomi Aratani. The nurse called George, who raced in his car over the icy roads to see his wife and meet his new daughter for the first time.

As was customary in the 1940s, Sakaye was hospitalized for a few days, and because of his work at the language school George couldn't always make it to the hospital during visiting hours. So he left letters for Sakaye with the nurses.

"Yea, and you look very pretty today," George wrote. "I don't have to be there in person to know that."

**Letter written by George Aratani to his wife Sakaye
in January 1946.** (43.1998.1)

Writing in large script, he unabashedly expressed his enthusiasm for his wife and child. "I'm very proud of you and the baby—and when you add them up, you have a mighty happy man in me," he wrote.

Back in the two-bedroom apartment, George and Masuko prepared a corner for the baby. "These past days at home were pretty sad and your coming home will be like lighting a dark room. Everything is all set for your homecoming," George wrote the day before Sakaye and Donna were released from the hospital.

Once they were home, the apartment filled with visitors. Within weeks Sakaye's mother had come to help. Sakaye's family had relocated to the

**Donna Naomi and Linda Yoshiko, born in 1946 and 1947,
complete the Aratani family portrait.** (99.30.82)

resort area of Delavan Lake, Wisconsin, after leaving Poston concentration camp in Arizona. Sakaye's father, a landscape man, tended the grounds at the resort, which had hired many Japanese Americans as cooks, pastry chefs, and housekeepers.

Hearing stories of Donna Naomi from her mother, Sakaye's little sister Vickie was anxious to see the new baby. In early spring she traveled by a bus and train by herself to come to Minnesota to see her newborn niece. She was captivated by Donna, from her tiny fingers to the dark spot on her back, typical of Asian babies.

Having her mother and sister with her was a bright spot for Sakaye on the bleak winter landscape. That was at least one good thing about Minnesota, George decided: Sakaye's family was nearby.

Like grains of sand shifting across the dunes of Guadalupe, during 1946 Japanese Americans constantly resettled in one town after another. Taking a first step closer to California, Toshitaro Ishikawa, the former All Star Trading head, and his family moved from their New York attic to Chicago.

Chicago was a popular destination for evacuees. At the beginning of 1946 more than 20,000—and perhaps as many as 30,000—Japanese Americans had resettled in the Windy City. The Quaker organization American Friends Service Committee (AFSC) had set up special hostels there, and the War Relocation Authority had an office in the city to provide job placement services. During the last months of the war, defense plants were more than willing to hire Nisei men; many times Japanese Americans found themselves working in Chicago's manufacturing plants alongside African Americans and European Americans. Mini-Japantowns, full of ethnic grocery stores and churches, sprouted in the Near North Side and on the South Side.

With the assistance of friends, the Ishikawas found an apartment in Chicago. Toshitaro, unfortunately, was still experiencing the lingering effects of valley fever, which made work impossible for a while even though he had many connections with trading companies in Chicago. One of these contacts was Seiichiro Shigeyoshi "Shig" Kariya. The son of a prominent Los Angeles trader, he had started a department store chain, the Saji-Kariya Company, with his brother-in-law. Their imported goods included chinaware from Nagoya, where the headquarters of the renowned Noritake Company were located.

Shig's father died in 1921, but his son inherited the family's business acumen, sharpening his own trading skills in Nagoya and the Pacific Northwest. Like George, Shig had been interned at Gila River with his widowed mother. The two men, surprisingly, had never crossed paths there, though Shig had been active in camp leadership as the head of Block 10.

Before the war ended he and his mother moved to Chicago, where he worked as a machine operator for Donnelly Printing, which at that time published *LIFE* magazine. Shig, however, had aspirations to work for a large New York–based trading company—more specifically, he wanted to get back into international trade, especially with Japan.

In Chicago, Toshitaro observed that Shig very much reminded him of George. The two young men were both in their early thirties, were only children, and had strong ties to Japan. Both could speak and write Japanese and were hard-working. Both had had strong male role models in their lives. Their fathers, exceedingly successful businessmen, had both died early, thereby intensifying the sons' desire to continue the family legacy of success.

Wouldn't these two make a powerful team? thought Toshitaro. Starting something new from the ashes of war would be risky; Toshitaro, with his credentials and contacts, would easily be able to get a secure job with a large company once trade was resumed with Japan. Yet something—perhaps the spirit of Setsuo Aratani—tugged at him. He knew that George had little business experience, but he sensed a potential in him which, once realized, might rival even Setsuo Aratani's empire. Maybe I can be part of realizing this dream, thought Toshitaro. He wasn't sure how, but he felt that it would somehow be possible.

⸻ ✦ ⸻

In the summer of 1946, the MISers found themselves released at last from their exile in Minnesota. "We're finally pulling out of this cold country," George wrote to a friend in Guadalupe. "The War Department has announced that this school will move to Presidio, Monterey."

George was ecstatic. Monterey, located alongside a picturesque bay surrounded by windblown trees, was only a two-hour drive from Guadalupe. Although he still wasn't sure what he would do after leaving the language school, he had been thinking about starting a business either in San Francisco or Los Angeles. Moving to Monterey would bring him closer to his goal.

The Aratanis—George, Sakaye, six-month-old Donna, and Masuko—piled into their car with their luggage and drove to the West Coast in June. They made their new home in a two-story fourplex within expansive Fort Ord. Now that they lived near the ocean, Sakaye and Masuko could again buy fresh seafood at Fisherman's Wharf, while George and his friends went crabbing in the bay.

The intense teaching schedule at the military school did not abate. "Because many of the enlisted instructors have been discharged, the civilians have a very heavy schedule for the current academic period," wrote George in July of 1946.

Once in Monterey, George began to see the resolution of his financial problems. A settlement with the Superintendent of Banks was being negotiated, but at a heavy price: George finally agreed to pay $60,000 in three installments over the course of a year. He would get the money from California Vegetable Growers, the trust set up to operate the Big Three farms at the beginning of the war. Through these payments on outstanding notes, George was also able to finally reimburse Chester Otoi for his share of the dehydrator. The siege of lawsuits seemed to be ending at last. George's mind was now free to consider new ideas and weigh new options.

George's friend Tad Yamada, ca. 1945. Tad served as an interpreter in the Army after World War II. (99.30.55)

It was at this point that he heard from his former All Star Trading associate, Toshitaro Ishikawa. Writing from Chicago on December 1, 1946, Toshitaro, in his elegant Japanese penmanship, subtly inquired about opportunities in Los Angeles.

"As you wrote in your letter," George responded a week later with a mixture of caution and encouragement, "the job and the housing situation are none too promising in Los Angeles, but on the other hand, one is apt to find something good if you're on the spot and hunt around."

George promised that he would look for "any good prospects" in Los Angeles during the Christmas holidays. "If I was in a position to start a business, I would have done so long ago and maybe this housing and job problem would have never existed as far as you're concerned. While on the subject of business, my Sumitomo Bank lawsuit may be settled some time in January and if so I may resign from my present job and do something more constructive towards my future well-being."

George hinted to Toshitaro that "something more constructive" might be "starting trade [which] has been on my mind now for a long time now."

In fact, the possibilities of international trade had been the subject of many late-night discussions in Minnesota with his Guadalupean friend Tad Yamada, also a civilian instructor at the MIS. When the language school had moved from Minnesota to Monterey, however, Tad had enlisted in the Army at the rank of sergeant. He was assigned to the American Translation Interpreting Service (ATIS) in Japan, where a number of Nisei and a contingent of Japanese staff members translated Japanese documents.

Before he left to go overseas, Tad and George discussed the future over drinks. "Geez, George, after the war, we've got to get together and do something," said Tad.

George agreed. "I'm thinking of reactivating All Star Trading."

Tad's eyes brightened. "Since I'm going to be stationed in Japan, you can come over and stay with us in our quarters and see what you can find."

In the Japanese capital and in the other large cities of Japan
there are vast stretches of open prairie; nothing
stands between the onlooker and the horizon but some jerry-
built shelters made of rusty corrugated iron,
the slender brick stacks that are all that remain of the public
baths, and some forlorn hulks that were once
banks or warehouses.
—John Kenneth Galbraith, "Japan's Road Back," *Fortune*, March 1946

What Tad and other Nisei GIs found were cities left in shambles. George still remembered the serene suburban home in which he had studied Japanese with Nakamura-*sensei*, but the reality was now quite different.

Beggars in rags could be found on many street corners. Factories, noisy with twirling spindles of silk before the war, were quiet and idle. City people swarmed in droves to the countryside, where they searched the dirt for sweet potatoes or any morsel of food that could sustain their families. The Keio University campus had been heavily damaged; only the library and the small Free Speech Auditorium were left standing. When classes resumed, they were held at a neighboring high school.

In the atomic aftermath of Hiroshima and Nagasaki, orphans warmed themselves at open fires in the streets. *Hiropon* (heroin) was rampant. *Panchan* (child prostitutes) sold their bodies for a few yen. Black marketeers flourished. A month after Japan's official surrender, rice sold for 47 times the wartime price; vegetable prices were up nearly tenfold; sugar, soy sauce, and salt were 82 times higher.

Under General Douglas MacArthur, SCAP initially decided to take a hands-off position concerning the reconstruction of the occupied nation. "The plight of Japan is the direct outcome of its own behavior, and the Allies will not undertake the burden of repairing the damage," the U.S. Post-Surrender Policy for Japan stated.

Essentially, Japan would "be permitted eventually to resume normal trade relations with the rest of the world," but raw materials or other goods purchased abroad and exports would be controlled. For months private trade was tightly restricted; in fact, it was "impossible for American firms to correspond with Japanese companies," by order of the U.S. Department of Commerce.

Finally, under the jurisdiction of SCAP, in December of 1945 the Japanese Board of Trade was established to oversee purchases of Japanese exports and sales of imports to Japan. Agencies were set up in a number of countries to handle the sale of restricted Japanese imports.

But SCAP found itself in a Catch-22 situation: a certain faction of the American public wanted to levy heavy reparations to punish Japan. At the same time, however, they didn't necessarily want to foot the bill for supporting an impoverished satellite nation.

Additionally, a perceived political threat from Russia caused lawmakers to be wary of alienating the Japanese citizenry. "An economic policy based on revenge, for instance, would almost certainly ensure failure of U.S. political policy," wrote Colonel R. C. Kramer, a businessman who served on General MacArthur's staff. He warned that "a starving people is not politically tranquil."

General MacArthur argued this point even more strenuously before the Appropriations Committee of the U.S. House of Representatives. In support of continued food shipments to Japan, he said, "To cut off Japan's relief supplies in this situation would cause starvation to countless Japanese—and starvation breeds mass unrest, disorder and violence. Give me bread or give me bullets."

These sentiments were apparent in the careful dismantling of the *zaibatsu*. The *zaibatsu*, comprising the most influential industrial families in Japan, controlled 75 percent of the country's commerce, banking, raw materials, and transportation businesses. The *zaibatsu*, which included the Big Four—Mitsubishi, Mitsui, Sumitomo, and Yasuda—had launched Japan's rise from a quasi-feudal state to a modern military power.

The *zaibatsu* owned trading companies, manufacturing plants, and financial institutions; it was Sumitomo's Los Angeles branch where Setsuo Aratani had borrowed money and made yen deposits. After the Manchurian Incident of 1931, Japan's banking system became "militarized" under strict governmental regulations. Plants that once made such consumer merchandise as dishes, shoes, and *tatami* mats were converted to produce military weapons.

While SCAP intended to decentralize the *zaibatsu*, it did not completely eliminate them. A month after Japan's surrender, Yasuda was the first *zaibatsu* to present a blueprint for its voluntary dissolution. Purges of business leaders followed—30,000 executives would be removed from their positions, and 250,000 barred from high economic positions.

American officials like Colonel Harry I. T. Cresswell, chief of Counter-Intelligence, expressed their alarm over such actions. They believed that, in light of tension between the U.S. and Russia, "Japanese industrialists would be our best friends."

The Deconcentration Review Board (DRB), an American panel responsible for screening the reorganization of firms, later concluded that "it is inadvisable to break up Yasuda, Mitsui, Mitsubishi, Sanwa, Sumitomo," as it would undermine "public confidence."

Instead, the answer to Japan's economic problems was simple, according to Colonel Kramer: "Japan must export services and manufactured goods; it has little else."

<hr />

During his two-week vacation from the language school in December of 1946, George visited a variety of small makeshift companies in downtown Los Angeles and San Francisco. "I discovered that every other guy I met is contemplating getting into trading with Japan and they are all working hard, very hard, to make the necessary contact to lay the groundwork for future operation," he wrote to a friend in Japan. "The one who works the fastest and accomplishes the most will no doubt cash in."

While many of these businessmen were hopeful, hardworking Nisei and Issei with direct ties to Japan, others were stationed overseas as part of the Occupational Forces. They might not even speak Japanese, but they had the advantage of daily access to Japanese companies. George, on the other hand, had to rely on his MIS friends and the Japanese postal service, which was in dire shape—a letter might take weeks to arrive at its destination in Japan. Long-distance telephone service was also out of the question. Somehow George needed to make a Japan connection, and fast.

He wrote to one MIS friend who had returned to Tokyo. "I've been doing some research on my own—checking on items most needed here in the States," he wrote. For the Japanese American evacuees who had suffered through years of bland army-style meals in mess halls, the answer was obvious: *Nihonshoku*, Japanese food. They craved the brown flakes of *katsuobushi* (dried bonito) on top of cold steamed spinach; *konbu* (flat strips of seaweed) to punctuate their miso soup and cucumber vinegar salad; Asakusa *nori* (dried paperlike seaweed), wrapped around rice balls. Also in demand were *takenoko* (bamboo shoots), shiitake (dried mushroom), *umeboshi* (red pickled plum), *rakkyō* (pickled baby onion), and *unagi* (eel).

"Japanese people who are practically all settled now [in the United States] and engaged in some work and living normal lives are starving for these savory Japanese foodstuffs," wrote George. He also wanted his Tokyo business connection to compile a list of goods, "big or small," needed in postwar Japan. "It is my hunch that this exporting of goods to Japan will be nothing to sneeze at," George predicted.

Nothing initially came of this inquiry, mostly likely because consumers in Japan were themselves starving—literally—for the very same foodstuffs. Undeterred, George continued to write letters on his manual typewriter in his duplex in Ord Village, while Toshitaro Ishikawa guided his fountain pen over rice paper stationery in his tiny Chicago apartment. Together, though separated by thousands of miles, they investigated leads with soldiers, friends, and bureaucrats.

Among those who responded to George's letters was a distant relative who was working at Toki Electric Industrial Company, which produced lightbulbs. His assessment of George's prospects was not encouraging. "As you may know well, the export trade of Japan is at present under strict control by SCAP Headquarters, and in the case of U.S.A., the import goods from Japan are handled exclusively by the U.S. Commercial Company," he cautioned.

The War Department continued to be responsible for procuring Japanese goods and shipping them, while a government-funded public corporation, United States Commercial Company (USCC), took charge of the "disposal in the United States of Japanese products" through domestic import companies. American exports, on the other hand, were also being handled by the War Department; these were limited to foodstuffs and "other commodities required for the maintenance of minimum subsistence levels among the Japanese people."

Under SCAP's strict regulations, private entrepreneurs like George could write or send telegrams to potential business partners in Japan, but communications concerning "contractual obligations" were forbidden. In other words, George could inquire about available products, but he could not directly forge a deal. Instead, a description of the proposed transaction—specifications of the product, Japanese producer, prices—had to be submitted to the USCC for approval.

Furthermore, as of the spring of 1946 Japan was still closed to foreign traders because of the shortage of appropriate housing, transportation, and food for them. General MacArthur's SCAP had taken over as their head-quarters all the premier hotels left standing. Japanese entrepreneurs could not leave the country, and foreign assets were "mobilized" for payment of reparations and restitution claims. As a result of these obstacles, face-to-face negotiations were impossible for private businessmen like George.

Further complicating the progress of trade after the war was the lack of a standard foreign-exchange rate. In Japan's faltering economy, different products were assigned different exchange rates, according to their demand overseas. It was a complex and unwieldy system. Textiles, Japan's prime product, were assigned a less favorable rate of exchange than less popular exports, some of which sold at 600 or 800 yen to a dollar.

In spite of these obstacles, George and Toshitaro worked furiously toward finding an opening in defeated Japan. Toshitaro contacted his former employer, Kokusai Suisan Kaisha, a company that had at one time exported seafood to America. He also asked his brother-in-law, Kazusada Kanda, about trade prospects; like George's relative, Kanda's response was a "bit on the pessimistic side."

"I suppose most traders in Japan today cannot help feeling that way judging from the present situation in that country," George wrote to Toshitaro. George was in agreement with other advocates of free trade: only by strengthening Japan's economy could the U.S. "scratch Japan off as her ward and thus save millions of dollars of U.S. taxpayers' money." "Furthermore," George wrote, "if U.S. military forces can be sent home and let Japan run her affairs as she sees fit and engage in free trade, not only will U.S. save money but she will gain by doing business with Japan."

Sharing the views of other American free-market capitalists, George believed that the U.S. government should exercise more aggressiveness in hammering out an acceptable peace treaty. "Russia seems to be putting the monkey-wrench in the machinery," George complained. In the end, however, he was convinced that America would prevail. "I feel safe to say that the resumption of trade with Japan is just around the corner."

As 1947 began, George and Toshitaro approached the new year with optimism. Their attitudes may have been fueled by naiveté, a lack of other viable options, or just plain guts. How could they compete with hundreds of start-up companies, not to mention men who had been in the inner circle of business and industry for generations?

Toshitaro Ishikawa smoothed out his slacks and readjusted his tie. He pressed down the sides of his thinning hair. Born in 1900, he would turn 47 this year. Unlike many men his age, who were securely entrenched in their careers, he was helping his "principal," George Aratani, start a new business.

Toshitaro had written a letter to C. G. Sellers, a representative of the Universal Foreign Service Company, custom brokers and foreign-freight forwarders in Los Angeles. The Universal Foreign Service Company was started by self-made millionaire Kay Sugahara—called the "Nisei Onassis of America"—who was the first Nisei customs broker in the mainland United States. Orphaned at 13, Sugahara would later make his fortune as a shipping magnate. During the war, he joined the Office of Strategic Services (OSS) and served in India.

As the manager of All Star Trading, Toshitaro had worked with Universal Foreign Service before the war, importing sake from Hiroshima. Now Toshitaro traveled from Chicago to Los Angeles, where the All Star Trading branch had once been located on East First Street.

Little Tokyo had changed drastically. Blues jazz clubs had replaced Japanese eateries. The once-majestic Nishi Hongwanji Temple on the corner of Central and First streets was now being used as temporary housing instead of primarily as a place of worship. *The Rafu Shimpo* bilingual newspaper had recently reopened with a skeleton crew, and readers picked up issues mainly to peruse the classified ads in search of jobs and apartments.

Compared to its heyday before the war, Main Street looked shabby. Toshitaro walked down to Fourth Street and stopped at the building whose sign read "Universal Foreign Service Co." He tried the door and turned the knob. Locked. He knocked—still no response. He checked his watch; it was ten o'clock in the morning.

Toshitaro returned two more times that day, to no avail. It was difficult to contact anyone with knowledge about restarting a trade business. Unable to stay any longer, Toshitaro returned to Chicago. There, at his apartment he found a letter from C. G. Sellers waiting for him. "Before the outbreak of war, your shipments consisted of Japanese sake and fertilizers," wrote Sellers. "We do not see any hope for the immediate future in the importation of these products." This negative response was certainly bad news, but George and Toshitaro were realistic about the hurdles they needed to overcome.

---

*Now, we on this side already have an
importing and exporting company which was engaged
in trading with Japan prior to the outbreak of war;
therefore, we on this side are ready for action.*
—**George Aratani, in a letter from Monterey,
California, 7 January 1947**

While many hoped to make their fortune from trade with Japan, in reality, progress was slow. In 1947 Japan's annual export trade was less than 10 percent of its level in the 1930s. Sixty percent of its postwar exports, mostly textiles, went to Asian markets. Production lagged; "two-thirds of all productive capacity is idle and deteriorating, research and development are forgotten, most businesses are bankrupt," reported *Fortune.*

Market demands had changed as well. While SCAP pushed the sale of raw silk—one of Japan's top prewar exports—American women were buying stockings made of a new tougher material called nylon. The Department of Commerce, in a press release issued on March 1, 1946, optimistically announced the availability of small stockpiles of antimony, tin, and rubber, as well as tea and art. It would take more than "small stockpiles," however, to jump-start Japan's stagnant economy.

To further complicate matters, certain American industries hoped that Japan, a fierce trade competitor, would never recover. The *New York Herald Tribune* quoted American textile manufacturers as stating, "It had been hoped, particularly among textile manufacturers in this country, that Japan would be kept down, if not eliminated, as a world competitive factor." Ceramics interest groups raised $200,000 towards a propaganda fund to prevent the Japanese from "stealing the bread out of American mouths."

In light of such attitudes and obstacles, some of the former partners of All Star Trading wanted to take a wait-and-see approach to reviving the company. This was totally unacceptable to George, who had already witnessed the loss of his father's farming empire to California Lettuce Growers.

"Time is now!" said George, as he met with his father's Issei colleagues at a stockholders' meeting in Los Angeles.

Impatient, he finally issued an ultimatum: "Regardless of what you want to do, I'm going into trading by myself if necessary." Finally, the stockholders relented: all except Tad Yamada sold their shares to George. Like a rookie hitter anxious to prove himself, All Star Trading was eager to enter the big leagues.

Meanwhile, on the domestic front, resettlement continued. Sakaye's parents, grandparents, and uncles moved from the Wisconsin resort back to Southern California. Amidst the strawberry fields of Gardena, their former home, her uncle Lloyd Nakayama established Lloyd's Nursery. Sakaye's father Eijiro secured a job as caretaker of the grounds of a Catholic school in Long Beach, just south of Gardena. The Inouyes made their new home in a little house next to the football field of St. Anthony's, a school in Lakewood. Within months George, Sakaye, Masuko, and little Donna left Monterey and moved in with them. Beds were set up in the living room, and the house was filled with people.

The household increased by one that autumn. On November 5 Sakaye gave birth to Linda Yoshiko Aratani at the Japanese Hospital on Fickett Street, where Setsuo Aratani had spent his last days. Although George and Sakaye had planned on "half a dozen" children, Linda Yoshiko would complete their family. Sakaye (who later underwent a bevy of medical tests and operations) could not bear any more children. It was disappointing for both George and Sakaye, but they learned to deal with it in their usual manner—with acceptance and by forging ahead with other aspects of their lives.

I have little to go back for in that valley,
and under the circumstances I must concentrate on some
other business in the future. Trading, I feel,
is good as any and now it is my desire to make
something big out of this.
—George Aratani, in a letter to Toshitaro Ishikawa, 15 May 1947

George had to find a home for his new business. Wandering the streets of Little Tokyo he ran into one of his father's old Issei friends, who let George use a desk in his office. He used this temporary space until he was able to sign a lease for Room 420 of the Taul Building (owned by businessman Taul Watanabe), which was located at 312 East First Street.

Once he had found office space, George needed to recruit and assemble his team. His right-hand man would be Toshitaro Ishikawa, the quiet, serious Issei who had worked two jobs in order to pay off his late father's hospital bill and secure a beautiful gravesite for his ashes. Tad Yamada, back in Tokyo as part of the American Translation Interpreting Service, could serve as their overseas scout; while civilians found it difficult to travel through the rubble of Japan, GIs in uniform could move around much more easily. Although George had not met Shig Kariya, Toshitaro's recommendation had impressed him. The Nagoya-born man was well qualified, and surely his contacts with the ceramics industry in Nagoya would prove useful.

George still had two others on his list of people to call. One was Yoichi Nakase, his Guadalupean buddy who had been called "Sunshine" in high school and "Mayor" in camp because of his congenial manner and caring demeanor. And of course, he couldn't forget Tets Murata, his childhood friend and neighbor, who had moved from Detroit to Bakersfield, a desert town north of Los Angeles. Tets, who now had a son and daughter, worked for a beer distributor in the area.

"It's not bad up here," Tets said when George called.

"C'mon, Tets. Join me. I need you on my team."

Tets was silent for a moment. He remembered his days spent calculating figures in the packing shed of Guadalupe Produce. He had had his own company car—functional, albeit used—and had been the envy of many a field worker. He didn't know if George could really make a go of such a longshot enterprise in a field that was already crowded with competitors. But on the other hand, why not?

"Okay," he finally agreed. "Count me in, George."

Back in his Little Tokyo office, George sat back. He recalled his father's advice given as they had traipsed through the rows of broccoli years ago: "Hire good people, loyal people. There are only 24 hours in a day—you yourself can do only so much." Now those words had special significance for him. Many of these men had already proven themselves on the farmlands of Guadalupe. But how would their experience in vegetables transfer to the concrete jungles of Manhattan, Los Angeles, and Tokyo? Did the team, earnest and hardworking as its members were, have what it took to survive the sometimes harsh and cutthroat environment of the corporate world?

9

The Voyage

George Tetsuo Aratani, head of All Star Trading Company,
located in the Taul Building in Little Tokyo,
left on the S.S. General Meigs *today for business purposes.*
He is expected back in two months.
—The Rafu Shimpo, March 1948

In August of 1947, one hundred foreign businessmen from the U.S., Britain, France, Holland, and Australia entered Japan under a special program sponsored by Japan's Board of Trade. Meanwhile, in a showroom on Madison Avenue organized by the United States Commercial Company in New York, traders were viewing samples of German- and Japanese-made merchandise. Like a champion boxer recovering from past injuries, trade was making a comeback.

Within months All Star Trading also entered the ring. In his Los Angeles office, George called a number in Chicago. "Shig Kariya? My name is George Aratani."

On the other end of the line, Shig responded warmly. "Yes, Mr. Ishikawa has told me a lot about you."

"Same here." George chuckled as he tapped his fingers against his metal desk. From his second-floor window he could see Studebakers and Ford trucks passing on First Street. Men in felt hats and suspenders hurried past

American Commercial, Inc., moves from the Taul Building to a storefront at 1144 Maple Street near Little Tokyo, Los Angeles, ca. 1946. From left to right: Toshitaro Ishikawa, George Aratani, Gary Kadani, Mas Mitani, and Yoichi Nakase.
(99.30.57)

the storefronts. Little Tokyo was regaining some of its prewar energy. "I plan to go to Japan," George said, as he explained how he wanted to pursue trade in the near future. "So Shig, I understand that you have some relatives in Nagoya who are involved with the ceramic business?"

"That's right."

"Do you still keep in touch with these people?"

"Oh, yes. Especially my cousin. His name is Mizuno."

"I know this is a bit unusual—we have not met officially—but I think you'll be a big help to me if you join my company. I mean, I've never met you; you've never met me . . . but what do you think, Shig?"

Shig had already been approached informally by Toshitaro Ishikawa. He had heard of the esteemed Aratani family, and he was willing to make a change. "I was just getting ready to move back to the West Coast. Chicago weather is too much for me."

The deal was struck without a contract or even a handshake. George was acting purely on the weight of Toshitaro's recommendation. For his part, Shig agreed to join the team without ever seeing All Star Trading's meager office space.

In a matter of weeks Shig and Toshitaro took a train out to Los Angeles to meet face-to-face with George. Shig immediately resigned from Donnelly Printing and prepared to sail to Japan. He left the port of San Francisco in February of 1948, with George following a month later.

As word spread throughout the Japanese American community that the head of the revived All Star Trading Company was going to travel to Japan—which was still a risky venture in 1948—phone calls and visitors became frequent. Issei and Nisei friends from all over Southern California showed up at George's in-laws' home in Lakewood or at his office in Little Tokyo; each brought parcels wrapped in brown paper. "George-*san*, can you take this little package? It's a small package. *Onegai, neh*. [We beg you.] It's for our relatives."

George couldn't refuse, and within two weeks he had two cratefuls of *omiyage* (presents) to deliver. How could he say no? Masuko had lost her sister and teenage nieces in the bombing of Hiroshima. She was anxious to send her mother some clothing and foodstuffs. Other requests came from business colleagues who could not be refused.

He had initially planned to fly on the Pan American Clipper, but now, faced with taking so many packages with him, other arrangements had to made. This trip would be very different from the four musketeers' experience 13 years earlier. Instead of a luxury liner, George traveled on a former military troop transport ship. Instead of comfortable accommodations, 12 men slept in bunks in each "room." Aside from one Chinese American businessman, all of George's roommates were originally from China and did not speak much English.

The voyage took two weeks. As the ship moved across the Pacific, George noticed the dejected expressions on the faces of the Chinese travelers. He approached the only other English speaker in his room, Howard Fong. "Hey, what's wrong with those guys?" George pointed to the other men. He had never seen a group of people looking so morose.

"Mao Tse-tung." Howard had been able to extract that much with his rudimentary Cantonese. "His army is overrunning China. Their families may have been killed."

George could sympathize. It seemed war never ended—as soon as one conflict subsided, another intensified.

———— ◆ ————

Shig and George, both of whom had been in Japan in the late 1930s, had expected to see a wounded Japan. Even so, they were not prepared for the extent of her injuries. George, normally not given to displays of emotion, felt tears come to his eyes when he saw Tokyo.

The city had suffered through a barrage of incendiary bombs from U.S. forces. On March 10, 1945, in the largest of the American firebombings in Japan, 1,700 incendiaries were dropped by hundreds of B-29 bombers. An estimated 83,000 to 100,000 people died in that one raid.

Newer buildings made from ferrous concrete survived the resulting fires, but residential areas, once crowded with wooden houses, were completely devastated. A mound protruded here and there, but what it had once been neither George nor Shig could tell.

Shig went straight on to Nagoya to meet with his cousin and begin investigating the porcelain industry. George spent a week at Grandma Aratani's home, where he stored the gifts he had brought from America. After seeing firsthand the aftermath of the war, he felt that his first mission was to see that the packages entrusted to him got delivered. The postal service was not reliable, and people were hungry.

Serving as a Nisei Santa Claus in spring, George traveled to his main destination: Hiroshima. The once lush seaside city had literally been flattened. Even the mountains above the city were now two-toned from the blast—black at the bottom, white higher up. George wondered how these people were going to survive.

After he made each delivery he would be asked to stay for a visit. Sparing a rare tangerine for their privileged guest, people sat George down on a *tatami* mat and asked about America: How were relatives in California? How were the children? George, spying fleas jumping on the mats, tried to answer as best he could. The survivors obviously wished that they could be transported to a land unblemished by war.

Returning to the train station, George watched as ragged people carrying chopsticks followed American soldiers. "GI, GI," they called. When the soldiers finished their smoke and tossed the cigarette butts to the ground, the people would pick them up with their chopsticks. Later the tobacco would be carefully taken from each cigarette butt, mixed, and then rolled into new cigarettes to be sold.

The yen had become so devalued that individuals were carrying suitcases full of paper money. Just making a simple purchase required a stack of bills. Under such conditions, the rebuilding of Japan would take a long, long time, George realized. The packages he had delivered would help a few people for a short time, but through the promotion of trade, George hoped to do his part to revitalize for the long term the country he had known before the war.

⁂

Foreigners doing business in Tokyo had only one place to stay—the Teito Hotel. A former governmental building that had housed the Department of National Parks, it did not boast plush accommodations, though its restaurant did offer the rare treat of ice cream. Pulsating and crowded with merchants, it was a grand marketplace full of gossip and news about all the latest wares available to be bought and sold.

Nearby was the Dai-ichi Building, the headquarters of General Douglas MacArthur, Supreme Commander of Allied Powers. A former insurance building, it looked like a large tomb; several stories high, it was constructed of cement blocks. It was from the Dai-ichi Building that MacArthur, clad in his tan uniform and with pipe clenched between his teeth, would emerge with SCAP aides; among them was Captain Cappy Harada, the former Santa Maria star athlete who now served as aide-de-camp to Major General William F. Marquat, chief of the Economic and Scientific Section of SCAP. Whenever General MacArthur would appear, the Japanese on the street outside would get on their knees and bow.

While MacArthur was harshly criticized in the American press for being too soft on the Japanese, George felt that the military leader was doing a good job of reviving a bankrupt country. Ignoring criticism from the U.S. Congress, he was helping Japan get on its feet again.

When the two principals from All Star Trading arrived in Japan in 1948, George found that the Japanese economy was still poorly organized. First he had to apply at the Ministry of International Trade and Industry (MITI) for his import-export licenses; potential traders were required to fill out additional documentation for each industry with which they planned to be involved, (i.e., chinaware, textiles, etc.). Quotas were strictly enforced.

The competition was intense: approximately three hundred trading companies had sprung up in Japan during the late 1940s, with many of their owners having been recently discharged from the U.S. Army. Instead of going home, these entrepreneurs stayed in Japan, especially if they knew the language.

Frank Kito, a former Little Tokyo attorney, was a case in point. Frank had helped George with the Guadalupe farms before the war. After his discharge from the military, he remained in Japan; now he was a judge advocate stationed in Tokyo, where he ran into George in 1948.

"I'm rubbing elbows with the prime minister and top business people," said Frank, a thin man with an angular face and high cheekbones. "If I go back to the United States, I might have to bum around with ordinary guys like you, George," he teased.

Also in Tokyo was Kay Sugahara, head of the Universal Foreign Service Company. Assigned to the Office of Strategic Services, he worked with an advisory group headed by Joseph Grew, later appointed Ambassador to Japan. Both Sugahara and Grew were among those who recommended that Japan's imperial system be retained in order to symbolically maintain national cohesion. Peter K. Okada, a former MISer, was assigned to the 108th Military Government Team in Osaka, where he gained valuable skills that later enabled him to launch a plywood importing enterprise, PWP Japan, Inc.

But while these men eventually succeeded, many more failed. The reasons were many: back in America, the label "Made in Occupied Japan" signified shoddy quality; U.S. consumers were apprehensive about buying goods from their former wartime foe; American textile manufacturers insisted that Japanese factories produce for Japan's domestic use only. And due to the country's miniscule production capabilities, orders often could not be filled.

Competition was fierce, and many times the Nisei, a minority both in America and Japan, lost out.

———— •·•·• ————

Every week the Teito Hotel posted in its makeshift lobby the names of all its guests. That list served as an important resource for the Japanese businessman, manufacturer, or entrepreneur seeking to make a connection with a foreign trader. One day a young Japanese banker noted a familiar name: Aratani.

The Sumitomo Bank officer had served in Los Angeles before the war and had traveled quite frequently to Guadalupe. He had been close to Setsuo, and when he saw George's name he was excited to meet his late friend's son. "George-*san*, I want to introduce you to the top man of Sumitomo Bank," he said. "Anytime that you're free."

"Hey, I'm free now," George said.

As they walked, the banker explained the current situation, "You know that since the breaking up of the *zaibatsu*, this man we're meeting is no longer chairman or president. The top men are being purged. His title now is not impressive, but he's still a very important man."

At the Sumitomo headquarters George was introduced to Shozo Hotta. Although he was prematurely gray and small in stature, he commanded the room with his distinctive, somewhat aloof manner. He gained George's respect immediately.

"You are a Nisei born in America?" Shozo asked.

George nodded. "*Hai.*"

"Then why is it that you speak Japanese?"

George answered in Japanese. "My parents sent me to Japan, and I attended Keio for three years."

Shozo was duly impressed with this young, articulate man from California. He shared with George how the country's financial institutions and framework had collapsed after Japan's surrender, causing banks to fail and inflation to run rampant.

George, for his part, shared his plan of action with Shozo. He and Shig weren't interested in importing Japanese trinkets like cheap jewelry boxes, toy pianos, or German-style figurines. They wanted to represent more substantial goods—in addition to dishware, George's eye was on frozen albacore.

Shozo Hotta listened carefully and then explained that the fishing industry was struggling. American fishing interests on the West Coast wanted

Shozo Hotta, head of Sumitomo Bank in Japan. (99.30.170)

Japanese fishermen out of Alaskan waters and their canned fish off American grocery store shelves. Korea also wanted Japanese fishing limited to the islands' immediate coastal waters. Japan needed to both feed its people and increase its balance of payments for trade purposes, but the country could not ignore the pressures of international politics.

"Careful how you approach people," Shozo warned. "Japan is still rebuilding. You'll need some introduction. In the past, this bank's recommendation was always respected. Don't hesitate to ask me in the future."

George was overwhelmed. This man, a virtual stranger, was speaking to him as if he were his son. He was taking time out of his schedule for a *shirōto*, an amateur. George promised to provide Shozo Hotta with a report after he returned from visiting some freezing-and-processing plants. He could not wait to share news of this fortuitous meeting with Shig, who was busy forging his own contacts in the city of Nagoya.

Today you can depart Tokyo on the bullet train and reach Nagoya in two hours. Located in Central Honshu, south of the nation's capital, it is currently Japan's fourth-largest city, an industrial metropolis known for its

Eijoh Mizuno (right), president of Nagoya's United China and Glass, with George Aratani, ca. 1948. (99.30.54)

wide, gridlike boulevards. Nagoya is a port city that regularly ships thousands of shiny new car models from Toyota, which is headquartered in a nearby suburb.

While executives involved in shipbuilding, food processing, and other industries frequent Nagoya, it is not a popular stop for tourists. For them, the city is merely a blip between Tokyo and the exquisite temples in Nara and Kyoto. As a student, George himself had bypassed Nagoya.

The Tokaido Railway, which operates the bullet train, follows the same path as the ancient Tokaido Road traveled by the samurais. In the seventeenth century, Nagoya's strategic location was not lost on military leader Ieyasu Tokugawa, who permitted his ninth son Yoshinao to construct a castle there as protection against the overlord who controlled the nearby city of Osaka.

A secretive master builder, Kato Kiyomasa, assembled the stone base of the fortress behind bamboo screens. Afterward, 200,000 men labored to construct the rest of the castle in a matter of weeks. Mounted on both ends of the roof peaks were a pair of prized dolphins; each reaching over 8 feet high, they had silver eyes and were covered with 560 scales of 18-carat gold.

With the Meiji Restoration in 1868, Nagoya developed as a city of commerce, and in 1907 its harbor was opened to international shipping. By the 1930s the city was supporting Japanese expansion into China with shipments of munitions and aircraft, the same weapons that would lead to its own eventual ruin: during World War II the city was bombed incessantly to cut off the flow of weaponry. On May 14, 1945, during a firebombing, Nagoya Castle burned to the ground. Destroyed were the symbols of its former maritime presence, the pair of golden dolphins.

It was to the charred remains of this Nagoya that Shig Kariya returned in 1948. Shig's cousin, Eijoh Mizuno, represented the spirit that would lead to the gradual resurrection of the destroyed Japan. A small man with heavy eyebrows and a broad nose, he had lost his trading company and office to the firebombs. Nonetheless, he continued to believe in the advantages of working with America, and he became one of the first international traders in Nagoya after the war. Contacting his former customers, Eijoh launched his own company, United China and Glass of Nagoya, from the basement of a battered building with no heat. During the winter employees had to wear overcoats and mufflers as they worked in the office.

Eijoh—known as Eizoh to Shig and Eiji to George—proved to be a valuable mentor. Compassionate, well connected, and kind, he instructed both Shig and George on the ins and outs of the chinaware industry. Like the master builder toiling behind bamboo screens, he helped to assemble the foundation for the new version of All Star Trading.

———•◆•———

Back in the twenties Setsuo Aratani had investigated the use of refrigeration in the transport of vegetables within the U.S. Twenty-five years later, his son George was exploring the world of frozen food in Japan.

While the average consumer today thinks nothing of dropping bags of frozen peas or entire frozen dinners into the grocery cart, in the 1940s the technique of quick freezing was still being perfected.

Fish for export needed to undergo the "quick-frozen" process, which usually took 15 to 20 minutes in the late 1940s. Few such freezing plants, however, were operating in Japan. Abandoned during the war, some were just starting to resume business in 1948. Hearing of a plant reopening near Yokohama, George went to investigate. He was not prepared for what he found: fat, apparently well-fed rats scurried across the concrete floors and through the aging equipment. As soon as he saw the unsanitary conditions,

George knew that this was not the factory with which to do business.

The other plants he was able to visit were operating on small six- or eight-cylinder motors whose limited capacities were sometimes inadequate to thoroughly process the fish. He knew that SCAP would never permit albacore to leave the country unless it was frozen completely.

There must be better plants somewhere, thought George. He traveled to investigate some facilities that had operated in Northern Honshu before the war. Unfortunately, the plants were now dormant.

Disappointed, George returned to Tokyo and the Teito Hotel, where he resumed his weekly lunches with his new "godfather," Shozo Hotta, the head of Sumitomo Bank. One evening they visited their favorite high-class geisha house together. Over the course of George's work in Japan, geisha houses would often be the venues in which business deals were forged.

The geisha spanned a wide range of ages. All wore splendid, ornate kimono, and the younger women wore elaborate wigs; white foundation covered their faces and any exposed skin. Trained in classical traditional arts, the geisha provided entertainment, and sometimes they lent a sympathetic ear. That night, the geisha plucked at the *shamisen*.

After eating the delicate arrangement of fish and vegetables served on small dishes and drinking his share of warm sake, George turned to Shozo. He explained his difficulty in finding adequate facilities for freezing albacore.

Shozo loosened his tie and took another sip of sake.

"Maybe I should concentrate on dinnerware. I have a man down in Nagoya," George said.

"Dinnerware." Shozo nodded. "We loaned some money to a company called Narumi; they produce fine china. I can introduce you to them, as well as the Nagoya branch manager. He'll help you out."

George held the tiny sake cup, now empty, above the low table, and he pondered his situation. He had known very little about the frozen fish industry, and like a mouse traveling in a maze, he had only encountered dead ends. With dinnerware he would also plunge into a strange new world—a world of Korean potters and samurai tea cups, a world of jiggers, slips, and tunnel kilns.

In 1616, the same year William Shakespeare died, a Korean potter by the name of Li Sanpei—better known by his Japanese name Kanae Sampei—discovered stone deposits in a mountain on the southern island of Kyushu.

This material was essentially kaolin, whose name is derived from the Chinese word *kao-ling*, meaning "high hills."

Kaolin is primarily comprised of kaolinite, the pure white clay mineral needed to create porcelain. In the porcelain-manufacturing process, the pulverized mineral is mixed with other clay and fired at high temperatures to give the final product its almost translucent quality. The best feldspar porcelain must be made up of at least 20 percent kaolin.

The Arita region of Kyushu dominated the Japanese porcelain industry for two hundred years. During that time kaolin was also discovered in North America in what later became the state of Georgia. A ceramics center was eventually created in a tristate area flanking the Ohio River; nicknamed the "Staffordshire of America," this area's production reflected the influence of English traditions. (The area's most prominent ceramics manufacturer, Homer Laughlin, launched his business in 1874.) While specializing in earthenware, a porous ceramic that is also referred to as pottery, American manufacturers never developed a strong porcelain chinaware industry.

Asia, on the other hand, excelled in the production of both porcelain and earthenware. Seto, on the outskirts of Nagoya, had produced simple, plain earthenware since the seventeenth century. *Cha-no-yu*, the tea ceremony, had so greatly impacted Japanese society that even samurai carried brown-glazed or celadon cups alongside their swords for one last sip of tea on the battlefield.

Then, early in the nineteenth century a Seto ceramist, Tamikichi Kato, moved to Arita, Japan's porcelain-producing region; there he studied the creation of chinaware for four years. He eventually returned to Seto where his characteristic style of blue-and-white ware (called *sometsuke*) made Seto the ceramics center of Japan and a major supplier of goods for exports. While Japanese consumers continued to prefer the austere and unadorned earthenware, Europeans and Americans developed a taste for porcelain.

Steeped as it was in this long tradition of ceramics, Nagoya seemed the obvious place to procure porcelain dinner sets for import to the U.S. Both Japanese and Westerners were familiar with Noritake, the largest dinnerware brand in Japan, a company founded by the Morimura family. This business's origins can be attributed to Baron Ichizaemon Morimura, a member of a Japanese trade delegation who established a trading company in Tokyo's Ginza in 1876. Exporting Japanese-style pottery, curios, and bamboo knickknacks, primarily to the United States, Morimura Brothers expanded its production of ceramics by working with a number of small factories in Japan.

In January of 1904 the Morimura Group founded its own ceramics factory, Nippon Toki Gomei Kaisha, in the area called Noritake within the city of Nagoya. Export goods—both tableware and "fancy ware" (giftware)—were nothing like the *shibui*, or spare style, valued by tea master Sen-no-Rikyu or the ancient samurai. Instead, ornate vases were characterized by classic or neoclassic shapes with swirling baroque handles. Seeking to appeal to Western tastes, Japanese designers hand-painted the items with images of landscapes, Victorian women in flowing dresses, and even a friar smelling a rose. Advanced techniques such as raised enamel and gold luster were also incorporated.

Rapid technological innovations impacted the productivity of both American and Japanese ceramics manufacturers in the 1930s, but because trends in dinnerware changed often, production could not be entirely mechanized. One season a certain shape or color would be all the rage, only to be abandoned for another style the following year. Mass producers such as the Homer Laughlin China Company, located in Newell, West Virginia, aimed to please "Her Majesty—The American Housewife."

In order to meet high production goals, the art of throwing pieces by hand on a pottery wheel (as practiced at smaller kilns around Nagoya and Arita) had long since been abandoned. Instead, slip—liquid clay—was poured into hollow plaster molds; the plaster absorbed the slip's water, leaving the clay to build up on the walls of the mold. After a drying period, the piece was removed from the mold, which could be used multiple times. Another technique, called "jiggering," involved placing clay on a rotating plaster mold and pressing a template against it. The mold formed the inside of the item, while the template shaped the outside.

Mechanical conveyers, production-line methods, and tunnel kilns were also incorporated into the manufacturing process. Tunnel kilns enabled carts of greenware (unfired ceramics) to move through the kiln continuously. The long, tunnel-like shape of the kiln also distributed heat in a way that optimized the firing process.

Such innovations were brought about in large part by the demand for ceramics engendered by the rise of such American discount merchandisers as Woolworth's in the twenties and thirties. The twentieth-century retailing revolution transformed the home furnishings business: now companies like Homer Laughlin could branch out into major chain stores, mail-order merchandising, and department stores.

For instance, if Quaker Oats needed 48,000 decorated bowls a week for a promotional offer, Homer Laughlin delivered. Noritake also got involved in the premium business through an affiliation with Larkin bath and laundry soap, which was marketed by mail order.

The increasing number of ceramic imports was not welcomed by American manufacturers, who had higher labor costs. Cheap ceramics from Japan, Czechoslovakia, and Germany had flooded the market during the Depression, contributing to American factory closures—now, after World War II, the last thing domestic producers wanted was for Japanese dinnerware to tempt "Her Majesty" again.

——•◆•——

Upon his arrival in Nagoya, George was met by both Shig and the Sumitomo Bank representatives. To travel to the ceramics factory they were to inspect, they hired a *mokutan jidōsha*, a taxi that burned charcoal instead of gasoline, which was then a rare and expensive commodity.

Loaded with passengers, the taxi strained up the side of a mountain until, finally, it stalled.

"Will all of you get out and push?" the driver asked.

George looked at Shig, shrugged his shoulders, and got out. Each man rolled up his sleeves and pushed the *mokutan jidōsha* up the steep road.

On another day they visited the Narumi dinnerware factory. George noticed that one side of Narumi's wall had been covered with camouflage paint. "From the air, it doesn't look like a building," an official explained.

Unlike Tokyo, the target of incendiary bombs, Nagoya had been hit with explosives. Because the devastating firebombs hadn't been dropped, fires did not rage through the port city. Instead, surviving structures stood in perfect condition right next to the cement-and-wood rubble of buildings that had taken a direct hit.

Dinnerware manufacturers like Narumi—which was Noritake's main competitor—had ceased production during the war, partially because no one in Japan used Western-style dinnerware. Moreover, Japan instituted an austerity program that prohibited the manufacture of extravagant consumer goods. Narumi, under military orders, had been taken over by Sumitomo Steel during the war—instead of fine china, the factory produced airplane propellers.

With the Occupation, operation of the factory was returned to Narumi's personnel. As soldiers of the U.S. 8th Army and Allied Occupational Forces continued to cram into buildings throughout Japan, they needed Western-style food as well as the flat plates and coffee cups with which they were familiar. Slip was mixed, jiggers whirled, and tunnel kilns were heated. Dinnerware factories were back in production.

As George and his group entered the Narumi factory, Yasuo Kimura, the manager, introduced himself.

"I'm in a bit of a bind," said Kimura. "Another American trading company came here recently, and our production is already committed to them."

"Oh?" George was curious. Who had beaten them to Narumi?

The company—which was a partnership of American soldiers—was called Amerex and was currently trading textiles. Through connections with a chinaware buyer at Macy's in New York and a Japanese trading company, the fledgling group was now planning to enter the dinnerware market.

"So, even though Hotta-*san* introduced you to Narumi, I must tell you that we're in no position to supply." Yasuo Kimura was sincerely regretful— in Japan, retaining "face" was all important in business relationships. Shozo Hotta's introduction carried weight, but it alone could not overcome production limitations. Like the frozen albacore venture, George's plan to import dinnerware seemed doomed.

Despite the seeming disappointments, these early trips to Japan did produce some valuable leads for George. He met with other dinnerware manufacturers through the efforts of Shig Kariya's cousin, Eijoh Mizuno. Shozo Hotta also encouraged George to visit a former college classmate who worked at the Noritake factory, but George was not excited about representing Noritake products in America. Eventually Noritake was going to do their own selling, he figured. Nevertheless, to accord Hotta-*san* the proper respect, he agreed to the meeting.

At Noritake's large manufacturing plant production was only at 20 to 30 percent of its prewar level. Equipment had been severely damaged, resources of raw materials had been drained, and the labor force had been reduced from 4,000 to 1,000.

However, once the U.S. Army established its procurement office to supply troops throughout the Far East, Noritake benefited from its long trade relationship with America. General Headquarters' Industrial Division, the Aichi prefectural military government, and other agencies stepped in and helped the company obtain raw materials, fuels, liquid gold, and packing material. A huge blanket order for dinnerware was issued to Noritake, which produced the dishes under the name "Rose China" because the company could not ensure the same high quality it had maintained in the past.

Rose China was distributed to post exchanges on American military bases throughout the region. For private traders, however, supplies were limited—in fact, the only items readily available were tea sets.

George still didn't know much about the American dinnerware market. "Can I sell these tea sets in America?" he asked a Noritake executive.

"Definitely. They're made for the United States," the executive responded.

George was now weary. Despite his best efforts, he had endured three months of dead ends and unrealized business deals. He could not return to L.A. empty-handed. He needed to have something to sell, and if it had to be Noritake tea sets, so be it. Without consulting Shig or his Los Angeles office, George placed his first order.

"Okay, give me five hundred sets." They were 23-piece sets, with a conservative floral design. (In the dinnerware industry, George learned, each piece—such as a sugar bowl's lid—is counted separately. A teapot with a lid is considered two pieces.)

At the time, goods from Japan could enter the United States through two routes. One was overland: the shipment would be unloaded in either Seattle or Portland and then travel by rail to the Midwest and Chicago. The other, cheaper alternative that George chose was across the Pacific Ocean, through the Panama Canal, to New York Harbor.

Even as George completed the transaction, he felt some apprehension. I'm going to compete with Noritake, yet here I am selling their merchandise, he thought to himself. Noritake had been producing goods since before World War I, even before he was born. He shook his head and thought: We've got a long way to go.

Returning to the U.S. in August of 1948, George had no more definite leads (aside from some Christmas merchandise he had ordered). Japan was in worse shape than he had imagined, but plenty of GIs still seemed hopeful and eager to make their fortunes once trade was fully reestablished; they were creating a very competitive arena in which to operate.

Importing frozen albacore did not seem a viable option, and who knew what would happen with Nagoya's struggling dishware manufacturers? In a letter to Leo McMahon at the end of August, he wrote: "Japan is still in a pretty bad mess economically and my guess is that it will take her quite some time before she can have a sound economy."

After returning from Japan, George decided to open an office in New York, America's business center. Buyers for nationwide department stores and discount merchandisers perused showrooms in the Big Apple first—only if they had any money remaining in their budgets did they consider purchasing goods from outfits based on the West Coast.

George preferred to stay in Los Angeles because of his remaining business ties in Guadalupe. Shig, on the other hand, would go to New York. Although he had never set foot in Manhattan, Shig had always dreamed of working for a large international trading company there. New York City was where six Issei trading pioneers had first arrived on the ship *Oceanic* in March of 1876, as Japan struggled to learn about the West to maintain control of its expanding economy.

Some five decades later, the All Star Trading partners also faced obstacles, but with some important distinctions from their predecessors: theirs was a tiny young Nisei company that could be squashed either by other larger American corporations with years of experience, or by the Japanese conglomerate—though temporarily hobbled by war wounds, it was certainly well equipped to bounce back. To achieve their goal, George, Shig, and the company's other principals would have to be persistent and committed, even when common sense might instruct them otherwise.

CHAPTER

10

Nisei in Manhattan

This is the land of the Great Dream.
Every Nisei is a dreamer who someday somehow hopes to
get on top of the ladder, though the
chances are a thousand to one against him.
—Roku Sugahara, "A Nisei in Manhattan,"
***Pacific Citizen*, 10 March 1951**

New York was the land of the Great Dream for both George Aratani and
Shig Kariya. It didn't matter that neither of them had ever set foot on the
island of Manhattan. It didn't matter that only five years earlier some
Brooklyn Heights residents—and even New York City Mayor Fierello
LaGuardia—had protested the establishment of a hostel there for Japanese
Americans released from concentration camps. Since the opening of Japan
in the late 1800s, pioneering entrepreneurs had set up shop in New York to
sell their racks of silk and stacks of chinaware. Now George and his Nisei
team planned to make their mark there too.

Shig was the initial scout. He arrived in New York in 1949 with his
$200 monthly stipend from George in his pocket. A tall, slim man with an
engaging smile, he thought before he spoke and chose his words carefully.
Like George, he was gutsy, and in his own understated way, ambitious and
extremely resourceful.

Shig Kariya in the New York City offices of American
Commercial, Inc., ca. 1950. (99.58.1)

Shig soon learned that $200 didn't go very far in Manhattan, the center of New York financial activity. In fact, in his column "A Nisei in Manhattan" in the *Pacific Citizen*, businessman and writer Roku Sugahara advised a friend from Japan that he should be prepared to come to New York with a expense account of $600 a month.

"Six hundred dollars?" The columnist's friend was shocked—the president of his corporation didn't make half that much money.

At the time of his arrival Shig had no idea about New York's cost of living. Not knowing anybody in the city, he headed for the New York chapter of the Japanese American Citizens League (JACL).

While many of the West Coast chapters of the JACL had begun before the war, the New York chapter was not launched until June 16, 1944. It was atypical in other ways as well. First of all, it was organized on an "inter-racial basis" and was open to all citizens "without regard to race, creed or color." Members of the first board of directors included Clara Clayman, who had worked in the War Relocation Authority office in New York.

"The reason for having others besides Nisei in an organization like this," explained Clayman, "is that no one minority group can live by itself. We need to think of every group and in so doing, we can solve our own problems. Otherwise, our own problems will be multiplied."

Vocal, politically savvy leaders such as Roger N. Baldwin, director of the American Civil Liberties Union, and Norman Thomas, leader of the Socialist Party, were among the JACL sponsors. Such unions as the Brotherhood of Sleeping Car Porters and the black newspaper *Pittsburgh Courier* also played a role in launching the organization.

The first president of the New York JACL was Al Funabashi, a Nisei businessman with blue-green eyes who would later play a major role in George's trading company. A captivating speaker with a larger-than-life persona, he lobbied for the continuation of the Fair Employment Practices Commission created in 1941 by President Roosevelt to combat workplace discrimination. Al liked to think big, and it was this large-scale thinking that, in time, would ignite George's dreams.

By the time Shig arrived, the New York JACL had full-time staff members and an office housed in a hotel. After setting down his suitcase, Shig approached the office manager. "Do you know of a good place to stay?" he asked.

The woman brought out a city map. "Well, a lot of Nisei stay over here." She pointed to an area northwest of Central Park, near Columbia University and not far from Spanish Harlem. The university attracted people from all over the world, and the Japanese Americans felt safe in such a diverse environment. Shig and George shared a room at Hotel Paris for some time while they surveyed their options.

Shig eventually found a YMCA on McBirney and 23rd Street which rented rooms for the period from six o'clock in the evening to eight o'clock in the morning for $2.80. This meant he had to pack up his suitcases every day and lug them to the JACL office, where he had arranged to use a type-writer and telephone.

After a month of this, Shig found an apartment on 110th Street, near Columbia University, and in time he rented a small office at Broadway and 26th Street. As he settled into New York life, he soon learned that he was not the only Nisei with big dreams. In 1949 at least 30 other companies—most of them virtually single-person enterprises—were scrambling to establish a toehold in the U.S.–Japan import market.

Like these other makeshift companies, All Star Trading was vulnerable: it could easily be squeezed out of what little business it could grab. Japan's manufacturing base and buying power were still greatly diminished, which limited the number of products that could be traded. However, once Japan's economy rebounded, any U.S.–based Nisei trading company could expect competition of the most deadly kind. The *kaisha* (Japanese corporations), with money, experience, and prestige on their side, would undoubtedly flood the markets.

Nisei relationships with *kaisha* were complex. On one hand, before the war the *kaisha* were sometimes the only place well-educated Japanese Americans could find white-collar work. "It was either the salt mines of the produce game or the restricted life of being a '*kozō*' [shopboy] for a Japanese corporation," observed columnist Roku Sugahara. At the same time, that path was often a dead end for the Nisei, because top management positions went to the elite who had been born and raised in Japan.

The individual Nisei trader would soon become an endangered species, predicted observers. "He may wind up, like his pre-war counterpart, as being a typist or an office boy for some giant corporation like Mitsui, NYK, or Mitsubishi," wrote Sugahara.

George and his team needed to be "smart, shrewd and cagey" to stay ahead of the game. But first, they needed money.

*As you may know, I am having a difficult
time in starting the All Star trading
business because of lack of working capital.*
**—George Aratani, in a letter to Naoichi Ikeda,
2 January 1948**

Although there were no detailed job descriptions, each person on the All Star team had a specialty: administration, accounting, sales. In addition to making contacts, George's job was to raise money and maintain a steady payroll. In the early days, this was no easy feat.

"In financing my foreign trade business with Japan I mortgaged my ranch property in Lompoc, the dehydrating plant, and other property in Guadalupe and have thus been carrying on my business," George wrote to Naoichi Ikeda and Ben Kodama, the former partners of Guadalupe Produce Company. He couldn't even afford to buy a house for his growing family. Building the business was his first priority.

Using some of his property as collateral, George had been able to secure a loan from the Bank of America, but he had already spent a large chunk of that money on the business trip to Japan. Then the merchandise he had purchased in Japan did not arrive in time for the Christmas shopping season; strikes in harbors on both coasts that year also slowed delivery. Unable to turn a profit from the merchandise fast enough, he had to default on his first loan payment.

Through a loan from Guadalupe Produce—which existed in name only—George was able to keep All Star Trading afloat. Other Nisei businesses were in the same predicament, because the U.S. government's attempts to artificially stimulate the Japanese economy were having negative ramifications for American international traders. In 1949 the exchange rate had finally been fixed at 360 yen to a dollar. Fueled by black marketeers, inflation was persistent, driving prices to record highs.

George, in his typical easy going style, attempted to maintain his optimism. His Guadalupe-nurtured demeanor inspired trust, which helped him convince bank officers to give him lines of credit. Unbeknownst to his business associates, however, the mounting financial pressures were taking their toll. At home in Los Angeles, George also had to handle such time-consuming chores as calculating corporate taxes and similar tedious yet vital paperwork. Sometimes he would forgo his own salary to maintain payroll. He developed ulcers and got in the habit of carrying antacid and arrowroot cookies (used to alleviate the pain of teething babies) to soothe his sour stomach.

Sakaye watched George with concern, but she did not want to disturb the peace of the household with questions. After a brief stay in her parents' small cottage next to the high-school football field, the Aratanis rented a house in Boyle Heights, next to East Los Angeles. There, with step-mother Masuko's help, Sakaye raised her two daughters; George was absent for long stretches of time, either traveling to New York or Japan. Because of his extensive travels, Sakaye began a collection of telegrams from George wishing her the best Valentine's Day, anniversary, and Christmas from cities like Chicago, Tokyo, Nagoya, and New York.

In an attempt to retain her immigration status as an international trader, Masuko had remained as the official president of All Star Trading until the summer of 1948. It was her name that appeared on letters to the Department of Commerce and other governmental agencies inquiring about eligible imports and exports to and from Japan. (Inevitably, the agencies would address their responses to "Mr. Masuko Aratani.")

However, Masuko and other Issei in similar immigration predicaments finally received relief: The Immigration Act of 1917 was amended to allow the attorney general to suspend deportation proceedings against certain aliens of "good moral character" who had lived continuously in the United States for seven years or more. The Issei would not attain full rights, however, until 1952, when the McCarran–Walter Act declared them eligible for citizenship.

— • —

Before filing appropriate papers and licenses, George often consulted with the former academic director of the Military Intelligence Service, John Aiso, who was now established in a thriving legal practice in Little Tokyo.

"What is this All Star Trading?" John asked. "Sounds like a sports team."

"It is." George laughed, explaining how his father had loved baseball so much that his crate labels had pictured home-run batters.

"Hmpf. That's no name for an international trading company."

Pragmatist that he was, George agreed. Still, he wanted something that started with "A" so that it would be listed at the beginning of the phone book. "American," he finally decided. This was an American company, after all. "American Commercial, Inc."

* * *

*Here in Manhattan, community spirit is something
that comes in bottles. Everyone is out to make a fast dollar
and quicker still to act the part of the caustic critic.*
—Roku Sugahara, "A Nisei in Manhattan,"
***Pacific Citizen*, 1 June 1949**

From its very beginning, American Commercial, Inc. (ACI) was a bicoastal operation. For weeks at a time George stayed in New York, either with Shig or in an inexpensive hotel near 90th Street. He commuted via subway to the company's small office, where he and Shig worked on the books, sometimes until midnight. Shig's mother, Masa, had moved to Manhattan, and she would often stop by at dinnertime with a Japanese *bentō*, a meal complete with rice balls, grilled fish, and pickled cabbage.

New York was a jarring experience for George, who was more familiar with open spaces and the congenial spirit of West Coast living. On his way to the subway one day, he stopped by a newsstand to look at the different newspapers and magazines offered in New York City. The proprietor, who was sitting close by a small heater, called out, "Hey you, I'm here to sell newspapers, not show 'em off. If you want to buy it, buy it. If not, keep movin'."

The next morning George was getting off the subway during rush hour. As the crowd pushed him up the stairs to the street level, he noticed a man lying facedown on the sidewalk. Normally George would have approached the man and asked if he were all right; instead, he followed the lead of everyone else in the crowd and merely stepped over him. Everyone was in a rush to get to the office on time.

George again experienced culture shock while shopping in the famous Macy's department store on Times Square. He expected a salesperson to ask if he needed help, but three saleswomen nearby continued to talk amongst themselves while George patiently waited.

"I want to buy this," he finally called out, raising a scarf he thought Sakaye might like.

The saleswomen continued their private conversation.

"Excuse me," George said a little louder.

"Did you say something?" one of them asked.

George soon learned the rules of the game. "If you want something, you have to ask for it," he told himself. "That's New York."

Instead of enjoying New York's exciting nightlife, George usually spent weekends alone, feeling homesick for his family. Shig, on the other hand, often attended the Nisei dances at the McBirney YMCA, a multistory building on 23rd Street. Though these events were frowned upon by some Issei parents, who felt that the JACL-sponsored dances attracted a fast crowd, they provided an opportunity for young people to socialize with their fellow Nisei. Indeed, it was at such a dance that Shig met Jean Ito, a stylish, engaging woman born in Oakland, California, who would later become his wife.

———— ·◆· ————

In the beginning, American Commercial, Inc., considered handling any product that might sell in either the U.S. or overseas—Shig had even been approached by a company in Japan which was seeking to stock the country's abandoned zoos with animals. It was a bizarre request, but Shig visited local zoos around New York and inquired about the availability of lions, tigers, giraffes, buffalo, and monkeys.

But in the end, zoo animals and tea sets weren't going to put food on the table, so George and his West Coast team turned to the market they knew best: the local Japanese American community. The most obvious product to supply was food, specifically semidried fish, which Issei warmed over an open flame. There was a ready market not only in Los Angeles, but in Hawai'i as well.

Soon a distributor in Honolulu approached American Commercial with another food request: "If you are handling sun-dried fish, we are looking for dried abalone."

Dried abalone. Just the thought of the chewy, delectable snack made George's mouth water. As a child, he had often gone into a store on Guadalupe Boulevard to buy a piece of dried abalone from a large jar on the counter.

The Chinese—and later the Japanese—had once monopolized the abalone harvesting industry. In 1929 abalone caught on with the larger population as a domestic gourmet food item. While abalone (a huge, flattened snail) was usually grilled at popular California eateries, the state's Asian population preferred it raw, canned, or dried.

One day George received a phone call from a supplier. "We have a shipment that came in here around noon from Mexico. We can show it to you."

"Okay, bring it over," George said.

"No, no, we can't get there until dark."

"Okay, how late? We'll wait for you."

"Seven o'clock."

As George hung up, he frowned. How strange, he thought. Why meet after sundown?

Later that day he learned that Mexico was restricting sales of its abalone to canneries—this shipment was probably contraband. Nevertheless, like agents on a covert mission, George and Toshitaro waited in their office in Little Tokyo. This pirated treasure of the sea would help to sustain their fledgling company.

⁕

The abalone deal had, of course, been only a momentary stopgap. George still needed to search for new products, which meant another trip to Japan. This time he visited Toshitaro Ishikawa's brother-in-law, Kazusada Kanda, who manufactured shell buttons in Osaka, a large city not far from Nagoya.

These buttons were made from large pink, black, and white snail-shaped Trochus shells, once plentiful in the Palau Islands, located about 500 miles from Manila. After being ground and polished, one iridescent shell could be made into 50 buttons for men's shirts or women's blouses and sweaters. There was a plentiful supply of Trochus shells because no one had collected them during the war, and the creatures had been left to propagate unchecked. However, the Palau Islands were now off limits to the Japanese.

Ishikawa's relative was attempting to revive his prewar button business, now reduced to a cottage industry carried on in sheds behind private homes. George and Shig visited these small makeshift factories and observed women operating machines that drilled holes into buttons with the press of a pedal.

As one of the experts in Japan's shell button industry, Kanda advised SCAP once a year on the total tonnage of Trochus shells that should be imported the following fiscal year.

"You should buy these, Aratani-*san*," he told George.

"I'll consider it, Kanda-*san*, but where do I go to sell them?"

"Go to Seventh Avenue in New York." Kanda had never been to the United States, but he knew all about the garment district. "You go there and show these buttons. If the price is right, they're going to buy them. Have no fear—there'll be a ready market."

George took a deep breath and ordered $35,000 worth of shell buttons.

Once American Commercial received its first shipment of buttons, George pounded the pavement, brazenly making cold calls on garment manufacturers along Seventh Avenue. The garment district was a lively and noisy area: trucks rumbled down the streets carrying bolts of fabric past dingy storefronts stuffed from hardwood floor to ceiling with button samples and ribbons.

American Commercial had no strategy or organized plan. Instead, the staff tirelessly contacted every business either in person or over the phone. They wore out the soles of their shoes and got sore arms and shoulders from carrying cases of samples from store to store. Usually they left samples with first-time customers, who then checked to see if the buttons would work well with their mechanized sewing operations. (Many of the buttons were of a shank type—shaped like a tiny mushroom with a hole in the stem—and could only be sewn onto garments using certain kinds of sewing machines.) Soon their persistence began to pay off.

Several months later George visited a large garment manufacturer. As the buyer was talking to another customer, the proprietor appeared from the back of his shop, his dark eyes flashing. "What's your name?" he asked.

"Aratani. My company's name is American Commercial."

"Where you from?" The dark eyes remained steady on George's face.

"The West Coast." George was getting a bad feeling from the man's tone of voice.

The button dealer brushed his hands along George's samples. "Where are these buttons from?"

"The manufacturing? Japan," George quickly replied.

The man's face grew red. "Get the hell out of here," he declared.

"What a minute—all I came to—"

"I said, get the hell out. If you don't, I'm going to have you thrown out."

"What did I say?" George wanted an explanation.

The owner took hold of George's suit collar, led him to the door, and literally shoved him out of the store.

George was shocked. Outside, back on the pavement, he tried to assess what had just transpired. He always avoided thinking about discrimination—if he worried about that, he would be too paralyzed to launch a business. No, the man must have had a son who was killed in the Pacific war. "Well, if that's the case, I sympathize with the guy," he told himself, picking up his case and trudging back to his office.

The next time George was on Seventh Avenue, he visited a friend, another garment manufacturer, and he related the recent incident. To George's surprise, the friend smiled. "You went over there?" The friend's smile became a laugh. "Imported buttons from Japan forced this guy to close his button manufacturing plant in New Jersey." So, instead of sorrow over a fallen son in the Pacific, it had been anger over the demise of his business. George could empathize: How devastating it would be to fail in a venture. Understanding how important it was to diversify one's business, he now turned his attention to dinnerware.

———◆———

The Noritake tea sets finally arrived from Japan. George was elated. The floral pattern was attractive, and the sets looked as good on delivery as they had back in Nagoya. In the same manner that he had tackled the button business, George enthusiastically began calling on department and discount store buyers. The answer everywhere was unequivocally the same: "Not interested." American housewives didn't want tea sets; if anything, they wanted a coffee service. Tea sets were for the consumer market in Great Britain and Australia, not for java-drinking households in the United States, George soon discovered. Crushed, yet undeterred from his goal, he knew that he would somehow have to make some sort of return on his huge investment.

Enter Al Funabashi, the oldest of three sons. Shig knew of Al's father, Kensuke, an enterprising Japanese immigrant who before the war had been a commissioned broker with Mitsui Trading Company, whose offices were in the Empire State Building. Kensuke had earlier worked as a butler in a large mansion on the outskirts of Boston; there he met his future wife, Catherine Horan, a housekeeper of Irish Catholic descent.

Interracial marriage between Japanese and European Americans was unusual at that time, though certainly not unheard of along the Atlantic seaboard. In California, antimiscegenation laws prohibiting unions between a "white" and "Negro, Mulatto, or Mongolian" were on the books. East Coast politicians were advocating "racial purity," and they expressed specific concern about intermarriage between European Americans and African Americans.

The Funabashi family eventually settled in Lyndhurst in suburban New Jersey, where the three Funabashi boys, with their light-colored eyes, tall frames, and pale skin, identified themselves as both Japanese and Irish.

Al (first row, center) and Maria (second row, far left) Funabashi host a party for employees and their families at their home in New Jersey in 1954.
Gift of Minoru Endo (99.59.1)

They, like any other Nisei, faced societal discrimination.

Kensuke intended for his eldest son to become an engineer, but Al wanted to be a lawyer. He enrolled in New York University but dropped out after a year to begin work at a trading company called National Merchandise. In a stockroom filled with boxes and crates, Al became acquainted with the dinnerware industry and the concept of replacements and fillers; ensuring a steady stock of fillers to replace broken goods was as vital as providing new lines of dishes. He also became familiar with Japanese dinnerware manufacturers like Meito.

Ever ambitious, Al approached his boss after he had worked at National Merchandise for some time. "If I complete my work in the stockroom in the morning, would you give me a chance at sales in the afternoon?"

His employer sized Al up. He was tall, gregarious, and knew how to talk; aside from his last name he didn't seem Japanese, but he fit in well in the presence of other Asians. "Why not?" he said.

During World War II Al and his two brothers were drafted, but a medical exam revealed that Al had an enlarged heart, which exempted him from military service. His younger brothers were assigned to the all-Nisei 100th/442nd Regimental Combat Unit.

Al had previously tried several other sales jobs, but limited opportunities for Japanese workers and other minorities meant that he was paid only menial wages—35 cents an hour—while others earned at least 70 cents.

A New Jersey factory that produced electronic insulation for radios provided Al the break he was looking for. Operated by a Quaker family, the business hired many Japanese Americans, who were resettling on the East Coast from the concentration camps. In time the shop was unionized, and the charismatic Al rose through the ranks to become union president. After the war he sold transformers for oil burners.

It was at this time that George made an inquiry of Tom Hayashi, a lawyer who was president of the New York JACL chapter. "You know any guys experienced in selling and trading?" George asked.

Tom smiled. "I think I have the guy for you."

George went to see Al Funabashi, and after several days of negotiation Al officially agreed to join American Commercial. His first task was to unload the five hundred Noritake tea sets.

Al explained to George that coffee sets, which featured a taller pot than the one included in tea sets, were more appropriate for the American market. Even so, within a short time Al had sold every last cup and saucer to the T. C. Green chain of variety stores. And George was duly impressed. Most of the managers of American Commercial were steady, taciturn men —the company really needed a powerful personality in order to break into the dinnerware market, because the challenge was great. Importers faced exorbitant duties that sometimes equaled 70 percent of the merchandise's value. Moreover, the lucrative hotel-and-restaurant market was virtually off limits to Japanese manufacturers due to a voluntary quota agreed to by representatives from Japan.

Al, however, could depend on a basic business principle: the value of personal contacts—he knew most of the buyers at the big New York department stores. George expected big things from his new sales manager.

George told Al how he had been kicked out of the store in the garment district.

Al nodded. "I know how it is."

"But you don't look Japanese."

"Hey, I'm Japanese too. My name is Funabashi. Just don't let it bother you—take it like a businessman."

George's worries were far from over, however, and he continued to take swigs of antacid and chew on his arrowroot cookies. Within the next two years, Nisei trading companies left and right would close their doors. At one time more than 30 such firms traded in products as diverse as pearls, silk, decorative objects, canned eels, mahogany lumber, orange juice, and plastic zippers. Five years later, only about five companies, including American Commercial, were still operating.

"It's all expense and not a dime in income," wrote Roku Sugahara in his column. "So these boys, like the Arabs, fold their tents and scurry back to the West Coast in search of a steady job or a new bankroll."

But George continued to dream. He didn't want to just sell to "gifty-nifty" dime stores—his sights even exceeded middle-echelon outlets like May Company, headquartered in St. Louis, Missouri, and S. S. Kresge Company, the predecessor to Kmart. Along with Al Funabashi and the rest of the team, he aimed for the brightest star, the largest department store in the world: Macy's.

11

Making It to
Macy's

Bringing it in is the easiest part.
Peddling it is another matter.
—Roku Sugahara, "A Nisei in Manhattan,"
***Pacific Citizen*, 13 January 1951**

By 1950 American Commercial, Inc., was located in a one-room office on Fifth Avenue. Unadorned and purely utilitarian, the space housed a set of metal filing cabinets, a large calendar from a local print office, and three desks piled with papers. In one corner sat the company's inventory—cases of shell buttons and dish samples.

Macy's Department Store, a more imposing structure, sat 30 blocks away at 34th Street and Broadway. George straightened his tie as he and Al walked up the subway station steps towards the blocklong storefront. Macy's, with its multiple floors, was a far cry from the "gifty-nifty" mom-and-pop stores that often sold imported goods. The department store had a history dating back to 1842. The Straus family, who acquired the store in the late 1800s, had in fact started their careers in Macy's profitable china department. Now George wanted to build his company in the same way.

A display of Mikasa dinnerware at an annual china-and-glass trade show in Pittsburgh in the late 1950s. Maria Funabashi is pictured. Gift of Maria Funabashi (99.56.4)

As they rode up the escalator to the china-and-glass department, Al tapped his fingers on the railing. "I don't know if he'll see us," he said. Even as George was admiring the well-dressed store clerks and attractive display cases, he was somewhat anxious, because he knew that Macy's buyers were renowned for their hard-nosed negotiating with suppliers.

In the china-and-glass department they met with buyer Jerry Stone. While they didn't sell any dishes to Macy's that day—they didn't give up hope.

The company continued to hone its blend of entrepreneurial spirit, efficient administration, and creative salesmanship. Al knew how to approach buyers, and he had an eye for chinaware design. The detail-oriented Shig, himself the son of a department-store entrepreneur, could handle the day-to-day demands of the office. George, on the other hand, understood Japan. But for American Commercial to operate at its optimum, each of these Nisei men would need to accept the strengths of the others.

So I say to these wiseacres from the glittering Ginza,
don't be too hard with the Nisei yokels who are
roaming the streets of Tokyo; your fellow countrymen look
just as foolish, naive and peculiar here
along the great white way. That makes us even.
—Roku Sugahara, "A Nisei in Manhattan,"
***Pacific Citizen*, 11 August 1951**

In 1950 Al went to Japan for two months with George, leaving his wife Maria to take care of their two children in New Jersey. It was Al's first trip to his father's homeland, and it wasn't an easy trip for him. His Japanese was very rudimentary; moreover, he had a New Jersey accent and his speech had a nasal quality. Worst of all, he wasn't used to being silent while others spoke. George, on the other hand, was a master linguist who seamlessly melded Western mannerisms with the Japanese language. Despite the foreign words flowing from his mouth, George nevertheless established himself as quintessentially American—maybe it was the way he greeted prospective Japanese suppliers with a firm handshake, or how he laughed and smiled so easily in group photographs.

Arriving at the first factory they were to visit, Al was amazed to see a mountain of plain white soup bowls, tied together with twine, sitting outside the main building.

"From Indonesia," George told him. "Their number-two export market since the war."

Neither man expected full-fledged factory tours; understandably, manufacturers wanted to keep certain techniques under wraps. They were invited, however, to observe the final painting process. Women with their hair tied back in kerchiefs and older men bent over blank white dishes moving along a conveyor. With a careful steady hand they decorated plates and then set the finished product on the conveyor belt. At the end of the process a quality-control person inspected the workmanship, flipping each plate over to check the stamp: "Made in Occupied Japan."

Afterwards Al and George were invited into the company office, where they were served cups of hot tea. George asked polite questions. "How are things now? Are you having any problems coming back after the war?" The manufacturer answered with equal politeness.

As his cup of tea grew lukewarm, Al shifted in his seat. George made a few more observations; the manufacturer added his. For Al this exchange of pleasantries was excruciating. What were they waiting for? He wanted to see drawings of sample dishes. Wasn't that the purpose of their visit? This small talk wasn't getting them anywhere.

Finally, the drawings were presented. Al, roused from his boredom, pounced on the designs. Most were conservative—a simple platinum rim with flowers. Al had hoped for something bold, modern, reflective of the postwar era. The more established chinaware companies had already cornered classic, traditional patterns, the sort that were passed on from generation to generation. He was hoping to target a younger market, those who were looking for something bright and innovative. He gave his input and the manufacturer nodded, but Al couldn't tell whether he was merely listening out of politeness or if he was truly interested in making changes.

"Well, please work on these designs," George said, concluding the meeting. "We'll be back in a couple of days."

At the next factory the same routine was repeated, and at the next and the next. Finally, Al—who wasn't too keen on green tea to begin with—had had enough. "George, how much time do we have to spend at each place? In the States we get down to business and then get the hell out of there; none of this tea-drinking foolishness," he said, exasperated. "When do we get down to prices and shipments?"

"Slow down, Al," George said, holding up one hand. "Japan has a long history, a tradition—there's a certain way of doing things over here."

Al Funabashi and George Aratani in Japan in the1950s. (99.30.62)

Al shook his head as he thought: These guys would be chewed up and spit out in a matter of minutes in New York. But then, he reminded himself, this wasn't New York.

Later they called on Shig Kariya's cousin, Eijoh Mizuno, who George had met on his previous trip to Japan. Mizuno, George explained, was the main agent for United China and Glass Company (UCGC), headquartered in New Orleans. This time, Al was duly impressed. UCGC was a leader in the ceramic "fancy ware" industry; fancy ware included porcelain statues, everything from kewpie dolls to elegant figurines in elaborate eighteenth-century costumes.

Attempting to assist his American cousin's associates as much as he could, Mizuno offered to set them up in an office and assigned two of his own staff members and two secretaries to work with them. More importantly, he provided business contacts and invaluable advice.

"You have to be patient," Mizuno explained to Al over a warm bottle of sake. The three men had gone to a Nagoya hostess bar, where George was hoping to teach Al some Japanese expressions.

"I'll try," Al said, "but it's—what's the word? *Muzukashii.*"

"Yes, it's difficult," Mizuno nodded solemnly. Although he kept his thoughts to himself, the veteran of the ceramic industry was hopeful. He had good intuition: because these two men balanced one another so well, they might just be more successful at selling dishes than the world had ever seen before.

HAPPY ANNIVERSARY
REGRET CANNOT BE WITH YOU LEAVING JAPAN
BY DECEMBER TENTH LOVE=GEORGE
—Telegram sent to Sakaye Aratani
on 24 November 1950

Meanwhile, back at the ranch—or rather, the rented house in California—the Aratani women were growing used to George's frequent absences. In fact, when George returned from his first business trip back in 1948, his younger daughter Linda, just a toddler at the time, didn't recognize him. George attempted to reach out for his daughter, but she shrieked in fear—who was this stranger?

Sakaye took the long separations in stride. Her parents, uncles, and grandparents were not far away, and from their first meeting Sakaye and Masuko had become fast friends. Sakaye never thought it a burden to live under the same roof with George's stepmother. In fact, in time she came to realize that she couldn't manage without her.

Masuko freed Sakaye to be more active outside the home. It was Masuko, who had studied at Nihon Women's University, who sat down with her granddaughters to oversee their mathematics, English, and Japanese-language drills. Never having had children of her own, Masuko was enjoying her role in nurturing and educating Donna and Linda.

The four Aratani women grew very close and became more independent during George's frequent absences. This proved to be the great divide in George's life: his professional time was spent in the male-dominated business world, yet the private world of his own household was run entirely by females. Like other Nisei women of her generation, Sakaye had always deferred to George's decisions and schedule. Whenever the entertainment of clients was required, even at the last minute, she stepped in without complaint. As she once told a *Los Angeles Times* reporter in the 1950s, she admired the virtues of Japanese wives. "They have one thing they respect—their husbands," she said.

Yet Sakaye maintained her own identity. Charming and vibrant, she knew how to forge a path to her dreams. While George was in Japan on one of his early business trips, she took it upon herself to move the family from her parents' home in Lakewood to a rental in Boyle Heights, just east of downtown Los Angeles and therefore closer to George's office. Toshitaro Ishikawa had just moved from Chicago but had not yet sent for his wife and son, so he lived with the family for a few months.

While the rental house was adequate, Sakaye eventually wanted to find a home they could call their own. And like most other American housewives in the late forties and early fifties, she wanted a house in the suburbs.

One day Sakaye pulled her hair back from her face in a neat bun and gathered her pocketbook and the keys to the blue Chevrolet. Driving around a number of exclusive neighborhoods in the San Gabriel Valley, northeast of downtown Los Angeles, she imagined Linda and Donna playing in the front yards of the respectable three-bedroom homes. "For Sale" signs clearly indicated their availability.

Stopping at a real estate agent's office, she met with a broker. "How about these houses?" she asked, pulling out addresses she had jotted on a piece of paper.

"San Marino. And Pasadena. Very nice." The broker smiled noncommittally and took a few notes. "I'll be right back."

Sakaye straightened out the creases in her flared skirt while she waited. When the broker returned, his face was a bit flushed. "I'm sorry. This is a bit awkward—but, well, I've been told that those particular neighborhoods don't sell to Japanese."

"Oh." Sakaye's heart sank, but she didn't allow her anger or disappointment to show. Discrimination had been woven into their lives, from the hardships of the Alien Land Laws to the brutality of the evacuation. It was not George's, Sakaye's, or even Setsuo's way to directly challenge the policies. Instead, they always sought an escape hatch, and they usually found it.

Sakaye, ever the optimist, was not discouraged for long. Getting back into the blue Chevrolet, she explored more neighborhoods.

East of Boyle Heights was the small community of Montebello. Although it was close to downtown Los Angeles, it still boasted green spaces and was bordered by sloping hills. On a corner lot across from the elementary school was a three-bedroom home for sale. As soon as Sakaye stepped inside, the house felt right. George would like this, too; Sakaye was sure of it. Although there were only a few Nisei living in the area, the residents seemed open to newcomers and less provincial than some in other neighborhoods. However, when she inquired at a real estate office, she was again refused: No Japanese wanted.

Sakaye was crushed. She had finally found her ideal house, but it was not within her reach. Somehow she would have to be satisfied with their rental home. Then a phone call came a few days later. "There's been a change," the broker reported. "The house is now available."

Sakaye didn't waste any time. She signed the papers without waiting for George's return from Nagoya.

She gave him the news over the phone. The line was filled with static. "I bought a house," she told him.

"What?" he asked.

"I bought a house," she said louder.

"What kind of house?"

"Nice. A nice house. Across the street from an elementary school for the girls. It has a big living room that can hold a grand piano."

"We don't have a grand piano."

"But we will someday."

George laughed; there was nothing he could do about it now. At this point they were barely making enough money from the dried abalone and the buttons to pay their bills. In fact, they had to dip into their savings. "Yes," he said. "Someday."

Dinnerware buyers eagerly sought out established companies such as Noritake; in fact, the Noritake salesmen usually sent customers their travel itinerary with the expectation that they would be met upon their arrival. Buyers who didn't drop everything and rearrange their own schedules might lose out on stocking the latest Noritake patterns.

Midsized and smaller American potteries and importers often found that buyers for large department stores were unavailable to meet with them. American Commercial—a very small fish in an ocean infested with sharks—had to be daring to get its foot in the door.

One place where a small company might have a chance of doing business was the annual china-and-glass trade shows. These shows consisted of booths set up in hotel lobbies (later in convention centers) which showcased the companies' best wares. Many million-dollar deals were sealed in the evening at elaborate receptions hosted by suppliers in hotel suites.

Al, savvy in salesmanship and dinnerware, knew that trade shows were the place to be. However, the china-and-glass association was a select club—only companies with an established track record were invited.

Moreover, importers were particularly disdained by the dominant Ohio Valley potteries.

One night in 1951, shortly after Al and George returned from one of their buying trips to Japan, they packed up their samples from the chinaware factories in Nagoya—Hira China, Aichi Kagaku, and Nagoya Shokai. Loading the boxes into Al's car, they prepared to crash the biggest dinnerware party of the year.

It was a grueling drive from New York to Pittsburgh; a raging snowstorm nearly forced them to turn back. When they finally arrived, they had to accept inferior accommodations at the Fort Pitt Hotel—known as the "Snake Pit"—along with the other importers who had already set up their booths in the downstairs lobby.

Al and George had not reserved a booth, so they created their own display space in their hotel room. Laying out their samples on the bed and the floor, they put their plan in motion. Utmost discretion was required. "Nobody knows us here," George worried. "We could be thrown out by the association."

Al reassured George that he had plenty of contacts with buyers. The plan was for him to stroll over to the William Penn Hotel and snag potential customers while George stayed in the room and watched the merchandise.

After a while, there was a knock at the door.

"Hey George, it's me, Al. Let me in."

George unlocked the door to let Al and the department store buyers in.

Compared to large companies like Noritake, American Commercial's prices were low. In addition, there was something a little different about their dishes—they were fresh, less pretentious. The buyers began to look interested. They could imagine young housewives with limited budgets setting their tables with this china.

———— •◆• ————

Tad Yamada, meanwhile, was still in Tokyo serving with the U.S. Civil Intelligence Section under the leadership of Paul Rusch, the former Japanese college professor and MIS recruiter. Tad had stayed in close touch with George, and the two men often got together during George's business trips overseas. He also periodically sent dish samples to ACI through the military mail.

During one of his trips to Tokyo, George told Tad how an executive from Mitsubishi Corporation had paid him a surprise visit at the Teito Hotel. "I first met him before the war, at a barbershop in Little Tokyo, Tom Umeda's folks' place. Imagine that." Accompanying the Mitsubishi executive had been Bunpei Maruoka, who worked for Kanegafuchi Chemical Company; like George, they were Keio men. A second meeting followed, and this time a young pharmacist and a physician came along; from them George learned about the state of Japanese medicine.

The doctor had been impressed with a U.S. Army field hospital's use of nitrous oxide—laughing gas—as an anesthesia for injured American GIs. Struggling Japanese hospitals, on the other hand, relied on ether, a highly flammable compound.

The two friends pondered the possibility of two men from the farms of Guadalupe selling medical supplies to Japanese doctors. In addition to importing dishes from Japan, would they also be able to bring highly technical equipment into the country?

George and Tad soon joined forces with the men George had met. After Tad received his discharge from the army, he set up shop in Bunpei's spacious living room in Shinagawa, in the southern section of Tokyo. Hanging a shingle that read "American Commercial" outside the house, in January of 1951 Tad became the first president of the company's Japanese division. He traveled back and forth between New York and Tokyo, and he attended medical conventions where he learned about inventions as diverse as heart valves and isolette rockers for premature babies. Tetsuo Sakata, the young pharmacist who had been present at that second meeting, also helped staff the Japanese office.

The U.S. Army field hospitals were using Heidbrink anesthesia machines, made by Ohio Chemical Company. George rushed back to America, where he discovered that the company was located in Madison, Wisconsin. When his long-distance efforts to contact an executive in the firm failed, George decided to book the next flight to Wisconsin. In Madison, he met the president of Ohio Chemical, Bill Lunger, and convinced him to go out to lunch.

"Now what's your outfit called again?" Bill asked, after ordering a couple of martinis.

"American Commercial, Incorporated."

He looked at George with some skepticism. "How many people do you have over there in Japan?"

"Well, we're just kind of starting out." George didn't add that the office had just moved out of Bunpei's living room into Tad Yamada's apartment in

Tokyo's Minato District.

As they continued talking, the martinis arrived. Then another round, and another. George's drinking skills, sharpened while he was a student at Keio University, were paying off.

"Okay," the president finally said, "I'll give American Commercial an exclusive distributorship in Japan for one year." The two men shook hands, and without signing any papers, they forged a deal. Even as he continued to push the development of the dinnerware business, George was also diversifying his nascent empire.

———◆◆◆———

When George and Al returned to Japan in 1951, George decided to try something different. Instead of staying at a Western-style hotel, he made arrangements for them to stay at a *ryokan*, a traditional Japanese inn, in an area of Tokyo near Sophia University. They wore *yukata* (cotton kimono) instead of suits and ties; they sat on *tatami* mats and gazed at pine trees in the garden. By making these changes George hoped to slow Al's internal clock so that he could better understand Japanese sensibilities and the pace of doing business. Although businessmen in Tokyo ran from appointment to appointment just like their counterparts on Wall Street, psychologically they approached deals with less definite assumptions. There was always a quality of *aimai* (ambiguity)—they kept their cards close to their chest. It was relationship, not finance, which ruled negotiations.

The development of relationships took place after hours, at discos and bars or on the Koganei golf course not far from downtown Tokyo. In fact, the course was operated by one of Toshitaro Ishikawa's former associates after being used by the U.S. Occupational Forces for some time. When a spot eventually opened up at the golf club in 1958, George invested the then small fortune of $2,000 to become a member. He had learned well from his father: golf was a valuable asset in doing business, and it proved to be as helpful in Japan as in America.

Al and George frequented nightclubs, primarily Mama Cherry's Copacabana in Tokyo. Usually a three-piece combo would be playing as the club's beautiful waitresses took orders, socialized, and danced with the patrons; George even learned a new dance called the Dodanpa, which he planned to introduce to Sakaye and his friends in Los Angeles. In a sense, the Copacabana's waitresses were modern-day geisha. As with traditional geisha houses, no other women usually entered cabarets and nightclubs. In

Japanese manufacturer Osao Yamaguchi (far left) and Yoshio Kato (far right) dine with George Aratani and Al Funabashi in Nagoya, Japan, ca. 1952. (43.1998.6)

fact, a customary pile of salt was strategically placed near the entrance in order to purify the establishment from the presence of women.

George and Al often stayed out until the wee hours. As they stumbled into the *ryokan* one night, they were met by the angry stare of their maid. Saying not a word, she prepared their bath. "I think we're in trouble," George commented. Al got the same impression.

The next day the proprietor of the inn spoke to her Nisei guests. "I can't condone this behavior," she said. "Your maid is in your charge. She is expected to prepare your breakfast and wait up for you in the evening. This staying out all night is not good for your health. You need your sleep." She then gave the adult men a curfew—10 P.M.

Staying at the *ryokan* had certainly given Al a taste of old Japan—and it had also effectively put a cramp in their nightlife.

<hr />

As he promoted a more relational approach to business, George noticed that exposure to Western trade was causing the Japanese style of business to erode rapidly. United China and Glass Company's management, for instance, demanded perfection from its employees. Because some of George's staff in Nagoya had previously worked for American-owned United China and Glass, they brought with them a hard-line approach.

Once George overheard one of his staff members berate a manufacturer over the phone for delivering substandard goods. Approaching the employee, George said, "Listen, take it easy. We can't talk to our manufacturers like that. If they don't give us the proper-quality goods, they get one more chance. If they still don't deliver, forget them; we won't use them again. But don't speak to them disrespectfully."

His Japanese employees viewed George's response as too good-natured. After all, they had been trained by officials at American trading companies, who had taught them to look down on manufacturers. When they said "Jump," the manufacturers should ask, "How high?" This George Aratani may have been born in America, but his philosophy was from the past.

This was only the start of the problem. During serious negotiations with manufacturers, George was unabashedly candid: "We've been studying how this new product would do in department stores. We plan to charge this retail price. From that you can figure out how much would be reasonable for us to pay you."

Both manufacturers and his fellow American Commercial executives were dumbfounded. What kind of negotiating tactic was this?

Soon these stories reached the ear of Al Funabashi, who pulled George aside. "Hey, George, they're saying that you're too easy on the factories." Al was never one to skirt the issue.

"Oh?" George was amused.

"They say that Aratani-*san*'s method is very unusual."

George shook his head. "Al, this is my thinking. Certain Americans have this condescending attitude towards Japan because we won the war; some even resort to dirty tricks to get the best deals from Japanese factories. I don't think that's the best way to go. It's more important to have good relations with the manufacturers. They know our markup; we might as well just be open about it."

Al listened carefully, then nodded. Maybe expecting the best out of someone wasn't the same as badgering them. If American Commercial was in this for the long term, its suppliers needed to be part of the team, too.

———◆·◆·◆———

Before they left Japan in 1951, George wanted to resolve one piece of unfinished business. He had thus far put off calling on his friend and former mentor Shinzo Koizumi, the former Keio University president. Part of his hesitation stemmed from the fact that his friends in Japan had warned him about the effects of Koizumi's injuries from an incendiary bomb. While not life-threatening, his wounds had marked him forever. The face that had once rivaled the most handsome *kabuki* actor's had been permanently disfigured.

But George often heard and read about Koizumi's activities. Highly regarded in both the East and the West, he had been appointed tutor to Prince Akihito. With the day of his departure approaching, George finally called Koizumi's home. "I'm Aratani, from America," he said.

"Aratani-*san*," Koizumi's wife answered, "by all means come by."

George brought along several bottles of whiskey as gifts. He found he was nervous about meeting his former mentor again, and despite the fact that he had tried to prepare himself, he was still shocked at the sight of his friend's appearance. Deep scars marked Koizumi's face, and numerous skin grafts had not been able to repair the damage.

As they spoke, however, all discomfort seemed to melt away. Koizumi's voice was the same one George remembered from his Keio days. The whiskey was opened, and they spoke of life during the Occupation.

"You have truly become one of the most respected men in Japan. I read about you in the papers all the time," George said.

"And you—how is your business?"

"It is called American Commercial, Incorporated. ACI." George told Koizumi about the new offices in Nagoya and Tokyo, which were handling medical supplies. "In December we'll be sending over the first nitrous oxide machine to Japan. It will completely revolutionize anesthesiology here."

Koizumi was delighted. "Your hands are in everything, just like your father's. Maybe one day you too will sponsor a sports team to Japan."

"I'd like to," said George, who had inadvertently switched to speaking in English. He poured more whiskey into Koizumi's glass.

Koizumi looked at George for a while before speaking. "You spoil me," he said in English.

George was at a loss as to how to react to Koizumi's statement. "*Kanpai*," he finally said, lifting up his glass. "Here's to a new era in Japan."

**The principals of American Commercial, Inc., in the 1960s:
(left to right) Yoichi Nakase, Tad Yamada, Tets Murata, Joe Orshan, Al Funabashi,
George Aratani, Ed Cooper, Min Endo, and Shig Kariya.** (99.30.84)

Although an increasing number of trading companies continued to close, ACI was beginning to grow. The New York office moved across the street into a much larger space. The accommodations at 212 Fifth Avenue were not plush, but they at least allowed for a proper showroom in which to display the expanding line of ACI dishes.

With more dishes came more executives, including Min Endo, a slim Nisei man with kind eyes who had served at both the Military Intelligence Service Language School and in the Occupational Forces with Tad Yamada. He was given responsibility for customer service and later was instrumental in streamlining ACI's order processing.

Al headed up ACI's front line. He recruited Joe Orshan, who brought merchandising expertise gained at Cox & Co., sales agents for the Southern Potteries of Erwin, Tennessee. And Al's younger brother, Ken, who had recently graduated from Bowling Green State University in Ohio, accompanied him on local sales trips to such discount stores as Kresge's in Newark, New Jersey.

On Friday nights, however, there was no selling. Instead, the executives of ACI rolled up their sleeves and cleaned the showroom. They unpacked the new shipments of china which lined the hallways and shined up new sample dishes for buyers, who often stopped by on Saturdays. Nobody had to tell them to trade in their paperwork for dust mops—they were a team.

Other than the salesmen, no one had a specific title, and no job descriptions were on file. Most of the Nisei had been raised in households where their parents said little but expected much. They knew how to operate without detailed instruction.

The same was true for the Los Angeles office, which handled the financial aspects of the business, as well as the shipping arrangements for West Coast outlets. The California headquarters had also moved into a larger office south of Little Tokyo, at Maple and 11th streets, occupying about 1,500 square feet of a brick warehouse. A small showroom in front displayed American Commercial's dish samples. George had a desk, and Toshitaro Ishikawa worked there as he dealt with suppliers from Japan. Tets Murata kept their accounts up to date, and various salesmen worked the telephones. A shipping manager oversaw the inventory in the back, where stacks of dishes were stored.

The movement of inventory was the bane of many trading companies. Before they left the port of departure, imports had to be paid for with letters of credit. Once they arrived in the U.S., the merchandise was usually stored for a time before being shipped to chain or department stores—which usually didn't pay within the standard billing period of 30 days. This long time lapse between paying and being paid meant importers were losing money.

Even the larger Japanese *kaisha* faced similar difficulties in New York. "Lack of adequate finance capital is one of the larger stumbling blocks facing the Japanese suppliers," wrote Roku Sugahara in a 1952 "A Nisei in Manhattan" column.

> In order to keep in operation, they must borrow funds at the bank and pay terrifically high interest rates. The payment of one percent interest per week is quite a common thing. In order to meet the relatively high payroll each week, the bosses must go out and borrow money, adding to their costs and financial instability.

ACI expected to cover their letters of credit prior to receiving money from their retail customers. George's responsibility—to forge congenial relationships with lenders—was not an easy task. Amerex, a competitor that had beat out American Commercial in a deal with one of Nagoya's premier bone china manufacturers, had already gone out of business. Why should any bank lend money to a small company in business fewer than five years?

With his straightforward style, George nevertheless managed to gain the confidence of both American bank executives and Japanese suppliers. Like a deft dancer, he could move in different circles without losing his momentum or equilibrium. In the office he had the ability to calmly smooth over cultural and generational tensions that occasionally arose between Issei and Nisei staff members. It was his sense of balance that won people over, including new employees.

Then, in 1951, just as George had secured a loan from Bank of America and ACI began to make serious inroads in the chinaware trade, his health began to deteriorate. This time he was diagnosed with hepatitis.

"Hepatitis?" George stared at his doctor with surprise.

"I suspected it from the beginning," his doctor told him. "The whites of your eyes seemed jaundiced. And now the tests confirm it. You may have contracted it from seafood. But at any rate, I'm admitting you to White Memorial here in L.A."

"How about my wife and daughters? Will they be okay?"

"If they're healthy, I'm sure they will be fine."

For the next 11 months George was bedridden, initially at White Memorial in Boyle Heights, where he could stand at his window and wave to his daughters in the parking lot.

"When's Daddy coming home?" they asked.

"Soon, soon." Even as Sakaye reassured the girls, secretly she was worried. She knew that hepatitis damaged the liver and could have irreparable effects; it might also return later in life. This time Sakaye did not have magic turtle's blood to cure her husband, but she did have a sister who could now help her husband on the road to recovery.

Sakaye's younger sister Vickie had blossomed into an independent woman who styled her thick, black hair in a flip and wore plastic-framed eyeglasses. George had already asked her to come work for him even while she was commuting at night to Metropolitan Business Junior College. She would be filling in for George's longtime friend and American Commercial associate, Yoichi Nakase, who had been called to serve in the Korean War. Now Vickie sat beside George's hospital bed as her brother-in-law dictated letters to banks, suppliers, and lawyers.

Not all the matters handled in George's correspondence were directly related to American Commercial, Inc. In fact, losses suffered due to the wartime evacuation still remained a topic of discussion in the Japanese American community. Some Japanese Americans had already collected money through the Japanese American Evacuation Claims Act, which had been signed into law by President Truman in 1948. Although well intentioned, the law was exceedingly limited—it only compensated for "damages to or loss of real or personal property" during the wartime incarceration. There would be no compensation for loss of profits or earnings. Furthermore, only individuals, not businesses, could file a claim. Finally, no awards could exceed the pitifully small sum of $2,500.

George had earlier filled out his form by the January 2, 1950, deadline under the guidance of attorney John Aiso. He included losses suffered due to the liquidation of the hog farm, fertilizer company, and wholesale produce company. He listed the $7,000 legal fees spent on the Sumitomo Bank lawsuit. At the bottom, he included the cost to replace his treasured trout- and surf-fishing equipment, stolen from the shed of his Peralta Street home. The total claim—excluding his interest in Vegetable Farms and Guadalupe Farms—exceeded $70,000. Only after an amendment widened the act's scope was George eligible to receive funds, but for less than 15 percent of the total amount.

Throughout his personal financial trials, George did not forget the years of service from those employees who had been connected with Guadalupe Produce and related ventures. He firmly believed in the system of *orei*, a gift of thanks, to individuals who had labored so long under his and his father's leadership. Even as he lay in his sickbed, he instructed John Aiso to process bonuses for former managers of Guadalupe Produce and Vegetable Farms. The checks were sent to him in his hospital room for signature in December of 1951.

Whether it be the team in Guadalupe or the one in Los Angeles and New York, George was fully aware that people had always been his best investment.

By the end of 1951 the New York office of American Commercial was gearing up to go to Pittsburgh again, this time for its official debut at the prestigious china-and-glass show. This time they would not have to resort to secret sales meetings in a hotel room—they would have their own booth on the convention floor. American Commercial was now a formal member of the association and a real player in the chinaware industry.

George was still sick in bed, so it was left entirely up to Al and the others to prepare the booth. Shig Kariya and Ken Funabashi were assigned to drive the merchandise to Pittsburgh, while Al traveled by plane. The drivers filled the entire backseat and trunk of Al's Ford with boxes and bags of samples; packages were even tied on the roof. As Shig and Ken headed west, they hit a blinding snowstorm. A drive that normally took a few hours stretched into 24. With backs and legs aching, Shig and Ken finally staggered out of the car and into the Fort Pitt Hotel.

Al was pacing the worn carpet in the lobby.

"What took you so long?" he asked.

I'd like to see you drive in this weather, Ken silently fumed. But as they all focused their attention on unloading the car, they felt a growing sense of excitement as they shook the snow from the bags on top of the car. Eyeing the booths other importers had already set up, they wondered how buyers would respond to the new merchandise introduced by American Commercial.

The show opened immediately after New Year's Day, an auspicious time for Japanese Americans. Back in California, Sakaye and Masuko were resting after preparing a traditional New Year's meal of fresh *mochi* (rice cakes), black beans, and other Japanese delicacies. In Pittsburgh, meanwhile, the men were snacking on stale pretzels and sipping scotch as they pitched their products to prospective customers. Whether due to the good luck of the new year or their skill and salesmanship, by the end of the show American Commercial had accumulated a pile of orders. Buyers were amazed at both the prices and the quality of their dishes.

On the last night, the men of ACI stayed up late and celebrated. While Ken was a blood relative, Al felt a similarly close affinity with all those connected with the company—they were an extended family. Al wanted to do well not only for himself, Maria, and his children, but also for all the families relying on a paycheck from American Commercial. He had been able to help some people during his presidency of the New York JACL and through his championing of the Fair Employment Practices Commission. As a principal of American Commercial, Inc., Al hoped to do even more.

— ◆ —

George recovered fully from his bout with hepatitis, and he returned to his Los Angeles office. Soon he was back to his fast work pace, sending letters of credit, meeting with lenders, and maintaining payroll. He continued to keep in touch with many of his old Guadalupe associates, including Butch Tamura, who had started a dry-cleaning business in Pasadena. News was not always happy: deaths, a suicide, and other tragedies had befallen many in his circle of acquaintances. Feelings of loss washed over George, but he simply buried himself more deeply in his work.

Meanwhile, on the home front, Sakaye had the difficult task of maintaining her family's household in a way that maximized George's comfort. She reared two young girls almost single-handedly. She entertained out-of-town guests at a moment's notice. She never complained of the demands placed on her as an international trader's wife, though these were not inconsequential: either George was gone on business trips for long periods of time, or her house was full of Japanese visitors or associates passing through Los Angeles. Fortunately, she had her mother-in-law, Masuko, to assist with child care and to also give instruction on Japanese etiquette, food, and culture.

Serving as a Sunday School teacher at Nishi Hongwanji Temple in Little Tokyo and assisting with the PTA at Eastmont Elementary School kept Sakaye absorbed in her two daughters' lives. She also began to socialize with the growing number of Nisei women moving into the neighborhood. These were the wives of white-collar, middle-class men who had started their own businesses, ranging from insurance agencies to grocery stores. These families were gradually climbing up the economic ladder, a rise that resulted not only in more material goods, but also new ways of socializing. While the men formed Optimist clubs and golf clubs, the Montebello wives decided to launch their own women's club; these social and philanthropic organizations were the jewels of every thriving suburban city in the fifties.

Montebello, in fact, already had such an organization, whose clubhouse faced the city park. This club did not explicitly bar Japanese or other minorities from membership, but the young Nisei thirty-something women—many of whom had been turned away from buying homes in other neighborhoods—felt more comfortable starting their own group. As a result, they organized the Montebello Japanese Women's Club in 1951.

Like other clubs within the California Federation of Women's Clubs, the Montebello group planned events that were both fun and which raised money for social causes—fashion shows and sewing contests, for example. But Sakaye kept thinking back to the Depression, when her mother had left food on the doorstep for wandering transients. There must be something that they, as the wives of successful businessmen, could do to help those outside their own circle.

**Sakaye Aratani (third from left) and members of the
Montebello Japanese Women's Club, ca. 1950s.** (99.30.177)

The women found their answer in a strange source: used nylon stockings. The Women's Welfare Service, a Los Angeles–based group dedicated to assisting Japanese war widows, was collecting discarded nylon stockings, still a rare commodity in Japan. The nylon material was shipped to Japan and used by the widows to make men's nonstretch hose, gloves, and decorative items for resale in the U.S.

This campaign, called "Nylons for Japan," electrified the interest of the American wives. Perhaps because most of their husbands had served with the U.S. Armed Forces during World War II, the women could readily identify with the losses of war. It was easy to picture the faces of forlorn women, younger versions of their own mothers. And if they could help while also being thrifty, all the better.

Led by Sakaye and Kimi Inadomi, whose husband was building a chain of grocery stores, the Montebello group helped to send letters to churches and organizations across the nation. Once a week they gathered in the Women's Welfare Service office in Los Angeles to bundle the nylon hose into gunnysacks which they then tied up with twine. Sakaye was responsible for driving the full sacks to Los Angeles Harbor.

One day, headed south on the freeway, she felt her car suddenly lurch unevenly. She pulled over to the side as cars sped past her. Dressed in pumps and a skirt, she examined her tires; sure enough, the left front one was completely flat.

"Need some help?" a man asked as he pulled up behind her.

Sakaye nodded, gratefully. "I've got a flat tire."

As she opened the trunk to find the spare, the man stared.

"They're stockings," she explained. "Used ones."

The man shook his head. "Whatever you say, lady."

Sakaye didn't bother to explain. She was devoted to her volunteer mission, one of many she would undertake.

———◦◆◦———

Tradition is the enemy of progress.
—Slogan on a plaque in Al Funabashi's office

To make it to Macy's and beyond, American Commercial, Inc., had to break some rules—not laws or moral principles, but traditions within the dinnerware industry. One of their first targets was the china closet.

Many middle-class housewives had china cabinets in their home which held the treasured china, the dishes with a special pattern which they had carefully chosen before their wedding day. Those dishes would usually be used only on special occasions, for Thanksgiving and Christmas dinners, anniversaries, or family reunions. On those days only adult women were allowed to wash the dishes; husbands and children were strictly prohibited, lest a slippery hand drop a valuable piece of china and break it. However, if such mishaps did occur, the housewife could rest assured that a replacement with the same pattern would be available, even 10 years after purchase.

American Commercial, on the other hand, wanted to change the whole notion of chinaware as something precious to be used only on special occasions. Instead of promising that pieces would be carried indefinitely—a method referred to as "open stock"—ACI sold their dinnerware in limited sets. When consumers became bored with their old patterns, they were encouraged to buy a new one, and the new choices offered were fun, full of colors and variety.

The design of ACI's dinnerware was a bilateral process between decorators in Japan and their counterparts in New York. While American designers knew their customers' taste, the Nagoya team understood what colors and patterns would be technically possible and cost-efficient. One key Japanese decorator even moved to New York to immerse himself in American culture.

This merging of creative forces soon led to innovative designs: A sketch of fresh-cut flowers splashed across the middle of a plate, with the stems close to the rim. Japanese-influenced crackleware. Highly stylized images that looked as if they'd been drawn with a Japanese ink brush. ACI's early best-sellers included Shasta Pine, which got them into Chicago-based retailer Marshall Field's, and Woodrose, which was available in four different colors. Eventually even the beautiful Maria Funabashi had a pattern named after her: "Bella Maria," dishes with a vibrant blue rim.

The aesthetic value of the dishes was not the only factor at play—merchandising, packaging, and marketing were also key to reaching the department stores. While many high-end chinaware companies in the 1950s sold items piece by piece, each with a lifetime-replacement guarantee, ACI instead packaged their dinnerware in sets of 12 place settings for the bargain price of $50. At that time 93-piece sets were the standard for imported china: 12 each of dinner plates, dessert plates, bread-and-butter plates, fruit dishes, soup bowls, sets of cups and saucers, a platter, a casserole dish with a lid, a baking dish, a gravy boat, and a sugar bowl with lid and creamer. Mastermind Al Funabashi added 5 more pieces, including vegetable dishes, to bring ACI's standard set to 98 pieces. Soon Al's 98 became the rage with other manufacturers as well until overseas labor costs rose; 53-piece sets for 8 were then introduced in department stores.

Such innovations caught the eye of Jerry Stone, the chinaware buyer for Macy's who had met with George and Al in 1950 but hadn't purchased anything from them. Macy's was experiencing its own postwar woes: traditionally known for its cut-rate prices—attainable due to the store's sheer size—Macy's was now facing competition from Gimbel's in pharmaceuticals, Gertz of Long Island in books, and Bloomingdale's in stationery and menswear. In 1952 the store posted the first annual loss in its history.

As a result of this downturn, Macy's began to rethink its sales strategy. The store, which had pioneered fixed prices on merchandise, had always followed a cash-only policy instituted by its founder, Rowland H. Macy. Now, with the rising popularity of purchasing on credit, the store began to offer charge accounts to its customers.

Macy's also changed its approach to dealing with suppliers. Instead of attempting to squeeze every drop of profit from its vendors, the store advocated a more supportive stance. Fortunately, chinaware buyer Jerry Stone followed that philosophy long before it became a company edict. He had begun visiting American Commercial on a regular basis to look over the inventory and talk shop with Al, but he had yet to make a formal purchase.

Then, one afternoon in the early 1950s he pointed to the display case and said to Al, "I'll take these sets."

From his corner of the office, Shig looked up from his papers—bills for inventory, orders for patterns, and sales commissions—and watched as Al offered one of his cigars to Jerry Stone. This sale would lead to even greater opportunities, he knew: once other stores saw ACI merchandise in Macy's ads, they would want the same patterns.

There was no official celebration that evening, just more work. It had taken three arduous years to make it into the largest department store in the world, but American Commercial, Incorporated, knew that this was still just the beginning.

Up to this point American Commercial had distributed dishes with various factory backstamps; it had no unifying single brand. George preferred it this way. The Japanese are proud people, he thought—if the merchandise they manufactured carried their names, it would certainly be of the highest quality. But he discovered that this strategy didn't always work.

On one of their trips to Japan in the 1950s, George and Al were introduced to a beautiful, unusual product. It was a coup design, the industry description for a plate that is slightly curved with a raised, flat rim; the entire rim of this particular plate was a solid, brilliant, cobalt blue. George wanted to ask about the process used to produce such an effect, but he knew he wouldn't get far. The retention of such technical secrets ensured the livelihood of a company.

"This is very attractive," George said. "Are you sure this shade of blue will be uniform? *Daijōbu*? [Will it be all right?]"

The manufacturer recoiled as if he had smelled something distasteful. "Are you trying to insult me? What I am showing you is what you'll receive." He seemed as proud as an ancient samurai.

Leaving the factory with the unique sample plate, Al was excited. "We can do a big national promotion."

George nodded. "We're going to make a pile of money on this thing." They agreed to order 2,000 93-piece sets, which would take the manufacturer an entire year to produce.

When they returned to New York, every department store—Macy's, Gimbel's, and Abraham and Straus—wanted the plates with the brilliant blue border. Finally, Macy's won the bid. "If you give us an exclusive," said Jerry

Stone, the Macy's buyer, "we'll take any number of sets that you can get."

Within a few months, the first batch of 400 sets arrived at New York Harbor; they were shipped to Macy's warehouse and from there to the customers' homes. In a matter of days, Macy's received a dozen phone calls: the color on the dinnerplates and other pieces didn't match. The sets were shipped back to the department store and finally landed in the American Commercial warehouse.

George took a swig from the antacid he had stashed in his desk drawer. Then he called the manufacturer in Nagoya. "Stop production," he said, "I'm coming to Japan."

Face to face with the factory executive, George explained the lack of uniformity within the dinner sets. The manufacturer shook his head. "I don't believe you," he said.

"Listen," George responded, "I'll pay for your round-trip ticket so you can see all the returned merchandise for yourself."

"I've never been to the United States, and I don't plan to go now. Everything we shipped out of our warehouse is good merchandise."

George could see that he wasn't going to get very far with this man. "Fine," he said. "I'm going to have to complain to Nagoya's MITI office."

MITI was the acronym for the Ministry of International Trade and Industry, a governmental agency established before the war to regulate economic activity. Accompanied by his Nagoya office representative, George went to the MITI office, where he displayed the sample dish alongside six pieces produced later—all were different shades of blue.

After the men discussed the matter for a while, George called the manufacturer. "The top man at MITI's Nagoya office is going to be the judge," George said. "I'm going to assume the cost of shipping back about 50 pieces of bad merchandise. Then the three of us—you, me, and the official—will look it over. We'll go from there."

Weeks later, after examining the faulty china the manufacturer finally admitted: "This is the best we can do."

"That's it," said George. "Cancel my order."

Because ACI dealt with various independent factories, costly production problems like this were a real possibility; however, contracting with multiple suppliers meant that American Commercial could take advantage of each factory's unique specialty and technique. While George had been happy with this direction, he came to realize that American Commercial needed to establish a unifying brand name. Salesmen didn't want to peddle wares with different backstamps, including the acronym "ACI," which lacked public recognition (some people referred to ACI, devoid of any visual image, as "Akki" or "Assi" dinnerware).

George wanted a name that was easy to pronounce and which would serve as a symbol of this new unified brand. He thought back to ancient Japan, when Nara was the nation's capital. The imperial family, with its high regard for poetry and literature, had looked towards the three-peaked mountain range in the distance. They called it Mikasa, meaning "three umbrellas."

Mikasa was also the name of a modern battleship that had been victorious in the Russo-Japanese War in 1905. The name also evoked the image of Prince Mikasa, Emperor Hirohito's youngest brother, who was a leader of compassion and integrity.

In December of 1957, a new brand name—Mikasa—was introduced by American Commercial, Incorporated. There was no fanfare, no press conference. It would hold up on its own, thought George. He was convinced of it.

12

Going Solid State

"Sayonara to the Stigma, 'Made in Japan'"
—Headline on Charles Lincoln's column
"The Stereo Scene,"
Popular Electronics, **July 1969**

One Christmas in Manhattan during the 1950s, George was passing out holiday bonus checks to the American Commercial employees. "I think that you should all consider reinvesting your bonuses as stock options in the company," he said.

No one spoke for a moment.

"We have to think in terms of the long run," George continued, as some of the executives in the modest offices of American Commercial looked at one another with skepticism. Would this company actually make it? And was ACI stock worth their families foregoing extra Christmas gifts?

While most Americans were riding the wave of the postwar economic boom, the Nisei were starting from scratch as they sought to figure out where, exactly, they fit into the American dream. In the Santa Maria Valley, the inheritors of Minami Farms had returned to Guadalupe with hopes of leasing more land beyond the 80 acres owned by Isamu Minami; they also set up an operation near Fresno with every intention of making a comeback on the Central Coast. The Tomookas of Santa Maria Farms had resettled in the area, but their soil was now being farmed by strangers. Ken Kitasako, the former manager of Santa Maria Farms, had returned to the area in

Groundbreaking ceremony for the Kenwood Americas facility on Clark Drive in Mt. Olive, New Jersey, ca. 1977. (99.30.160)

1951, this time as the head of a small shipper, Pismo-Oceano Vegetable Exchange, a venture run predominantly by Japanese American farmers.

George was also feeling the financial pinch. Maintaining the cash flow for the dinnerware business continued to be a struggle. Department stores, still the best distribution outlets, took months to pay for their orders, while the Japanese factories required payment before shipping goods. George had to be creative, sometimes even borrowing from Sakaye's mother to keep the business going.

In spite of such financial concerns, he was always open to new ventures. Corporate diversification was nothing new: by 1960, General Electric—a company whose origins stretched back to Thomas A. Edison and the invention of the lightbulb in the nineteenth century—was producing jet engines, supporting television networks, and selling two-door refrigerators. Even Setsuo Aratani himself had sold both agricultural products and sake, although most of Setsuo's multiple ventures had been interrelated in some way, with a connection between the fertilizer plant, the packing shed, and the dehydrating plant. In the late fifties and sixties, George would be risking capital—and, in fact, the future of Mikasa and American Commercial—on innovations that would virtually define their times.

———◆———

[Nuclear reactors] are thus an important
preparation for the time, not too far distant, when this
nation must supplement conventional sources of
energy with nuclear fuels, and for the still more imminent
date when other nations in the free world must do this.
—W. Kenneth Davis, director,
Division of Reactor Development,
U.S. Atomic Energy Commission, 1958

In 1959 George received a highly unusual phone call from Tad Yamada, who was by now back in New York heading up AMCO, the medical equipment division of American Commercial. This arm of the business was flourishing, with a branch in Osaka and plans for a new, larger office in Tokyo. AMCO's catalogue of equipment primarily featured U.S.–made goods, including an artificial respirator. The company also exported one of Japan's first automatic blood-cell counters.

But Tad's call had nothing to do with disease, or even medicine. "They want to bring a nuclear reactor into Japan," Tad told George.

"What?" George thought maybe he wasn't hearing right.

"It would be a training reactor for educational purposes," Tad went on. "They want to go critical."

The proposal had come from American Technology Laboratory (ATL), a subsidiary of American Standard Radiators; the company was based in California, their offices near Stanford University, George's alma mater. Because ATL believed that nuclear energy was the wave of the future, they wanted to convince the leaders of Japan—the only country to have suffered atomic warfare—of the reactor's safety and effectiveness. By "going critical," the reactor would release energy after the splitting of uranium atoms.

George drummed his fingers on his desk as he listened. He was painfully aware of Japan's allergic reaction to nuclear power, even for peacetime use; his own relatives had died in the Hiroshima blast. Would involvement in this project lead to financial ruin? Wouldn't bringing in a nuclear reactor cast a dark shadow on their medical-supply business? He wasn't ready to give Tad a definite answer until he had spoken with the principals of ATL and his own Tokyo staff.

At American Standard, the laboratory's parent company, George met with executive Harold Miller. "It's very unfortunate that Japan had to be the first victim of the atomic bomb," Miller said, "but nevertheless, atomic energy will inevitably play a part in their peacetime endeavors. This demonstration will be important to the growth of Japanese industry."

Despite his fears, George discovered that his own staff in Tokyo also heartily endorsed the project. "Don't worry, Aratani-*san*," they said. "This will be good for our image. We'll be seen as a pioneer. Japan does not have many sources of energy. This nuclear reactor will put us on the map."

Japan was not a total stranger to the peacetime use of nuclear technology. By 1955 the publisher of the *Yomiuri Shimbun* newspaper, Matsutaro Shoriki, had invited two American nuclear-power experts to lecture on the atomic age. Japan had already established its own Atomic Energy Commission, and an independent nuclear research project was underway northeast of Tokyo.

The general public, on the other hand, was still unwilling to embrace anything nuclear. When it was announced in 1957 that Uji City in Kyoto was to be the site of a research reactor, local residents protested. Three hundred people crowded into an elementary school to hear details of the project, which was cosponsored by Kyoto and Osaka universities. They pointed out that the Uji River was not far from the proposed site. "If the radiation-laden waste leaks, our water supply will be polluted," predicted a worried professor from Osaka University who resided in the area.

Japan's antinuclear movement grew as more academics voiced their protests. Then, in October of 1957, the core of a reactor located in the Northern England town of Windscale suffered a meltdown of its uranium fuel rods. The damage was eventually contained, but large amounts of radioactive isotopes had polluted the atmosphere and the ground where cattle grazed, not to mention the water used to cool down the core. Two million liters of milk were feared contaminated, and they were dumped into the surrounding rivers.

When news of this accident reached Japan, nuclear safety commissions were set up in Uji City and other locales throughout Japan, and student groups demanded that nuclear reactors be kept away from populated areas. There was a general backlash, and talk of new nuclear reactors died down— that is, until George Aratani arrived back in Tokyo in 1959.

As usual, George didn't let ideological, political, or emotional concerns rule his decision. Like a high-precision scale, he weighed the pros and the cons. Once he received positive feedback from his Tokyo staff, the scales were definitely tipped in favor of the project.

Working together with American Technology Laboratories, American Commercial had already identified a likely site for the proposed reactor demonstration: the International Science Exhibition scheduled for May, to be set up near Tokyo Bay. It was largely up to George to get clearance from both the U.S. and Japanese governments to bring over a rod of uranium for the demonstration.

To forge a plan for the construction of the uranium tank, George again depended on people he knew. This time it was Tom Umeda, the Nisei Caltech graduate who had traveled to Japan immediately before the outbreak of war.

Tom, who had suffered job discrimination in the U.S. despite his scientific genius, had found recognition in Japan. He had worked for the Mitsubishi conglomerate before war broke out, and he had worked on designs for the Zero fighter plane. He was now employed by one of the larger chemical companies in Japan, Chiyoda Kako.

George brought out the blueprints for the tank, which would span more than 15 square feet. "It's too expensive for us to ship this over," he said. "Do you think that you can make it?"

Tom glanced at the specifications. The tank was a simple cylindrical steel structure that would hold the uranium rods. This was a boiling water reactor, similar to one already in full operation in Vallecitos, California, 40 miles southeast of San Francisco. The most crucial part of its construction was the welding of the tank, as all seams needed to be totally secure to prevent radioactive leakage.

"We can't foul this up," said George. "It would cause an international incident."

Tom nodded and rolled up the blueprints. "We can do it."

Workers at Chiyoda Kako were kept very busy during the next few months as they toiled to complete the tank on time. The two-week exhibition was to open on May 5, with the demonstration of the nuclear reactor scheduled for May 12. As the day approached, the usually calm George Aratani was becoming agitated. They had only one week to assemble the reactor, which arrived from California in separate pieces. A diesel generator had to be brought over from an American military base. And finally the uranium, protected in a tube and carefully crated, arrived via airplane.

The tank was transported from the construction site south of Tokyo to the exhibition hall. While the city's inhabitants slept, highways were closed as the tank made its slow, four-hour trip with a police escort. George stayed up until four o'clock in the morning to watch the large truck haul the tremendous tank.

On May 12, the 1.8 million visitors and conferees at the International Science Exhibition were all abuzz. Emperor Hirohito arrived at 9:45 in the morning. George, his hands clammy, watched the emperor closely; this was the same monarch the 11-year-old George had peeked at during his coronation march decades earlier. This was the same Emperor Hirohito who had walked through the flattened, charred rubble of Hiroshima and Nagasaki just 14 years ago. And today, on May 12, 1959, history was again being made.

The emperor, who was wearing a white gown over his austere suit, inspected every inch of the reactor. When he walked up the ramp, the lid to the tank was uncovered temporarily for his perusal. Finally, the critical moment arrived.

George held his breath. At a signal from an American Standard executive, a technician flipped the switch, and the reactor was put into action. The demonstration was over in a matter of minutes, but those few minutes had safely and successfully propelled Japan into a peaceful new atomic age.

Meanwhile, back in the States, it was business as usual. By the late fifties a cadre of trading companies and determined *kaisha* men had opened the door for Japanese imports in the U.S. market. Instead of selling trinkets and clothing, many entrepreneurs had begun to market cameras and audio equipment. They included a Japanese engineer who had first come to the U.S. marketing a tiny $29.95 transistor radio, a Nisei couple who had operated a gift store in Okayama after the war, and a youthful trader and Keio graduate who would later marry George's half sister's daughter. These individuals would eventually rank among the titans of the next wave of consumer products: Akio Morita, the cofounder of the Sony Corporation; Tad and Elaine Yamagata, who launched A & A International, now a subsidiary of RadioShack Corporation; and Sadahei "Sam" Kusumoto, chairman emeritus of Minolta Corporation, American distributors of Japan's Minolta cameras and business equipment.

Also working within the electronics trade was George's former Minnesota colleague, Bill Kasuga, who had remained in the Military Intelligence Service until 1958. Bill was born in San Francisco, but had been raised in the high altitudes of the Japan Alps. His father had been a barber; there was no family wealth to speak of. But what Bill lacked in money, he made up in compassion and kindness. (In fact, as a young man he had saved a nine-year-old boy from drowning near his brother's Sausalito Bait Shop.)

Like the men of American Commercial, Bill also knew how to use his Japanese-language skills to full advantage. After his discharge from MIS, he took a job with A & A Trading, a New York–based company begun by Tad and Elaine Yamagata. At A & A Trading he became acquainted with two brothers who shared his surname, Kasuga, and who were, coincidentally, from the same Japanese village where he had grown up. The Kasuga brothers had joined forces with their brother-in-law to form a company—Kasuga Musen, later renamed Trio—which specialized in audio equipment

Trio was established in Japan in 1946, the same year as another Japanese manufacturer, Tokyo Telecommunications Engineering Corporation, the predecessor to the Sony Corporation. Using a combination of their own factories and subcontractors, Trio produced amplifiers, tuners, and other sound equipment for two American outlets: Lafayette, a respected audio company; and RadioShack, a chain of audio equipment stores which also sold its own Realistic brand.

GIs who had served overseas were well acquainted with the Japanese audio products sold at the post exchanges, products made by such companies as Pioneer, Sansui, Sony, and TEAC. In the U.S., however, these companies were making few inroads into the industry, even as lesser-known manufacturers supplied import companies with less-than-stellar products. Because American buyers were combing Japan for cut-rate products and Japanese manufacturers were hungry for their business, the cheap merchandise flowing into the U.S. was bound to be inferior. Thus, "Made in Japan" became a catchphrase for "shoddy products."

The audio equipment Trio produced, on the other hand, was of high quality. In his work at A & A Trading, Bill sensed the untapped potential of Trio and its products. Sitting in his New York office on Fifth Avenue, just blocks away from American Commercial, Inc., he began thinking about George Aratani, his former MIS colleague and golf buddy. Somehow George—a budding entrepreneur and skilled international trader—might be able to raise Trio up to the next level.

Back on the home front in Los Angeles, in 1958 the Aratanis moved from their suburban tract house in Montebello to a custom-built home in the Hollywood Hills, overlooking the glassy blue reservoir called Lake Hollywood. The site was first discovered by Sakaye's sister Vickie, who, after serving as George's personal assistant while he was confined with hepatitis, had graduated from the University of Southern California with a teaching degree. Vickie was now married to architect and World War II veteran Henry Tetsuo Nakabayashi.

Henry designed George and Sakaye's dream house, according to their specifications, and he supervised every detail of the construction. Retaining a Japanese flavor in both its exterior and interior design, the new home had three bedrooms and a special eight-mat *tatami* room, which opened into a small Japanese garden where Masuko could practice the tea ceremony. The family moved in just as Donna and Linda were entering junior high school.

The Aratanis' house soon became the focus of the society pages in the Japanese American vernacular newspapers. "Straight out of 'House Beautiful,'" according to Kats Kunitsugu in her column "Carrousel," published in the *Kashu Mainichi.*

ACI manager Toshitaro Ishikawa and his wife, Komano, made an early visit to the new home in the relatively undeveloped neighborhood. Toshitaro, in his characteristically reflective manner, went from room to room, silently relishing the success of his former employer's son.

A few months later, on November 30, 1959, Toshitaro died of an aneurysm at the age of 59. He had relinquished his Japanese citizenship and had become naturalized as soon as the McCarran-Walter Act was signed in 1952. "I have no plans to return to Japan," he had told Komano. In spite of long years in Gila River, he harbored no bitterness toward his adopted country. He was buried in Forest Lawn in the Hollywood Hills, a few miles from the new Aratani home, not long after the mortuary opened its gates to the Japanese for the first time.

The new way of listening that has seized so quickly and vigorously on the American imagination can be identified in a brief but magical phrase—high fidelity.
—John Conley, editor of *High Fidelity* magazine

Whenever George was in New York, Bill Kasuga would drop by the American Commercial office to visit his old MIS buddy. "George, you have to get into the audio business," said Bill, who had added some weight to his slight frame.

"I have my hands full with the dinnerware business." George was used to people approaching him with new projects ranging from real estate to motion pictures. Requests had grown even more frequent right after the Los Angeles vernacular newspapers reported on his purchase of a site in Tokyo for a three-story building to house AMCO, the medical-supply business. He had also bought a slightly larger tract of land in Nagoya for AMCO and American Commercial.

George didn't seriously consider Bill's comments at the time, but he later recalled that Tad—who had served with both men in the MIS— encouraged him to diversify the business into this arena. Music was now the rage, even back in Japan. Everyone bought 33⅓ LP (long-playing) records of such performers as Nat King Cole, Perry Como, and Elvis Presley. These records were played on high-fidelity systems (hi-fis) and stereos.

Long gone was the antiquated phonograph with its heavy needle and scratchy sound quality; no longer did households have simple monophonic systems with one channel and a single speaker. Now the standard gear typically included amplifiers, tuners, and stereos with two loudspeakers. Audiophiles collected needles, vacuum tubes, wiring, and speakers to create their own one-of-a-kind hi-fis.

At first, George didn't understand why anyone needed two speakers.

"They're to accommodate two signals," an engineer explained. "More like how we hear things with our own two ears. When you listen to an orchestra, you can pick up all the different instruments balanced together."

After doing his own research, George understood that this new way of reproducing sound was indeed revolutionary, analogous to the jump from an automobile's standard shift to automatic transmission. The electronics industry definitely had the potential to be much bigger than dinnerware, but George also realized that the competition in the field, fueled by image and advertising, was exceedingly fierce. It's dog-eat-dog, he thought; I can't enter this field just halfway. He called Bill Kasuga and said, "I want to meet these Kasuga brothers."

Without signing any formal documents or contracts, in 1961 George sealed an agreement giving him exclusive distributorship of stereo equipment manufactured by Trio. Bill Kasuga left the trading company he had been working for and moved into the New York office of American Commercial, Inc., as head of the new electronics division.

After George returned from a trip to Japan to inspect the Kasuga brothers' manufacturing facilities, he raised the question of changing the company's name. "Trio" was fine in Japan, but there was already an antenna company in the U.S. called Trio—besides, George wasn't keen on the name, which had a theatrical connotation that didn't appeal to his conservative taste.

"Kasuga" was out of the question, even though it was the surname of the manufacturers and Bill. The name had to evoke an American or even British image as in the case of their successful competitors (Scott, Fisher, Sherwood, and McIntosh); Japanese electronic products were still viewed as inferior.

Thus began the search for a perfect moniker. American Commercial even held a contest among their employees to come up with a suitable name; the winner would receive a Trio table radio. A Japanese staff member won the prize, but the winning submission turned out to be unsuitable.

George spoke to everyone he knew who was involved in advertising or related creative fields. Personally, George liked the name Sherwood, but it was already taken. A late-night brainstorming session resulted in another option. The managers were consulted and they agreed: the new name would be Kenwood. Once the name was officially registered, the real work began.

Kenwood's debut product was the KW-60 receiver, which had an integrated AM/FM stereo multiplex tuner and a 60-watt amplifier. While some audiophiles in the 1960s still preferred to purchase individual components and assemble their sound systems themselves, many consumers, seeking simplicity, preferred integrated units.

As the KW-60 receivers arrived from the factory, Bill began to approach prospective retailers. "Where's this made?" one asked.

"Japan," Bill replied.

"No thank you," the buyer answered.

At the end of the first day Bill had no orders, only an aching back from carrying the heavy KW-60 from store to store. He knew he would have to change his tactics.

The next day he entered stores without the receiver. Bill had decided to first sell himself before pitching his product. He told prospective buyers about his work with the Military Intelligence Service, how he had been rejected by the U.S. Army because he was underweight, how all Japanese Americans on the West Coast had been placed in camps. By the end of the conversation, the retailer would inevitably ask, "What are you selling, by the way?"

"Receivers."

"Well, bring one by sometime," they said.

Once Bill had established a relationship with his customers, he began demonstrating the KW-60. "Compare this item with Fisher, Scott, or McIntosh equipment, and you'll see the difference," he said confidently, as he put a record on a turntable.

One storeowner folded his arms and listened intently. "Hey, that's not bad. How much is it?"

"At least 15 percent cheaper than a Fisher or Scott—and the performance is better."

The owner asked to keep the equipment on consignment for a couple of days, but Bill insisted on a purchase order. "If you don't like it, I'll take it back," he promised. A week later he returned to the store and received orders for three more units. His sales strategy was working.

Meanwhile, sales representatives for West Coast audio equipment stores were loath to take on an unfamiliar brand because their living depended on commissions. As a result, George, like Bill, had no alternative but to once more pound the pavement himself, along with his team: salesman Rudy Stoklos, who had operated his own audio business in downtown Los Angeles, and former Guadalupean Yoichi "Mayor" Nakase, George's long-time trusted confidant.

"I've never heard of this Kenwood," one dealer said. "Is it made by Kenmore?"

"No, no," explained George. "Kenmore is Sears, Roebuck. We're in a different class, a higher class."

In the early 1960s, the audio retail business was extremely localized; there were no national chain stores specializing in electronics as there are today. Selling to each local small mom-and-pop audio store was time consuming and labor intensive, and George recognized the need for some national exposure to promote the Kenwood name. When he heard about a well-known audio engineer who had gone into the retail business in Seattle, he flew immediately to the Pacific Northwest. This audiophile also wrote for *Stereo Review*: if he gave the KW-60 his stamp of approval, the company would be well on its way to establishing a respected brand name.

"I've never heard of Kenwood," the Seattle retailer said, "but I'd like to check it out. Do you mind if I hang on to it for a few days?"

"Go right ahead," said George, grateful to receive even the slightest bit of interest in the KW-60. "I'll leave this unit with you for as long as you like. You can even take it all apart if you want and junk it afterward."

On the third day, the retailer called George in Los Angeles. "I'm ready to place an order," he said.

George hopped a plane back to Seattle. "What made you decide to buy the KW-60?" He had to ask.

The engineer told him that he had left the receiver on for three days straight, and the machine had not burnt out. In fact, it was still working perfectly and continued to sound good. This was an important test: for 50 years vacuum tubes had controlled the electric current to adequately amplify sound in equipment ranging from telephones to hi-fi systems. However, one of the weaknesses of vacuum tubes was that they got extremely hot; unless the product was well engineered, the heat caused malfunctions. After 72 hours the Kenwood receiver was so hot "you could fry an egg on it," the engineer told George. "Yet the sound remained clear, without any distortions."

George beamed. Like his chinaware, the audio equipment he was selling was of top-notch quality, but was still affordable by the average person. And favorable reviews of the KW-60 began to be published in *Stereo Review*, *High Fidelity*, and other trade journals.

"Sound is priceless" became Kenwood's slogan in 1963, and somehow, even as they jostled with the more-established brand names, Kenwood products were finding a place in the market. In the ever-changing world of audio technology, however, things could change overnight. Kenwood had to release something other than the KW-60—and soon.

* * *

As George continued to accumulate his fortune, the Aratanis gained increased exposure as public figures in the Japanese American community. In 1960 they opened their home as a venue for the first-ever swimsuit competition in the Nisei Week beauty pageant: young third-generation Japanese American (Sansei) women, their hair curled and teased, strolled across the family's lawn in one-piece swimsuits and high heels. After the judging the contestants lined up for a publicity photo opportunity with their hosts, George and Sakaye.

For Donna and Linda, the move from middle-class Montebello to the hills of Hollywood had been an easy adjustment. Donna was more introverted, like Sakaye; neat and well mannered, she enjoyed shopping with her mother. Linda, on the other hand, was a tomboy who preferred to box with her father.

On the driving range with George at his exclusive country club, Linda once inadvertently let go of her golf club as she took a swing, and her father expressed his displeasure with her. That was the angriest she ever saw her father, because, like Setsuo, he now expected his children to always take the game very seriously.

Surprisingly—and unlike the usual situation in many other Nisei households—the Aratani girls were not subjected to their parents' high academic expectations, though their grandmother Masuko continued to tutor them in various subjects, including English grammar. Because Donna and Linda were female, they were not expected to carry on the family business that their father George had struggled so hard to build.

The pressures placed on them were thus lessened, giving them time to fully enjoy a wide variety of school activities; they participated in everything from the drill team to the honor roll. And every accomplishment was lovingly documented with the 16mm camera George had inherited from Setsuo.

Delegating responsibilities to members of his household, George approached his fatherly duties in much the same way as he worked with his staff at American Commercial. He felt fortunate that the capable Sakaye supervised their home life, so he did not have to become overly involved in details. And he always exhibited the utmost confidence in his girls.

For example, shortly after Linda obtained her driver's license, George asked her to drive home from her grandparents' house in Gardena, about 35 miles away from the Hollywood Hills. Linda had never driven on a freeway before. She was nervous, and her hands were clammy. She kept her eyes glued to the road as cars zoomed past. Pulling into their driveway, she finally glanced over at her father—and he was fast asleep.

Donna's patient nature complemented George's love of fishing, and they took trips to fish the waters of Lake Tahoe. However, as American Commercial began to achieve some financial success, family excursions became more elaborate. For their first trip to Europe, George booked two separate flights: one for him and Donna, and another one for Linda and Sakaye which departed 45 minutes later.

"Why can't we all fly together?" the girls asked.

"We don't have many relatives," their father reminded them. He explained that if they all perished in an airplane crash, it would be the end of the Aratani clan (at least in the United States). As Setsuo and Yoshiko's only child, George felt an immense sense of responsibility to preserve the family name. The Aratanis continued to travel in this manner until Donna was married.

The local citizenry went the formal route the other night and found that white tie and tails isn't so bad after all.
—From an article entitled "Local Community Supports First Deb Ball, 600 Attend," *Kashu Mainichi*, 23 February 1965

As George saw it, his job was to multiply his earnings and grow his business for his family. As her husband stayed busy with his ever-expanding companies, Sakaye became more involved in community service. Unfortunately, she suffered a degeneration of her hearing, the result of childhood mastoiditis so severe that she had been hospitalized at Children's Hospital. Years of powerful medicine to treat the condition had torn holes in her eardrums. An inner-ear transplant had helped, but her hearing remained poor even with the assistance of hearing aids.

This condition frustrated Sakaye. She wanted to be a good hostess, but often she could not hear what people around her were saying, especially at large social events. Moreover, as a former singer, she loved music, and she missed being able to fully experience it. That she couldn't enjoy all the nuances of music pained her, but it didn't stop her from being involved with

**The first Japanese American debutante ball sponsored by
the Japan America Society in 1965.** (43.1998.3)

groups such as the Japanese American Symphony. And she continued her
philanthropic work; she just had to make sure that she had a seat up front
during club meetings so that she could adequately hear the proceedings.

In the sixties Sakaye was involved with planning fund-raising dinners
for the Japanese American Community Service (JACS), a group organized
to improve social welfare. She also helped to sponsor lectures on culture and
art for the Japan America Society of Southern California.

The Japan America Society, founded in 1909, boasted an eclectic roster
of members. In the 1960s the director of the Coca-Cola Bottling Companies,
a Nisei Episcopalian priest, and various Japanese government dignitaries were
among the 450 members dedicated to maintaining and strengthening the
relationship between Japan and the U.S.

Today the organization has multiple branches across America, and
their focus has become more corporate. However, when Sakaye was active-
ly involved, the Society did much more than examine trade relations. In
fact, they made history by organizing the first Japanese American debutante ball, which was held at the famous Cocoanut Grove in Los Angeles's
Ambassador Hotel.

When the debutante ball was announced in the beginning of 1965, the
concept initially seemed a bit curious to many in the Japanese American

community, including Linda and Donna. The Aratani daughters were now young women in a decade filled with social changes brought about by the civil rights movement and the Vietnam War. In its own way, the proposed ball was sending its own timely message—it heralded the effort of upwardly mobile Nisei women to create their own social networks and identities.

Although their families had now achieved some degree of financial stability, the women still encountered racial barriers. They sought to initiate their children—particularly their daughters—into high society, even if it was limited only to their ethnic community.

Wearing white gowns and gloves, Donna, Linda, and 32 other Sansei women were presented to the audience. All were daughters of prominent businessmen and professionals. Vickie's husband, Hank, escorted Donna onto the stage, while George, dressed in a tuxedo, came out with Linda, who was no longer the tomboy of her youth.

The debutante ball would continue for two more years, until it became too difficult to recruit enough young women willing to participate. Times were changing: the Yellow Power movement was gathering strength, and the younger generation was becoming more interested in social protests and rock music.

—◆—

*Transistors have won, hands down; the sound of
Sixties from now on, and probably for
decades to come, will be solid-state sound.*
—High Fidelity, October 1966

George's recent venture into the hi-fi business was about to undergo dramatic change, and the source of this revolution was a small piece of metal no bigger than an aspirin tablet: the transistor, also known as the semiconductor. The transistor had first been developed by scientists at Bell Telephone Laboratories in the late 1940s, and it was soon used in hearing aids. In 1954 a small electronics company called Regency released the first transistor radio, just in time for the Christmas season.

The transistor worked by means of solid-state physics. Bell researchers had discovered that the flow of electric current could be controlled through small chunks of solid material rather than by a vacuum created in glass tubes. Sony Corporation, then only about 10 years old, immediately saw the potential for creating compact products that used transistors; they released their first $29.95 pocket radio in 1955.

While Regency, the first company to market such a product, didn't survive, Sony continued to grow. The company branched out, developing tape recorders and televisions—by 1960 it was experimenting on a semiconductor picture tube for television receivers. However, despite their rapid growth and diversification, Sony had yet to enter the hi-fi market.

Initially, Trio and Kenwood were hesitant to retool their factories for production of solid-state components—it was an expensive proposition. And some skeptical consumers, still fans of the dependable vacuum tube, pointed to the weaknesses of semiconductors: they were oversensitive, they tended to blow out, and they sometimes shrieked unpleasantly. But as the transistor was further refined, its advantages became clear.

Hans Fantel wrote in *Popular Electronics* in 1965:

Compared with tubes, the transistor is smaller, draws less power, develops practically no heat, takes no time to warm up, doesn't change characteristics with age—in fact, doesn't wear out.

Unlike tubes, transistors don't produce noise when exposed to vibration—they are not microphonic—and shrug off accidental knocks. Besides, transistors are virtually hum-free, so that the music sings out against a background of almost complete silence.

In 1965 Kenwood was virtually the only "made-in-Japan" producer to make headway in solid-state components; Pioneer, Sansui, and even Sony trailed behind. Early that year Kenwood had started production on a variety of solid-state components, including the KT-100 all-transistor AM/FM automatic stereo receiver, the TK-500 transistorized automatic FM stereo tuner, and the TK-400 all-transistor stereo amplifier. A higher-quality line—the KW-55A receiver, the KW-220 amplifier, and the KW-550 FM tuner—was introduced in 1960s at the Los Angeles Hi-Fi Music Show, a key trade event for launching new products and making large sales. Within months, the luxury model TK-80 FM multiplex stereo receiver—with a silicon power transistor and 80 watts of power—was being heralded. By introducing this high-quality solid-state stereo equipment, Kenwood led the way in breaking down consumers' stereotypes of Japanese hi-fi equipment.

Even as Bill was being encouraged to play more of a public-relations role in the industry, he was initially denied membership in its trade organization, the Electronic Industries Association (EIA)—no importers were allowed to join. Within two years, however, the group's doors creaked open for Kenwood. The EIA could see that, in order for the organization to survive, it would have to accept the new kids on the block: the Japanese manufacturers.

—•◆•—

They worked miracles with transistors in tiny TV
and radios. Engineered today's most popular tape recorders.
Gave you the home video tape recorder.
What is Sony up to now?
—Sony ad in *High Fidelity*, 1966

For more than two years, Kenwood, with its direct and unpretentious advertising slogans, was the sole Japanese importer in the U.S. high-fidelity market. But soon the gloves came off: the manufacturing giants of Japan awoke and prepared to dominate the audio-component trade "with a vengeance," according to *High Fidelity* in June of 1966. Sony was introducing an amplifier, turntable, and three-way-speaker system for the "well-heeled, quality-minded listener," while Pioneer, one of the largest manufacturers of loudspeakers in the world, was finally going to sell its products on U.S. shores. Panasonic, owned by the Matsushita corporation, was also entering the compact modular field the same year with the release of its Model SG-870 stereo.

Now American companies—Fairchild, Texas Instruments, and General Electric—were rapidly registering patents for integrated circuits (IC), systems in which numerous transistors and other electronic components were combined in a single block. "In the opinion of some Japanese manufacturers, the American IC's [*sic*] now constitute a very serious menace to the Japanese electronics industry," reported *Popular Electronics* in November of 1966.

As a result of increasing competition in the electronics industry, by 1966 the Japanese government was allocating $80,000 annually to aid six Japanese semiconductor firms (including Mitsubishi Electric, Toshiba, and Hitachi) in their research-and-development efforts. Having recovered from the wounds of World War II, the Japanese were catching up fast. Within three years, one hundred manufacturers were producing tape recorders and high-fidelity components in Japan. Japanese companies doing business in the U.S. now included Aiwa, Akai, JVC, NEC, Oki, Sanyo, Sharp, and Yamaha.

While George and Bill had first encountered much skepticism about the quality of Japanese goods, the country's hi-fi units were now considered even more reliable than units manufactured in North America. "The stronghold of Japanese supremacy has been in top-notch quality control. They go to extremes to make sure that the products work before they leave the Japanese warehouses," wrote *Popular Electronics* columnist Charles Lincoln during his 1969 visit to Japan.

In spite of increased competition from Sony and other large Japanese corporations, Kenwood experienced a surge of business at the end of the sixties. In 1969 both Mikasa and Kenwood moved their West Coast administrative headquarters from the old 15,000-square-foot space in Los Angeles to a new $500,000 45,000-square-foot building in the city of Gardena, once home to the largest number of Japanese Americans in the continental U.S. The West Coast headquarters for both Mikasa and Kenwood employed more than 45 individuals. No sooner had they settled in then they had to begin plans for an even larger space.

George threw a huge party to celebrate the grand opening of the new building. Everyone was there: Al Funabashi. Tets Murata, George's constant right-hand man, the person who patiently trained new recruits. Shig Kariya, Tad Yamada, Bill Kasuga, Min Endo, Yoichi Nakase. Sakaye, Masuko, and Donna, recently graduated from USC with a major in sociology, were among the honored guests. (Linda was pursuing her degree in occupational therapy up north in San Jose.) The food was sumptuous, drinks flowed freely, and the media's flashbulbs popped.

Before the night was over, the Mikasa managers lined up for a photograph. It had been more than 20 years since George and Toshitaro Ishikawa had written letters back and forth from Minnesota and Chicago. At that time, the establishment of an international trade company amidst the harsh residue of war, destruction, and displacement had been but a dream. The boys from Guadalupe and the boys of the MIS, fused together in friendship and determination, had somehow made it come true.

Within weeks of the grand celebration, a crisis hit. Store representatives were calling the Kenwood office: "Where the hell is George Aratani?" Yoichi, officially the key liaison between Kenwood's East and West Coast offices, explained the problem: "Trio can't make the stereo components fast enough," he said. "The Christmas orders are exceeding supply."

George furrowed his brow. This was a potential disaster—they couldn't disappoint their customers. After George spoke with Trio managers in Japan,

**George Aratani and Al Funabashi at the opening of
the new administrative headquarters of Mikasa and Kenwood
in Gardena, California, in 1969.** (99.56.2)

units were soon being assembled at record speeds. But there was still a transportation problem: How would they make it to the U.S. by December, the busiest season for overseas shippers?

George made phone call after phone call to his Japanese contacts; after years of doing business there, he'd built up a considerable network. Pan American Airlines finally agreed to provide Kenwood with an entire cargo plane, an expensive proposition. "This is costing us a hell of a lot of money," George told Yoichi.

In the midst of these negotiations, another problem arose: George discovered that the 80,000 backlogged units wouldn't all fit into a single cargo plane—now they needed two planes. Again, Pan American cooperated. The first plane left on November 24, near Thanksgiving, while the second took off from Tokyo on December 8.

Kenwood was going to lose money on the deal, so George tried to somehow capitalize on the event. He conferred with advertising director Kei Inouye, and when the Pan American plane landed on the runway at Los

Angeles International Airport, photographers were ready. As the delivery was being unloaded, clearly visible was a large banner draped across the stacks and stacks of Kenwood boxes. Its message: "Merry Xmas." This shipment was indeed a Christmas present to their customers at every level.

George breathed a sigh of relief. In the cutthroat world of electronics, late delivery of products could break a company, especially during the all-important holiday season. Unlike the tableware business with its steady customer base, the electronics industry was totally dependent on name recognition and corporate trends fostered by advertisements in men's magazines like *Playboy* and the sponsorship of high-profile sporting events.

He had reliable teams in place for Mikasa, Kenwood, and AMCO, but George felt his attention being increasingly divided. And he began to embrace a new passion during this stage of his life: philanthropy.

13

Rebuilding
the Community

Although the facts in the case are not simple,
the injustice arising from them is clear. More than 300,000
persons have lost all or part of their fortunes
located in the United States.

—From the brochure "Seven Reasons for Return,"
by James Finucane, executive secretary for the Committee
for Return of Confiscated German and Japanese Property

With the United States' entry into the Vietnam War and the growing civil rights movement, the next generation of Japanese Americans, the Sansei, began to struggle with issues of ethnic identity. How could the promise of American democratic principles be reconciled with the government's anti-Asian policies of the early 1900s? What about Executive Order 9066, the presidential edict that had led to the wartime incarceration of their parents and grandparents? Seeing parallels between those experiences and the poor treatment suffered by other ethnic minorities in America, some Sansei activists joined the Third World strikes taking place at San Francisco State University and UC Berkeley in the late 1960s, strikes that would lay the groundwork for the establishment of ethnic studies programs. Revolution was in the air.

Other than sporting longer sideburns, George reflected little of this era of protest and change. Yet in his own way, in courtrooms instead of on col-

George and Sakaye Aratani honored in the 1980 Nisei Week Parade in Little Tokyo as the annual festival's 40th grand marshals. (99.30.89)

lege campuses, he attempted to redress a wrong that had been committed against him and his family. He leaned on the strengths sharpened by his business dealings—including the ability to raise capital—to revitalize a community that had been stripped of their civil rights during World War II. Although George and his colleagues enjoyed economic success, many other Japanese Americans were never able to recover all that was lost. If restitution could not be fully realized by the government, it was up to the private sector, George figured, starting with capitalists like himself.

---

*The essence of the administration of justice in the
United States is the concept of "due process of law" and the
principle that no person should be deprived of
his property without such due process.*
**—Petition filed by attorneys for George Aratani
on 31 July 1963, in the Supreme Court of the United States**

Fifteen years after its passage in 1948, the Japanese American Evacuation Claims Act had still not fulfilled its mandate to compensate Japanese Americans who had lost property because of the forced wartime removal. Because as written it was severely limited in scope, the act had later been amended to allow for payments greater than $2,500. As a result, Butch Tamura and Miyokichi Matsuno, as the two partners of Vegetable Farms, had filed large claims with the help of the JACL. While these claims were pending, there was also the matter of the unrecovered yen deposits confiscated by the Alien Property Custodian.

Setsuo had originally deposited yen deposits in Sumitomo Bank's Los Angeles branch before the war as collateral for company loans, as a personal investment, and to be a source of funds for George while he was studying in Japan. These deposits were frozen after the bombing of Pearl Harbor, and now, many years later, the Office of Alien Property was offering a payback at the postwar rate of 360 yen per dollar rather than the prewar exchange rate of 4 yen per dollar. Instead of the $175,957.40 that Setsuo had originally deposited, George stood to receive only $1,952.96.

In the 1950s JACL leader and Washington lobbyist Mike Masaoka had attempted to address the issue of wartime vested property, including yen deposits, in a legislative bill before Congress. George chose another route: the courts.

Although he had been warned by two Washington, D.C., attorneys—Thomas Caroyan and Philip Amram—that the case would be difficult, requiring literally hundreds of legal hours, he nonetheless agreed to be the lead appellant in a class-action suit. *George Aratani* v. *Robert F. Kennedy, Attorney General of the United States* was formally filed with the United States Court of Appeals, District of Columbia Circuit, in 1958. Five years later, as the case was one step away from being heard by the U.S. Supreme Court, George's attorneys called. "The government wants to settle," they said.

The Department of Justice agreed to compensate George and the plaintiffs at the original exchange rate of four yen to a dollar. There was one catch, however: total payments could not exceed the amount held by the Office of Alien Property—approximately $1,500,000—in the liquidated proceeds of Sumitomo Bank. Ultimately, although George and the other investors received only 25 percent of their money, that sum was still 40 times more than what the government had initially offered them.

———◦◦———

After all of his disheartening experiences with the legal system, George was more convinced than ever that people couldn't depend on the government to build up and support the community. It was up to individuals to make a difference. Men like his father Setsuo had set an important example with their tireless efforts toward early community building in this country earlier in the century. His wife, Sakaye, had already received public accolades, including recognition as 1965's "Nisei of the Year," from a Japanese American newspaper; she was honored for her contributions to a string of endless activities ranging from organizing cultural events to entertaining Japanese dignitaries. In 1965 she also assisted Madame Miki Sawada, a Japanese philanthropist, in the collection of shoes to be given to children of mixed heritage in Brazil. Now it was George's turn to focus on strengthening his community.

Before the war, Setsuo and George had both donated funds to the Japanese Hospital on Fickett Street where Setsuo had succumbed to tuberculosis. The facility had since fallen into disrepair, so a new building was purchased by a nonprofit group in 1962. However, this facility for Japanese-speaking patients, called City View Hospital, was not enough to meet the health-care demands of the community. The Issei, who had established the foundation of their lives in the United States, were growing old—what was most needed was a nursing home to house an increasingly infirm elderly population. As a result, the Keiro Nursing Home Drive began. Keiro—meaning "respect for elders" in Japanese—became the guiding axiom of the project's fund-raisers, including George, one of the home's directors. The people who would live in the new facility had suffered uncountable traumatic losses during the war years. Now, 20 years later, they deserved tender care, peace, and tranquility.

Fred I. Wada was a successful produce businessman who had been instrumental in securing the 1964 Olympics for Tokyo, and he and George headed the Keiro fund drive. Together, the two Nisei traveled to Japan in the fall of 1964 to see what they could collect.

As they moved from corporate headquarters to the offices of politicians, they often received some peculiar responses to their request. "Such a worthy project!" one donor claimed, as he presented them with a crateful of canned *mikan* (Japanese tangerines). Other "donations" included samurai swords and helmets. During a meeting with one mayor, George and Fred were shown into a room containing hundreds of ceramic tiles decorated with brush paintings of Mt. Fuji. "I'm willing to donate all of this to you," the politician said proudly.

George bowed respectfully. "That is much too generous a gift," he said in Japanese. "Perhaps something less?"

"No, I insist," the mayor said.

"Really, it is too much."

"No, no, I only want to help."

In the end, all the Nisei fund-raisers got for their efforts were crates of such souvenirs to ship back to Los Angeles. Although the trip left them in the red, George was undeterred. "The Japanese are not accustomed to contributing to charities," he told the committee. "Somehow we have to educate them. We can't rely solely on capital from Japanese Americans. Our base over here is too small."

As he had during the development of Mikasa and Kenwood, George continued to always think big. He sought to push the community beyond its present status quo and out of its comfort zone. He recognized the dignity associated with mom-and-pop operations and their important role in the community, but he firmly believed that money—and lots of it—was the key to propelling Japanese American institutions into a bigger league. Whether he would be able to raise the funds and rally community leaders, however, was another issue altogether.

In the mid-1960s George received a call from his old friend Shozo Hotta, the valuable contact he had met back when charcoal-burning cars had operated on the roads of postwar Tokyo. He and Shozo had become close over the years; George, in fact, had enabled Shozo's children to study in the United States, and he had even counseled them on love and marriage.

"The president of Sumitomo Bank of California wants to move into a new building; they plan to work with Kajima Corporation to develop a high-rise in the U.S. I'm giving them your name as a contact," Shozo said.

The Kajima Corporation was a well-known Japanese construction company that now planned to build a 15-story office building, luxury hotel, and shopping mall in Los Angeles's Little Tokyo. Such development projects were changing the face of the area. Residential hotels that had once housed low-income single male immigrants were being razed to make way for buildings oriented to wealthy Japanese tourists.

A Nisei drugstore proprietor, worried about his rising rent, approached George with his concerns. "With all these new developments, won't my rent go sky high?" he asked.

George listened carefully. "This construction boom will be good for Little Tokyo," he pointed out. "The area is becoming rundown, and it needs something new."

Japanese American community activists and certain small merchants disagreed with him: as business leaders, politicians, and dignitaries proudly participated in groundbreaking ceremonies for new construction, protests were staged around the old buildings marked for destruction. The future of Little Tokyo—and the larger Japanese American community—was at a crossroads. What would the Little Tokyo of the future look like? Who would it be for—the individuals who had struggled through generations of discrimination in the U.S., or the well-heeled tourist population?

George remained characteristically calm in the midst of these disputes. Believing that the area needed refurbishing, he continued to serve on the boards of Kajima International and East West Development, which oversaw construction of a new luxury hotel in Little Tokyo. But he also donated large sums of money to the various social service agencies and grassroots organizations that protested the Japanese-financed projects.

In terms of his philanthropic activities and financial donations, George never operated purely from a political or religious ideology. For example, while he faithfully gave to the Nishi Hongwanji Temple in Little Tokyo and the Institute of Buddhist Studies at UC Berkeley, he also contributed to St. Mary's Episcopal Church in Uptown, a former Japanese community west of downtown Los Angeles, and the Centenary United Methodist Church in Little Tokyo. In addition, he served as one of the fund-raising chairs of a Christian organization started by Paul Rusch, his old Military Intelligence Service colleague and the Episcopal lay leader he'd met as a student in Tokyo.

The Guadalupe of his youth had been filled with Buddhists and Christians, day laborers and large farm operators; his world had become larger now, but he still believed that all of its diverse pieces were needed to make a community.

✦✦✦

We will have a world in which competition can be more fair.
—Excerpt from President Richard M. Nixon's speech
in support of an international monetary accord, 19 December 1971

As George concentrated on philanthropy and community building with fresh gusto in the 1970s, his companies faced new challenges. The growing U.S. trade deficit with countries like Canada and Japan had led President Nixon to coin a phrase: "Buy American." The government introduced a 10-percent surcharge on imports in 1971.

Tariffs were not a recent phenomenon in the chinaware industry—in fact, as long ago as the opening up of Japan to trade in the late 1800s, manufacturers such as Noritake had felt pressure from American companies to limit their imports. Countless negotiations and hearings were held in the 1950s and 1960s, most of them involving the lucrative hotel-and-restaurant market. Finally, in 1971 a hearing on the dinnerware industry was scheduled before the Tariff Commission in the nation's capitol.

Japanese chinaware did not compete directly with American companies, which primarily produced earthenware; nevertheless, the low prices of the Japanese products were viewed as a threat. To the average uninformed male legislator, dishes were dishes—they weren't aware of the different properties of earthenware, porcelain, and bone china. It fell to the leaders of Mikasa—specifically president Al Funabashi and national sales manager Joe Orshan—to educate them.

Al, the former New York JACL leader, had interacted with various governmental bodies before. This time he had a determined adversary: popular North Carolina radio commentator Jesse Helms, who had been solicited to speak for some of the domestic manufacturers. Could the men of Mikasa effectively convince the bureaucrats that exorbitant tariffs—sometimes as high as 60 percent—were not the answer?

Joe, a former Air Force pilot during World II, testified first. "We don't just do work with Japanese importers," he explained. "We also represent a factory in Illinois, Stetson China."

The lobbyists for the U.S. companies fumed in their seats; this was not what they wanted to hear. They'd hoped to represent the issue as black and white.

Al came next. He carried a dish with him to the microphone. "You see, there's different kinds of tableware," he said. He explained about porcelain: consisting of 10 to 25 percent kaolin, its glassy surface was a result of a vitrification process in which the clay was fired under intense heat. "That's different than earthenware," he explained, dramatically breaking a dish to reveal its inner structure. "This is more porous; there's more absorption. Just use your tongue and you can tell." He stuck his tongue on the earthenware and held it there for all of the bureaucrats to see. The chamber filled with laughter.

Al Funabashi had once again charmed an adversary, this time the Tariff Commission. With a simple ploy, he showed the committee members why high import fees were unnecessary. Tariffs already imposed on the industry were slowly lowered from 60 percent to 55, and then to 35 percent. (Today import duties on chinaware average around 6 percent.)

* * *

While Al continued his lobbying efforts, he did not neglect his duties in New York. He still worked closely with Mikasa's designers, and in the seventies his tastes became increasingly linked to women's fashion. In fact, Al made tableware history in 1973 by partnering with fashion designer Vera to create patterns for plates, glassware, and gifts. "The biggest single problem we had with Vera designs was solving the technical problems inherent with the bright colors," Al wrote in *Home Furnishings Daily* in 1972, the year after the designs' launch. Bright reds, oranges, and yellows—like those in the Vera-designed patterns—usually required paint with a high lead content, and Mikasa had to be careful that their products met Food and Drug Administration safety guidelines. (The company would later face similar problems with crystal imports from Europe.)

In New York, the company continued its search for more space. Mikasa's warehouse was now in New Jersey but the operational headquarters remained in Manhattan, and the two needed to be consolidated under one roof. Tad Yamada and Al began looking west, across the Hudson River to a town called Secaucus, which had once been home to a hog farm that in its day had permeated Manhattan with a foul smell. A landfill had replaced the surrounding swampland, and Secaucus was being transformed into a state-of-the-art business development called the Meadowlands. Mikasa became one of its first tenants.

With the company's expansion in the 1970s came unions. The always soft-spoken Shig Kariya, senior vice president, was caught in the middle of a competition between two local shops, the Teamsters Union and the International Dock Workers Union (IDWU) to represent Mikasa workers. How things had changed since Shig had single-handedly opened the first New York City office while living at the YMCA. Mikasa warehouse workers ultimately joined the IDWU, the union that Shig had favored.

The constant demands of running an ever-expanding business were taking their toll, however, on Mikasa president Al Funabashi, once energy personified. He and his wife Maria had purchased a condominium in Florida, and he hoped to retire soon and spend his days playing golf. "Maybe I'll stay involved as a consultant, but I've got to get out," he told his younger brother Ken in confidence.

Then, on a summer day in 1976, a month before the nation's Bicentennial, Al suddenly collapsed at his home in Woodcliff Lake, the site of many American Commercial picnics. Death followed swiftly; Al had suffered a fatal heart attack at the age of 59, just 3 years before his retirement.

The entire Mikasa team was stunned with grief. Young men and women Al had mentored over the years openly wept at the office upon hearing the terrible news. George, back in Los Angeles, was of course shaken, but he succeeded in maintaining his unflappable demeanor. He immediately flew to New York, where he made sure that an announcement was published in the *New York Times* the next day, on June 3, 1976:

FUNABASHI—Alfred W. The Board of Directors and Staff of Mikasa join the family with great sorrow at the death of our associate and colleague, and President of the China and Glass Association, who served with great distinction during his career in the ceramic industry.

Ever since the deaths of his parents, emotional loss had always been difficult for George to express. He was never the type to become melancholy or depressed, but he was affected all the same. It would take some time before George recovered from the loss of his Nisei partner and friend.

On the morning of Al's funeral, mourners filled the sanctuary of Our Lady, Mother of the Church, in Woodcliff Lake. Maria Funabashi looked for the last time at the face of her beloved husband, who she had teased about being named after Alfred the Great and William the Conqueror. One of Al's favorite expressions had been "*Yamato-damashii*" (Survive and win in any circumstance and never be easily defeated); he had learned the phrase from his father, a native of Ichinomiya, a town near Nagoya. The same weak heart that had kept Al from military service years ago had finally defeated him.

———— ◆ ————

Who could replace Al? It was a question no one wanted to contemplate, especially George. He sought the counsel of Ken Kolker, an executive with the Abraham & Straus department store and one of Al's closest associates. "Don't wait too long before appointing a successor," Kolker advised. "In the small world of the housewares industry, competitors may take advantage of your leadership void and seek to hire away your other good Mikasa executives."

George nodded. They both knew who the best candidate was: Alfred Blake. An Austrian immigrant with a flare for product development and marketing, Alf had worked for Mikasa since 1965 and was now head of the national sales division. Driven to succeed even as a teenager in Canada, he had worked at a drive-in restaurant, the White Spot, in Vancouver, British Columbia, where he quickly graduated from dishwasher to tray loader for the carhops. Alf then entered a managerial training program of a prestigious Canadian department store, Hudson's Bay, where he quickly moved up the ranks to become assistant manager of the china-and-glass department. He eventually transformed the department, moving it from its emphasis on traditional English styles to fresher, more youth-oriented products.

A Japanese Canadian agent for Mikasa informed George about this innovative buyer in 1967, and it wasn't long before he offered Alf the western regional sales manager's position at Mikasa's administrative headquarters in Los Angeles. It was a gamble: while Alf was very familiar with Mikasa's products, he didn't know much about the company itself, and it meant a relocation for his wife and three children. Nonetheless, he jumped at the opportunity, and the bet paid off. Within five years Alf had relocated to the New York office to serve as the company's national sales manager.

Like his father Setsuo, George had an intuitive sense about who would successfully become a hardworking member of the corporate team. However, while Setsuo had gravitated towards quiet, self-effacing men who complemented his own charismatic personality, George tended to seek out strong, colorful figures like Al Funabashi. Now the stage was set for Alf Blake, the enterprising Austrian immigrant, to step into Al's shoes and become the president of Mikasa.

In October of 1975 the Japanese Consulate in Los Angeles contacted the Aratani household: both George and Sakaye were invited to meet Emperor Hirohito and Empress Nagako during the couple's whirlwind trip through Los Angeles.

Meeting Japanese royals was not new to either one of them. Through George's friend Shinzo Koizumi—the former president of Keio University who later became Prince Akihito's tutor—the Aratanis had met several members of the Imperial family. And of course, George had briefly greeted Emperor Hirohito at the demonstration of the nuclear reactor at Harumi back in 1959. But this was different: the meeting would take place in George's home territory, Southern California.

A small group of Japanese American community leaders chosen by the Japan Consulate gathered at the Music Center in downtown Los Angeles. They formed a line, and one by one they shook hands with the emperor. He had aged considerably since George's first glimpse of him at the Showa coronation in 1928—his hair and even his bushy eyebrows were speckled with grey. The empress stood demurely behind him.

Later George would learn that when Japanese business leaders who were temporarily assigned to U.S. subsidiaries met the emperor they also stood in a line, but they bowed instead of shaking hands. "That's the difference between us," explained George. "We're American, and they are Japanese—two distinct ways of doing things."

While Mikasa's move to Secaucus had been a successful one, Alf Blake and other members of the management team saw a strategic need to maintain a presence in Manhattan. The showroom, they determined in 1978, should return to the center of the Big Apple. But that move left open space within the showroom next to the warehouse in Secaucus. Why not use it to sell certain Mikasa products to the public? they thought. The receptionist was

The Board of Directors of the Sumitomo Bank of California, with Sakaye Aratani, its first woman director, in 1978. (43.1998.7)

given a cash box, and with that Mikasa launched its first factory outlet store with a minimal financial outlay of $4,000. It was one of the first factory outlet stores to sell household goods in the nation, and certainly one of the first in Secaucus.

While the chinaware business continued to make an impact in the dinnerware market, Kenwood was being heralded by leaders in the electronics industry. In 1977 George learned that he would be inducted into the Audio Hall of Fame, an award organized by the magazine *Audio Times*. The fourth member of the Hall of Fame, George was lauded as a pioneer who had introduced Japanese high-fidelity equipment to the U.S. market. Howard Ladd, a pioneer in developing tape-deck technology, was honored the same year as George. Previous inductees included Avery Fisher, who founded Fisher Radio in 1945, and Joe Tushinsky, an optical-engineer-turned-executive who had launched Sony tape recorders into the U.S. market.

In heralding George's accomplishments, *Audio Times* underscored his management style. "He uses a team approach," stated the article, "getting the best out of carefully picked experts in every facet of his company. His particular expertise lies in corporate management decisions, financial planning, and marketing strategy.

"George is an incredible judge of character, his friends will tell you."

One day in 1978, a Japanese Sumitomo Bank executive came to the Aratani house. "I'll get George," said Sakaye, after they'd exchanged some pleasantries.

"No." The executive shook his head. "I came to talk to you."

He went on to explain that the bank was seeking a woman to serve on their board of directors. More specifically, they wanted Sakaye.

Sakaye shook her head. "I don't know anything about financial matters." Those things she usually left up to George.

"No, we think you're the person." After discussing the position with Sakaye for some time, the executive left a stack of papers—including a huge tome on banking law—with her. "Just look over the material," he said. "You could serve for just a year. If you're uncomfortable, you're perfectly welcome to resign."

Sakaye consulted George, as she always did. "What do you think?" She expected him to tell her to refuse.

"Why don't you try?" he said instead.

So Sakaye traveled to a monthly board of directors meeting held at Sumitomo Bank's California headquarters in San Francisco. There she met 16 men, all of whom held leadership positions within corporations in California and Japan. "They went out of their way to make me feel comfortable," said Sakaye, who made history as the first woman to serve as a director of Sumitomo Bank of California.

More surprises would follow in the coming years. In 1983 Sakaye was notified by the Japanese Consulate in Los Angeles that she was the recipient of a *kunshō*, a medal from the Japanese government, awarded to her for her work in fostering better relations between the United States and Japan during the previous 20 years.

The *kunshō* was a highly revered honor among the elite Japanese, both in the U.S. and Japan. Sakaye and another Southland resident, Peggy Kaoru Nakaki, were among the first Nisei women to be cited by the Japanese government in 1983. George was delighted for her, but Sakaye felt a bit self-conscious about receiving the honor before her husband did.

George dutifully accompanied his wife to dinners hosted by various Japanese and Japanese American organizations. In at least one article he was merely identified as an honoree's spouse looking on "from behind."

As part of the 1980 Nisei Week celebration, Los Angeles Mayor Tom Bradley honors (from left to right) Shozo Hotta of Sumitomo Bank, Little Tokyo merchant Mitsuhiko Shimizu, Sakaye and George Aratani, and Issei leader Katsuma Mukaeda. Also pictured is Darlene Kuba (second from right), assistant to Los Angeles City Councilman Gilbert Lindsay. (99.30.172)

"She beat me to it," George says with a smile. Sure enough, five years later he received his own medal, the Order of the Sacred Treasure, Gold Rays with Rosette.

George and Sakaye continued to give more and more generously to the Japanese American community, and the community continued to honor them. In 1980 they were chosen to be the grand marshals of the Nisei Week Japanese Festival, an annual summer event in Little Tokyo dating back to 1934. Their longtime friend, Shozo Hotta of Sumitomo Bank, would join them as the parade marshal. As George and Sakaye sat in the open car that would carry them down the parade route, the sun beat mercilessly on their faces and backs. The parade had become delayed. George watched concerned individuals approach Los Angeles Mayor Tom Bradley, who sat in the car just in front of them. "Mayor, are you going to be all right?" his aides asked.

That got George thinking: Yes, what about this heat? Their granddaughters Melissa and Stephanie were with them. Would any of them collapse from heatstroke?

"Hey," someone called out. It was Fred Wada, George's fellow business-man and philanthropist, his gray hair almost blinding white in the sunlight. He waved a bouquet of roses toward Sakaye and then brought out a para-sol. "It's so hot," he said. "I thought that this would help."

As the parade finally began, George, Sakaye, Melissa, and Stephanie enjoyed waving at the people lining the streets of Little Tokyo. This com-munity had become George's new Guadalupe. It didn't matter that he lived at least 20 miles away in the hills of Hollywood, and it didn't matter that his businesses were headquartered 30 miles south in Carson and Long Beach—this was the place into which he had infused literally millions of dollars for its redevelopment and revitalization.

Philanthropy was not always easy; the process was sometimes fraught with heated conflicts and controversies as each community member expressed his or her own individual priorities and ideologies. Despite dis-agreements, George never let those debates damper his enthusiasm. During his young adult years, he had witnessed the virtual erasure of the Japanese American community from the West Coast. Whatever it took, everyone needed to band together to bring it back and make it stronger than ever.

14

A Second Look

If George didn't do all this, I don't know
what would happen to the Japanese community.
Everyone waits for George to lead.
—Shig Kariya, in an interview on 4 October 1997

George Aratani, a man who has dined in the presence of sultans and emperors, enjoys eating hamburgers at the local fast-food franchise a mile away from his Hollywood Hills home. It's a typical Hollywood eatery, located on a busy street filled with commuters employed by the entertainment industry and frequented by young people attempting to recover from a hard night of wild carousing.

At more than 80 years of age, George still stands erect, and his black hair—which is not dyed—bears the fresh marks of a comb. He wears tan slacks and a short-sleeved shirt; his face is slightly tanned from a recent excursion to Martinique on a luxury yacht. Decades ago, a man sitting beside him on a plane thought that the name "Aratani" was perhaps Italian.

"I was born in California," George told his fellow passenger. "My family moved to a place called Guadalupe, California. I went to school with a bunch of Italian and Portuguese kids. Their names were Tognazzini, Bonetti, Rossini, Filipponi, Capitani. I fit right in: Mussolini, Aratani."

The Aratani family on the occasion of George and Sakaye's 50th wedding anniversary in 1995: (from left to right, behind Sakaye and George Aratani, seated), Jann Yusa, Joy Yusa, Linda Kimura, Jeff Yusa, Masuko Aratani, Donna Kwee, Liong Tek Kwee, Allison Kwee, Stephanie Kwee, Melissa Kwee, and Evan Kwee.
(99.30.169)

"What is your background?" the passenger asked.

"I'm Japanese American."

"Really?" the man said. "I didn't know there were people like you."

George is used to having an ambiguous identity. Right now he stands in front of an impatient teenager working behind the counter, who has punched George's order—a plain hamburger and large coffee—into her electronic cash register. George rattles his pocket for coins; he wants to get rid of his pennies. He carefully counts them one by one and deposits them in the girl's outstretched palm. The rest is paid for with a fresh $100 bill. As she clears out $20 bills from her register, the teenager glances again at the man in front of her. George Aratani requires a second look.

* * *

George is semiretired now—emphasis on "semi-." As chairman emeritus of Mikasa and chairman of Kenwood Americas, he still closely monitors corporate developments and often helps with evaluating candidates for high-level positions. He still has his own parking space in front of the California headquarters of Mikasa and Kenwood. His Mikasa office is small, perhaps just a little larger than the office in the Guadalupe Produce packing shed he had once inherited from his father. But while the packing shed had reverberated with booming male voices and the sounds of vegetables being chopped and flung, the Mikasa office is stone quiet, aside from the hum of central air-conditioning and the occasional buzz of the telephone. In the warehouse area, men wearing black nylon back supports around their waists operate small forklifts as they move fragile boxes of chinaware and crystal from containers that originated in Japan, Malaysia, Germany, and a score of other foreign countries.

Since the revival of All Star Trading in the late 1940s, George has played a major role in the amazing transformation of the company, which currently does $400 million worth of business each year. In 1994 Mikasa, Inc., became a publicly traded company on the New York Stock Exchange. An earlier leveraged buyout was financed by Japanese institutions, led by Tokai Bank. The original American Commercial team members, some of whom had reluctantly purchased Mikasa stocks with their Christmas bonuses, were now able to retire comfortably after decades of long and dedicated service. (However, George's former Guadalupe neighbor Tets Murata, at 80-plus years of age, still goes into Mikasa's Long Beach office Monday through Friday.)

In September 2000 Mikasa entered into a merger agreement with France-based J. G. Durand Industries, the parent company of the world's largest glass-and-crystal maker, Verrerie Cristallerie d'Arques. This new partnership, in which Mikasa will become a privately held subsidiary of J. G. Durand, will help launch Mikasa products into additional overseas markets. The management of Mikasa will remain unchanged, and many executives, including George, remain the company's major shareholders.

Mikasa's mode of operation will also continue as usual. "Noritake has a factory, and what do we have?" George rhetorically posits. "We have a warehouse. It's a shell; it's empty. We have to go to one factory after another and bring merchandise and fill the shell."

In terms of production control this can be a liability, but in the changeable world of dinnerware this weakness has turned into a strength. While other prominent dinnerware manufacturers—Noritake, Lenox, Royal Doulton, and Wedgwood—can point to long histories spanning at least 100 years, it is Mikasa that transformed the industry. In a recent survey, Mikasa had a stronger brand recognition than any other dinnerware company. This is all due, according to founder George and other principals, to the company's larger team, a team that began in the fields of Guadalupe and has extended to Los Angeles, New York, and South Carolina: from land to table.

While George and Al Funabashi once traveled back and forth between the U.S. and Nagoya, Mikasa's current chairman, Alfred Blake, tours the globe perusing new patterns and inspecting merchandise in factories. With their expansion beyond the tableware industry—their product line now includes such products as bathware and decorative items—Mikasa has forged contracts with manufacturers in 35 countries, including the Philippines, Malaysia, Thailand, Mexico, Czechoslovakia, and Austria, Blake's homeland.

Only 15 percent of Mikasa's chinaware is still made in Japan. The company continues to work with Narumi, the manufacturer of fine bone china which George visited via a charcoal-fueled car in 1948. And in the 1990s, the Japanese chinaware business came full circle: Yamago Togyo Ltd., a ceramics manufacturer based in Gifu prefecture in Japan, now operates a state-of-the-art chinaware-decorating factory, Golden State Porcelain, in Santa Maria, where George attended high school. Isamu Minami of Minami Farms was instrumental in introducing Golden State Porcelain's president, Isamu Oku, to the productive local labor force, which Oku finds to be among the best in the world.

New outlets for sales and distribution have changed the ways in which Mikasa's wares reach their customers' homes—gone are the days when department stores were the only vehicles for success. Mikasa now controls a substantial portion of its own distribution, a development that has proved invaluable, according to chief executive officer and president Ray Dingman, who is based in the corporate headquarters in Secaucus.

Since Mikasa's first factory outlet store opened in Secaucus, hundreds of others have sprung up outside metropolitan cities across the United States, Canada, and Europe. Due to their success in selling directly to the public, Mikasa is testing home stores in retail malls throughout the nation. These stores strengthen Mikasa's brand recognition and enable corporate executives to instantly monitor sales patterns through computerized cash-register receipts.

Kenwood Electronics has also gone through its share of changes. In the 1980s it was sold to its Japanese manufacturers so that George could focus his full attention on the chinaware business, but he still remains connected to the company as chairman of the holding company, Kenwood Americas. Bill Kasuga, his fellow MIS instructor, continues to work as a senior advisor of the Japanese subsidiary, Kenwood USA.

Competition in the constantly changing electronics field has been especially fierce and vigorous with the growth of computers and the video format. In 1993 Joe Richter was appointed president of Kenwood USA and he currently leads the company—best known today for communications equipment and home and car audio—from its headquarters in Long Beach. Annual sales exceed $600 million.

The medical supply business, AMCO, is now Japanese-owned, and it exports instruments to the United States and many other countries. Initially begun in an executive's living room almost 50 years ago, AMCO currently boasts more than 10 branches and approximately 250 employees.

Most of the surviving American Commercial team—aside from Tets Murata—have since retired, and none of their children work for any of the corporations. Yet, in spite of the recent mergers and sales, the new generation of executives has not forgotten the companies' genesis. "If you had to put a picture of an individual next to the name Mikasa," says Dingman, "it would be George Aratani's. He's very much the public face of the company."

Mikasa still retains the flavor of George Aratani's original team, according to Dingman. "We have kept much of that culture, in terms of how we deal with issues and [our] respect for other people's feelings." The team is stressed above all, rather than the individual. As a result, when Mikasa's new warehouse facility was opened in Charleston, South Carolina, the company's publicity department was hard pressed to pull together enough information to create profiles of individual key executives.

George and Sakaye still live in the same house designed for them in 1951 by Vickie's husband, Henry Nakabayashi. The neighborhood, once a collection of bucolic hillsides, is now crowded with homes. Other than a deluxe condominium at the PGA West golf resort in La Quinta near Palm Springs, this is their only residence.

"George is a very unusual man," says Alf Blake, speaking from his office in New Jersey between intercontinental business trips. "He's lived modestly; he's never lived at the high level he could. Money itself was never his prime goal. His philosophy was that money would come later; he always had long-range thinking. Very few people have this philosophy. In fact, I haven't yet met anyone like him."

George is perfectly content with his 50-year-old house. He loves the view of Lake Hollywood, the reservoir that sometimes shimmers blue-green during rare smogless summer days. The interior of the home, which has been remodeled over the decades, is tastefully decorated with pastel-colored paintings. In the family room attached to the kitchen are examples of Sakaye's *chigiri-e*, Japanese paper art, and photographs line the counter space. These images are not of dignitaries and celebrities, but of children and grandchildren. In the couple's bedroom is a painting of George at age 11 in the Aratani team baseball uniform: a reminder that he is the quintessential American son.

Notably absent from the house's decor are the Japanese medals of honor, and the plaques, trophies, certificates—most likely numbering in the hundreds—which he and Sakaye have garnered over the decades. There is one piece of memorabilia, however: it chronicles George's proudest moment, which occurred on September 7, 1993. That was the day he shot his age—76—in a golf game at Rolling Hills Country Club, an exclusive course near the Pacific Ocean.

Unlike his golfing companions, George was not immediately elated after achieving this once-in-a-lifetime milestone. "I was numb for a while," he says.

**George and Sakaye Aratani out on the golf course
with Mrs. Yayoi Tanaka and Japanese Consul General
Tsuneo Tanaka in 1982.** (43.1998.5)

Whenever he is home, George keeps his cordless phone close by his side—there are many calls to answer and things to be scheduled. There are golf games with the Japanese consul general and attorney friends; board meetings of nonprofit groups; multiple fund-raisers and dinners; and of course, socializing with out-of-town guests. Every appointment is recorded in his simple pocket-sized calendar, one that is given away free by banks or stationery stores. Needless to say, each day of the month is filled with George's scrawl, which he boasts that only he can decipher.

There are calls from CEOs of Japanese corporations, who may be responding to a donation request—perhaps a 36-inch color television—for one of George's many charities. A former actor and producer schedules a lunch meeting to pitch his dream of taking the history of Japanese Americans in baseball to the Baseball Hall of Fame in Cooperstown. Everyone wants—or perhaps even needs—a slice of George Aratani's time.

In 1994 George and Sakaye formally established the Aratani Foundation, an endowment that currently provides money to more than 40 nonprofit organizations and will continue to do so in perpetuity. As long as the project is for the greater good of the Japanese American community—whether postwar immigrants, the elderly, Nisei friends, children, or business expatriates—it has the support of George and Sakaye Aratani. "It is my philosophy," he explains, "to help the ones hurt by the mass evacuation. I myself lost the family business. Eighty-five to ninety-five percent goes to Japanese American organizations."

Though he is a registered Republican, George has little use for politics or ideology. He has given money to the Republican National Committee while also contributing to the political campaigns of all major Japanese American candidates, no matter their party affiliation. "They are solidly Democrats over there in Hawai'i," he notes with dismay. Yet that does not deter him from sending checks at election time.

Abraham Lincoln, who aligned himself with the newly formed Republican Party in the 1850s, is one of George's political heroes; he claims that Democrats, on the other hand, are wishy-washy. He also notes that President Franklin D. Roosevelt, who signed Executive Order 9066 and thereby authorized the incarceration of Japanese Americans during World War II, was a Democrat.

———— ·•· ————

George is often surrounded by people, but few really know him. Not surprisingly, Sakaye probably understands him best. Their long and loving partnership has been a traditional one marked by respect and compromise (the latter usually on Sakaye's part). She has successfully maintained a harmonious household and supported family members in ways not readily apparent to the general public. When Masuko suffered a stroke some years ago, it was Sakaye who stepped in as the primary caregiver. That daughter-in-law and mother-in-law can faithfully work and live together under the same roof for more than 50 years is evidence of their commitment to put family unity first.

Although George has spent months at a time away from home, he never stopped articulating—especially in cards, letters, and telegrams—his love for his wife. Husband and wife share similar values, as well as a passion for international travel and golf. "A man has a dream," says George, explaining his hectic schedule and long hours of work. "He is trying to achieve that dream not only for himself but his wife and his family."

Sakaye listens and gives feedback on various daily matters ranging from fund-raising projects to dinner arrangements. Yet in the end it is George who makes the decision. He readily acknowledges his wife's strength, however, and in fact, he firmly states his belief in the strength of all women. He refers to a survey taken of British survivors of German missile attacks on London during World War II. "Women withstood these harsh consequences better than the men did. The women didn't crack up; they endured," he comments.

George's own endurance has sustained him through rough times. Although he would be the last to admit it, his own life has been filled with loss, tragedy, and struggle. "He's had a lot of pain," says one person close to him. From his football injury in high school to the valley fever in camp to his bout of hepatitis, his own health has failed him when he needed it most. Beloved family members died early in his life. The outbreak of World War II led to incarceration in a concentration camp, loss of the family businesses, and a relentless effort by the Superintendent of Banks to recover money for business loans extended to George's father.

George does not dwell on these moments of tribulation; in fact, like the skillful golfer that he is, he expertly drives them away. Were it not be for a box of old documents dating from the 1940s, memories of his wartime struggles and the genesis of his early trading business would be lost forever.

"I really struggled," George says, glancing at some papers. "I did a lot of detailed work."

Later, he admits in an interview that he and his colleagues were gutsy. His younger daughter, Linda, speaks of his intuitive strength. She relates advice he gave her when he attempted to teach her how to drive in the parking lot of the nearby Hollywood Bowl. "Just go forward as fast as you can," he told her. He knew that was the best way to overcome your fears.

◦ ◦ ◦

Although George has spent much of his time developing his business and raising funds for worthy causes, these activities do not supercede his devotion to his family. His eldest daughter, Donna, married her college sweetheart, Liong Tek Kwee, a Chinese man raised in Southeast Asia. The couple make their home in Singapore, where Tek's family has a prospering real-estate development enterprise. Donna and Tek have four children: Melissa, Stephanie, Evan, and Allison. The eldest daughter, Harvard-trained Melissa, continues the family's philanthropic legacy; she is the cofounder of

Project Access, which organizes leadership training programs for young women in Asia. Stephanie graduated from Stanford University, her grandfather's alma mater, and she is seeking to combine her passion for social work in the Third World with her interest in management. Evan hopes to become an entrepreneur like his father and grandfather, and he is currently studying business at Babson College in Massachusetts. Allison is continuing her studies in Singapore.

George and Sakaye's younger daughter, Linda, is taking her interest in health care into the business arena by starting Joint Effort Rehab, a Southern California company that provides physical and occupational therapists to hospitals and nursing homes. She has three children: Jeff, Jann, and Joy. Both Jeff and Jann are currently attending college in San Diego, while Joy attends prep school in Rolling Hills, where she is a top volleyball player.

Most of George's energy these days is consumed by his efforts to raise money for his latest philanthropic project. During a recent fund-raising trip to Japan, he worked so hard that he came home in a wheelchair and had to go straight from the airport to the hospital to address some back problems. As many community groups in Los Angeles can readily attest, George Aratani is a one-man fund-raising machine.

Japanese firms have changed their attitudes about corporate giving; no longer do they merely offer samurai swords or tiles with Mt. Fuji motifs. The Keidanren, a Japanese consortium of financial and industrial companies, is responsible for the formation of the Council for Better Corporate Citizenship (CBCC).

In conjunction with the Ministry of Finance, the CBCC issues tax credits to charitable and nonprofit institutions. Unlike the situation in the U.S., gifts to such organizations—even universities and churches—are not necessarily tax-deductible, so all fund-raising campaigns must first present their aims and intentions to the Keidanren before corporations can benefit financially from the gifts they bestow. Solicitation of donations from the Japanese corporate sector requires someone savvy about Japanese manners and culture. After receiving a special status from the Keidanren, George and other fund-raisers have been able to raise literally millions of dollars for Keiro Services, Japanese American National Museum, Japanese American Cultural and Community Center, and most recently, a Washington, D.C., monument celebrating Japanese American patriotism during World War II.

George explains the ins and outs of approaching the Japanese for money. He tells a favorite story about the time he took two Sansei leaders of a Japanese American nonprofit organization to Japan. During their presentation to a Japanese steel company, one of the executives closed his eyes, merely nodding his head once in a while.

"We need your support," George ended his visit. "*Yoroshiku onegaishimasu.* I'm indebted to you."

As they left the executive's office, one of the Japanese Americans, an attorney, expressed outrage. "George, that guy was so rude. He slept while you were making your pitch."

George chuckled. "No, he wasn't sleeping. He was in fact listening very carefully."

"But his head was even wobbling."

George laughed again. "I guess you haven't seen any *kabuki* plays. He'll be considering our presentation very seriously. We'll just have to wait."

Within Japanese companies no one person makes a decision about donating money, he went on to explain to his colleagues; it must be made by consensus, as a group. There was no doubt that the executive would be taking their request to a larger group of people. Sure enough, several months later, the Sansei attorney received a check in the mail from the steel company with the "sleeping" executive.

Speaking about his latest fund-raising trip, George concludes, "It's not a good time right now." The economic crisis suffered by Japan in the late 1990s has led to a nosedive of the yen; bankrupt executives have leapt from office buildings; a shamed prime minister resigned from office. George's own golf membership at Koganei Country Club has even taken a tumble from its high value of $5,000,000 in 1990 to $850,000 (still considerably more than the $2,000 George paid in 1958).

Will Japan recover?

"Oh yeah," he says with confidence. He has seen much, much worse.

George no longer goes to Guadalupe much. He occasionally travels there to visit friends, attend funerals, or stop by his parents' Guadalupe gravesite. He did end up moving a portion of his parents' ashes to Southern California, originally to a columbarium next to a memorial honoring baseball folk hero Casey Stengel within Forest Lawn Memorial Park in Glendale. Now the Aratani family has its own sarcophagus within the expansive cemetery.

Mounted on the marble memorial is a Greek-inspired sculpture of a man, seated on the ground, whose hand reaches out to a child supported by a woman kneeling behind him.

Another son of a former "Big Three" farmer, Isamu Minami, still lives in Santa Maria. He serves as managing partner of Security and El Dorado Farms, which annually ships three million crates of produce from its three-thousand-acre holdings. H. Y. Minami & Sons also remains in operation, annually distributing four million crates of refrigerated produce, including broccoli, cauliflower, and strawberries, throughout North America and the Pacific Rim.

Butch Tamura, whom Setsuo had recruited from Los Angeles to Guadalupe, died in his Pasadena home following a severe stroke in 1984. His youngest son, Dennis, continues Butch's prewar agricultural legacy as an organic farmer in Watsonville, bordering California's Silicon Valley.

George still stays in close touch with the only son of Ben and Toyoko Kodama. Kody Kodama, who now resides in Rancho Mirage, California, vividly recalls his childhood in his parents' boardinghouse on Guadalupe Street. His sinewy legs are tanned from hours spent on the golf course, and Kody explains that it was Setsuo Aratani who had first introduced him and other Guadalupeans to the game of golf.

Ken Kitasako—or "Youngu," as Setsuo called him—still lives north of Santa Maria in Arroyo Grande. After retiring from Pismo-Oceano Vegetable Exchange after 26 years, Ken served as a board member of Kyowa Bank, an appointment that George arranged. Ken's beloved wife Muts, Butch's sister, died in 1997, but Ken still faithfully eats dinner at the kitchen table in front of her photograph.

Guadalupe has gone through its own ups and downs. In the 1980s Los Angeles newspapers reported on sting operations targeting the increasing number of prostitutes in town. On a positive note, groups such as the Rancho de Guadalupe Historical Society work to build civic pride by restoring old adobe buildings that represent the area's past links to Mexico. In the years since World War II, strawberries—which provided the foundation for Setsuo's initiation into farming—have proven to be one of Santa Maria's most profitable crops. And in the summer of 1999, a new Amtrak railroad station was completed on Guadalupe Street, thereby sparking hopes of economic revival.

Fires have destroyed some of Guadalupe's downtown buildings, but the Royal Theatre, originally financed by Chuhei "Charles" Ishii and some Issei partners, has survived, and it continues to screen movies on their last release before going to video. Also remaining is Masatani Market, now operated by Harry and Kimiko Masatani and their two sons, Steve and Brian. Although they stock some Japanese foodstuffs such as tofu and pickled radishes, more constant sellers are chorizo, tripe, and packages of tortillas.

Once a year, the past and the present meet in Southern California. The doors of George and Sakaye's Hollywood Hills home are opened wide to the men and women of Guadalupe; former comrades with the Military Intelligence Service; children and grandchildren from Southern California and Singapore; Japanese dignitaries and business contacts; and the Mikasa, Kenwood, and AMCO teams. As Sakaye and Masuko artfully prepare traditional dishes, George welcomes each guest with a drink, a handshake, or an embrace. In recent years the flow of visitors has diminished, but their hosts' hospitality and good wishes remain the same. The Aratanis and their guests usher in the new year, forever hopeful that their community, planted by leaders like Setsuo Aratani in places like Guadalupe, will survive for many more generations.

Sources

The photographs reproduced in this volume are from the collection of the Japanese American National Museum, gift of George and Sakaye Aratani, or from the private collection of George and Sakaye Aratani, unless otherwise indicated.

Chapter 1: Big Boss

Interviews with George Aratani, Masuko Aratani, Ken Kitasako, Sam Maenaga, and Masasuke Oishi. Also helpful were conversations with Jose Rubalcaba and Shirley Boylston, both of the Rancho de Guadalupe Historical Society, Donna Crippen (curator of the El Monte Historical Museum), and Masakazu Iwata.

Nancy Araki's interview of George Aratani (2 March 1994, Sun City, Calif.), Japanese American National Museum.

Key sources

Masakazu Iwata's *Planted in Good Soil: A History of the Issei in United States Agriculture* (New York: Peter Lang, 1992) provides an excellent overview of Japanese American farming before World War II. I am also indebted to Mr. Iwata for writing a two-page recollection of Setsuo Aratani. The *Guadalupe Gazette* (1 January 1931 issue) gives a unique view of life in Guadalupe, specifically the relationship between the Japanese immigrants and European American residents. Copies of the *Gazette*, which ceased publication before the war, were obtained from the Rancho de Guadalupe Historical Society and Richard P. Weldon.

Santa Maria Heigen Nihonjinshi (Guadalupe: Guadalupe Japanese Association, 1936), compiled by Kyugoro Saka, a former teacher at the Guadalupe Japanese School, chronicles a good, broad picture of the valley and its Japanese residents. Not only were certain chronologies valuable, but also brief profiles of prominent male leaders included at the end of the book. Yoshito Fujimoto has translated an abridged English-language version called *Santa Maria Valley Japanese History*, available at the Japanese American National Museum.

Yearbooks by Japanese vernaculars proved useful in verifying addresses, names, dates, and details of certain individuals and enterprises. They include *Sangyo Nippo*'s commemorative book published in 1940, and *The Rafu Shimpo Year Book* (1914–15). The Buddhist publication *Bhratri* also gave details on Setsuo Aratani's life.

Jane Imamura of Oakland generously provided a copy of her mother's book *Higan: Compassionate Vow*. Written by Shinobu Matsuura, it was translated into English by the Matsuura family and privately published in 1986 in Berkeley. Mrs. Matsuura was the wife of Buddhist minister Issei Matsuura, who was assigned to Guadalupe before and after the war. The book contains wonderful accounts of life in the Santa Maria Valley.

The Japanese American National Museum has a collection of 16mm home movies of the Aratani family. Through footage recording various events involving Guadalupe Produce and the Japanese community in the valley, this collection captures the charisma of Setsuo Aratani and the recreational activities of George Aratani.

Finally, Kent Haldan has documented and interpreted his extensive knowledge of Guadalupe and Santa Maria in his UC Berkeley doctoral dissertation, "'Our Japanese Citizens': A Study of Race, Class and Ethnicity in Three Japanese American Communities in Santa Barbara County, 1900–1960." I highly recommend that interested individuals refer to his work for a more academic treatment and analysis of the Issei farmers' impact on the area.

Other Sources

Edward Behr, *Hirohito: Behind the Myth* (New York: Villard Books, 1989).

Jerry Bunin, "Paul Kurokawa Remembered for His Contributions," *Telegram-Tribune* (San Luis Obispo, Calif.), 19 January 1999.

Frank F. Chuman, *The Bamboo People: The Law and Japanese-Americans* (Del Mar, Calif.: Publisher's Inc., 1976).

Gordon S. Eberly, *Arcadia: City of the Santa Anita* (Claremont, Calif.: Saunder Press, 1953).

Michinari Fujita, "The Japanese Associations in America," *Sociology and Social Research* 13, no. 3 (January–February 1929): 211–28.

Hashimoto, ed., *Nankashu Nihonjin* (The History of the Japanese in Southern California) (Southern California Japanese Association of America, 1916).

Robert Higgs, "Landless by Law: Japanese Immigrants in California Agriculture to 1941," *Journal of Economic History* 38 (March 1978): 205–25.

Lane Ryo Hirabayashi and George Tanaka, "The Issei Community in Moneta and the Gardena Valley, 1900–1920," *Southern California Quarterly* 70, no. 2 (summer 1988): 127–58.

Yuji Ichioka, "Japanese Associations and the Japanese Government: A Special Relationship, 1909–1926," *Pacific Historical Review* 46 (August 1977): 409–37.

Yuji Ichioka, "Japanese Immigrant Response to the 1920 California Alien Land Law," *Agricultural History* 58, no. 2 (April 1984): 157–78.

Masakazu Iwata, "The Japanese Immigrants in California Agriculture," *Agricultural History* 36, no. 1: 25–37.

Masakazu Iwata, "San Fernando Valley and the Issei Legacy: Or Rambling Thoughts from a Sun-Baked Farm Boy" (unpublished, 10 August 1994).

Lawrence C. Jorgensen, ed., *The San Fernando Valley: Past and Present* (Los Angeles: Pacific Rim Research, 1982).

Robert George Ketron, "Locational and Historical Aspects of the Quick Frozen Vegetable Processing Industry of California" (master's thesis, University of Arizona, 1968).

Dan Krieger, "Paul Kurokawa: A Lifetime of Service to the Central Coast," *Telegram-Tribune* (San Luis Obispo, Calif.), 6 February 1999.

Kango Kunitsugu, "Grand Marshal Kay Sugahara," *Nisei Week 1983–43rd Annual Japanese Festival* (Los Angeles: Nisei Week Festival, 1983).

Jackson Mayers, *The San Fernando Valley* (Walnut, Calif.: John D. McIntyre, 1976).

Pat McAdam and Sandy Snider, *Arcadia: Where Ranch and City Meet* (Arcadia, Calif.: Friends of the Arcadia Public Library, 1981).

Carey McWilliams, *Prejudice—Japanese Americans: Symbol of Racial Intolerance* (Boston: Little, Brown and Company, 1944).

Tessa Morris-Suzuki, *Showa: An Inside History of Hirohito's Japan* (New York: Schocken Books, 1984).

Moving Memories (video, 31 min.), prod. Karen L. Ishizuka (Los Angeles: Japanese American National Museum, 1992).

Kaizo Naka, "Social and Economic Conditions Among Japanese Farmers in California," (master's thesis, University of California, Berkeley, 1913).

Kerry Nakagawa, "Opening the Door," *The Rafu Shimpo*, Section B, 18 July 1997.

Musho Nakagawa, *Zaibei Toshiroku* (Los Angeles: Hakubundo Shoten, 1932).

Takeshi Nakayama, "A Place Where People Could Be Japanese," *The Rafu Shimpo Magazine*, 17 December 1994.

Owen H. O'Neill, ed., *History of Santa Barbara County* (Santa Barbara: Harold McLean Meier, 1939).

The Rafu Shimpo, 15 July 1928; 22 July 1928; 29 July 1928; 21 October 1928; 19 November 1928; and 23 December 1928.

Santa Maria Daily Times, 18 January 1924; 19 January 1924; 20 January 1924; and 1 September 1933.

Fumihiko Shirota, "Moxa Treatment," in *Encyclopedia of Japan* (New York: Kodansha Ltd., 1983).

Ronald Takaki, *A Different Mirror* (New York: Little, Brown and Company, 1993).

Junichi Takeda, *Zaibei Hiroshima Kenjinshi* (History of the Japanese from Hiroshima Prefecture in America) (Los Angeles: Zaibei Hiroshima Kenjinshi Hakkosho, 1929).

Koyoshi Uono, "The Factors Affecting the Geographical Aggregation and Dispersion of the Japanese Residences in the City of Los Angeles" (master's thesis, University of Southern California, 1927).

Noritake Yagasaki, "Ethnic Cooperativism and Immigrant Agriculture: A Study of Japanese Floriculture and Truck Farming in California" (Ph.D. diss., University of California, Berkeley, 1982).

Chapter 2: Let It Roll

Interviews with George Aratani, Ken Kitasako, Tets Murata, Kody Kodama, Isamu Minami, Masayoshi Tomooka, Masasuke Oishi, Sam Maenaga, Cappy Harada, and Masato Inouye.

Key Sources

The effect of the Depression on the Japanese American community is covered in Roger Daniels's "Japanese America, 1930–1941: An Ethnic Community in the Great Depression," in *Journal of the West* (October 1985). Moreover, Noritake Yagasaki's UC Berkeley doctoral thesis (see notes, Chapter 1) illuminates the strength of Japanese cooperatism and collectivism in withstanding harsh economic conditions.

As recommended by Cal State Fullerton professor Arthur Hansen, journalist Gene Oishi's memoir *In Search of Hiroshi* (Rutland, Vt.: Charles E. Tuttle Company, 1988) gives a more sobering view of life in Santa Maria Valley.

Past issues of the *Santa Maria Daily Times*, now called the *Santa Maria Times*, were extremely helpful in piecing together a timeline of events, in particular the labor strike of 1934.

Other Sources

Dennis and Jeanne Burke DeValeria, *Honus Wagner: A Biography* (Pittsburgh: University of Pittsburgh Press, 1998).

Santa Maria Union High School Yearbook, 1932; 1933; and 1934.

Samuel Walker, *In Defense of American Liberties: A History of the ACLU* (New York: Oxford University Press, Inc., 1990).

Chapter 3: Japan Journal

Interviews with George Aratani, Masato Inouye, Masako Aratani, Tad Yamada, and Sister Mercedes M. Martin (Maryknoll Sisters of Monrovia). Telephone interview with Haruyo Ogawa Kuroiwa, the widow of Dr. Daishiro Kuroiwa, the Japanese Catholic convert who purchased a sanatorium for the Maryknoll community.

Key Sources on Japan

Most valuable was a detailed daily journal kept by Masato Inouye. Moreover, *Amerasia Journal*'s winter 1997–98 issue, edited by Yuji Ichioka, was extremely helpful in shedding light on Nisei in Japan and Manchuria during the 1930s and 1940s. I referred to articles by Yuji Ichioka ("Beyond National Boundaries: The Complexity of Japanese-American History"); John J. Stephan ("Hijacked by Utopia: American Nikkei in Manchuria"); and Frank Hirata's "Fifty Years after the Pacific War: 'Molded to Conform, But . . .'").

In terms of the effects of Japan's military policies on its people, I've found Thomas R. H. Haven's *Valley of Darkness: The Japanese People and World War Two* (New York: W. W. Norton and Company, Inc., 1978) very insightful in terms of the "everyday" man's and woman's perspective.

For information on Nisei students in Japan, I found some interesting details in journalist Toshiyuki Ijiri's collected articles. The English version, translated by Ben Kobashigawa and Osamu Wakugami, has been published under the title *Paul Rusch: The Story of KEEP and What a Man with Vision Can Do* (Yamanashi, Japan: Yamanashi Shimbun, 1991).

Other Sources on Japan

Iris Chang, *The Rape of Nanking: The Forgotten Holocaust of World War II* (New York: BasicBooks, 1997).

John W. Dower, *Japan in War and Peace: Selected Essays* (New York: New Press, 1993).

John A. Harrison, *China Since 1800* (New York: Harcourt, Brace and World, Inc., 1967).

W. Scott Morton, *China: Its History and Culture* (New York: Lippincott and Crowell, 1980).

Edwin M. Reingold, *Chrysanthemums and Thorns: The Untold Story of Modern Japan* (New York: St. Martin's Press, 1992).

Haru Matsukata Reischauer, *Samurai and Silk: A Japanese and American Heritage* (Cambridge, Mass., and London: Belknap Press of Harvard University Press, 1986).

Santa Maria Union High School's *Breeze*, 1935.

H. P. Willmott, *Empires in the Balance: Japanese and Allied Pacific Strategies to April 1942* (Annapolis, Md.: United States Naval Institute, 1982).

Key Sources on Maryknoll Sanatorium

Unfortunately, I could not include here the breadth of information regarding the Maryknoll congregation's long connection with the Japanese American community in Los Angeles. In addition to the sanatorium, which is now a retirement home for Maryknoll Sisters, the mission also established a school and orphanage. The Maryknoll Japanese Catholic Center is now located on the outskirts of Little Tokyo, where the school once stood.

Sister Mercedes M. Martin of the Maryknoll Sisters kindly provided a tour of the site of the Maryknoll Sanatorium, now a retirement home for the Sisters. Prepared by the Sisters in 1961, a document entitled "A History of Maryknoll Sanatorium" can be accessed through the Maryknoll Archives.

The Monrovia Public Library has a good collection of books on the city's history. References include *Monrovia Blue Book*; Peter Ostrye's *Monrovia Centennial Review* (Monrovia: Monrovia Centennial Committee); and John J. Wiley's *History of Monrovia* (Pasadena: Press of Pasadena Star-News, 1927).

Tuberculosis specialist Dr. William Stead of the Arkansas Department of Health provided information on the disease, both past and present.

Last of all, Setsuo Aratani's death and funeral were comprehensively covered in the *Santa Maria Daily Times* (19 April 1940, 22 April 1940, and 25 April 1940). In the 22 April 1940 issue, the newspaper published an editorial, "Setsuo Aratani—Leader!"

Other Sources on Maryknoll Sanatorium

Charles F. Davis, *Monrovia-Duarte Community Book* (Monrovia, Calif.: Arthur H. Cawston, 1957).

Harry K. Honda, "Maryknoll at 75," in *Nisei Week 1987* (Los Angeles: 47th Annual Japanese Festival, 1987).

Maryknoll Mission Archives, *Maryknoll Sisters: Toward a Distant Vision* (New York: Maryknoll Sisters, 1992).

Chapter 4: Taking Over the Farm

Interviews with George Aratani, Ken Kitasako, Mary Tamura, Tets Murata, Kody Kodama, Komano Ishikawa, and Masato Inouye.

Key Sources

This chapter could not have been written without access to George Aratani's personal papers regarding his father's business. Among his papers is correspondence, as well as legal and business documents.

Regarding Stanford University and Japanese Americans, Professor Gordon Chang is a knowledgable resource. I referred to his book *Morning Glory, Evening Shadow: Yamato Ichihashi and His Internment Writings, 1942–45* (Palo Alto, Calif.: Stanford University Press, 1997) to understand the social climate for Nisei students in the 1930s.

Past issues of the *Santa Maria Daily Times* (January–December 1940) provided important accounts of labor struggles, the lettuce prorate committee (31 May 1940), Future Farmers of America activities (24 April 1940), draft information (September–October 1940), and the enterprises of Issei leaders such as Chuhei "Charles" Ishii (10 August 1930, 30 August 1930).

Coverage on the Santa Barbara County Fair included promotional advertisements, photographs, and articles (23 July 1940, 24 July 1940, 29 July 1940, 26 July 1941).

Other Sources

Beikoku Nikkei-jin Hyakunenshi 1860–1960, Shin Nichibei Shimbun Sha, 532.

The Rafu Shimpo Yearbook and Directory, 1939–40.

Julia Sommer, "Pre-War Japanese Students Give Scholarship," *Stanford Observer* (November 1987).

Chapter 5: Let Us Not Be Witch Hunters

Interviews with George Aratani, Mary Tamura, Komano Ishikawa, Ken Kitasako, Tad Yamada, Sam Maenaga, Masayoshi Tomooka, and Masasuke Oishi.

Key Sources

Again, the personal papers of George Aratani provided a paper trail that revealed how George and his business associates had to respond to news about the evacuation of all Japanese Americans from the West Coast.

The *Santa Maria Daily Times* was useful for information regarding the arrests of prominent Issei and impending evacuation of Japanese Americans (7–8, 10–12, 15, 24, 29, and 31 December 1941). Moreover, editorials provided perspectives from prevailing non-Japanese leaders. Especially revealing was "We Have a Ticklish Task Here" on 10 December 1941.

The History of Santa Barbara County, published in Santa Barbara in 1939, also contains useful profiles of prominent prewar business leaders.

Other Sources

Leonard J. Arrington, "Utah's Ambiguous Reception: The Relocated Japanese Americans," in *Japanese Americans: From Relocation to Redress* (Salt Lake City: University of Utah Press, 1986).

Frank Y. Chuman, *The Bamboo People* (see notes, Chapter 1).

John Culley, "The Santa Fe Internment Camp and the Justice Department Program for Enemy Aliens," in *Japanese Americans: From Relocation to Redress*.

Gary Y. Okihiro and David Drummond, "The Concentration Camps and Japanese Economic Losses in California Agriculture, 1900–1942," in *Japanese Americans: From Relocation to Redress*.

Something Strong Within (video, 40 min.), prod. and dir. Karen L. Ishizuka and Robert A. Nakamura (Los Angeles: Japanese American National Museum, 1994).

Marilyn Schobel, "Internment: Remembering Wartime Fear and Shame," in *Sagas of the Central Coast* (Santa Maria, Calif.: R. J. Nelson Enterprises, Inc., 1994).

Kanshi Stanley Yamashita, "An Island in Time," *The Rafu Shimpo Magazine*, 14 December 1991.

Chapter 6: Losing Guadalupe in Barracks 57-10-B

Interviews with George Aratani, Ken Kitasako, Masuko Aratani, Komano Ishikawa, Sakaye Aratani, Vickie Nakabayashi, Tets Murata, and Tad Yamada.

Key Sources

Here again, personal correspondence received and sent by George Aratani was pivotal in reconstructing the events during this tumultuous wartime period. Carbon copies of letters he typed on his typewriter have been retained, as well as business correspondence from the Santa Maria Valley.

Professor Arthur Hansen again offered valuable resources regarding Gila River concentration camp and the JACL chapter that was formed within it. Resources included "Return to Butte Camp: A Japanese-American World War II Relocation Center," prepared by the Bureau of Reclamation, Arizona Projects Office, by Archaeological Consulting Services, Ltd., 30 November 1993. Essential was "Development of Gila JACL," a report written by Charles Kikuchi in Chicago in July 1943. The report, which also contains board minutes, describes leaders and briefly mentions George Aratani.

Gila News-Courier, the official newspaper of the Gila River War Relocation Center, was helpful in tracing camp activities. The 12 September 1942 issue included a brief profile on George under the heading "Stars in Our Midst" on the sports page. Santa Maria Valley news was included on 29 December 1942, 29 June 1943, 25 January 1944, and 27 January 1944.

For an in-depth description of the camp, also refer to the final report submitted by community analyst G. Gordon Brown, who was assigned to the War Relocation Authority, Gila River Project, July 1945.

Other Sources

Gila River River Relocation Center, 1942–1945: 50-Year Reunion Souvenir Booklet (1995).

Claire Gorfinkel, ed., *The Evacuation Diary of Hatsuye Egami* (Pasadena: Intentional Productions, 1996).

Arthur A. Hansen, "Cultural Politics in the Gila River Relocation Center, 1942–43," *Arizona and the West*, no. 27 (winter 1985): 327–62.

William Minoru Hohri, *Repairing America* (Pullman, Wash.: Washington State University Press, 1984).

Bill Hosokawa, *JACL in Quest of Justice: The History of the Japanese American Citizens League* (New York: William Morrow and Company, Inc., 1982).

Peter Irons, *Justice at War: The Story of the Japanese American Internment Cases* (New York: Oxford University Press, 1983).

Pamela Iwasaki, "We Must Endure . . . A Look at Health Care in the Japanese American Internment Camps" (paper, University of California, San Diego, School of Medicine, 1988).

JACL Jonas Subcommittee on Claims Committee of the Judiciary House of Representatives, H.R. 7435 (Evacuation Claims Amendment).

Mike Masaoka, with Bill Hosokawa, *They Call Me Moses Masaoka: An American Saga* (New York: William Morrow and Company, Inc., 1987).

Second Year in Rivers (Rivers, Ariz.: Gila-News Courier, 1944).

Paul R. Spickard, "The Nisei Assume Power: The Japanese Citizens League, 1941–1942," *Pacific Historical Review* 52, no. 2 (May 1983): 147–75.

Dorothy Swaine Thomas, *The Salvage* (Berkeley and Los Angeles: University of California Press, 1952).

Michi Nishiura Weglyn, *Years of Infamy* (Seattle: University of Washington Press, 1996).

Chapter 7: Lines of Communication

Interviews with George Aratani, Sakaye Aratani, Masuko Aratani, Bill Kasuga, Tad Yamada, and Min Endo.

Nancy Araki's interview with Shig Kihara (2 March 1994, Sun City, Calif.), Japanese American National Museum.

Vince Tajiri's interview with John Aiso (1987, Los Angeles), Visual Communications.

Key Sources

Masaharu Ano provides a good overview of the language school in his article "Loyal Linguists: Nisei of World War II Learned Japanese in Minnesota," *Minnesota History* (fall 1977): 273–87.

For photographs and a chronology of the school and its various departments, I referred to the *MISLS Album*, which was produced by the school's staff in 1946. It has since been reprinted (Nashville: The Battery Press, 1990).

Other Sources

Stanley L. Falk and Warren M. Tsuneishi, eds., *MIS in the War Against Japan: Personal Experiences Related at the 1993 MIS Capital Reunion* (Washington, D.C.: Japanese American Veterans Association of Washington, D.C., 1995).

Joseph D. Harrington, *Yankee Samurai: The Secret Role of Nisei in America's Pacific Victory* (Detroit: Pettigrew Enterprises, Inc., 1979).

Jean Ishii-Marshall, "The Portraits on Grandma's Walls," *Japanese American National Museum Quarterly* (Japanese American National Museum, summer 1996).

James Oda, *Heroic Struggles of Japanese Americans: Partisan Fighters from America's Concentration Camps* (North Hollywood, Calif.: KNI, Inc., 1981).

James Oda, "John Aiso and the MIS," *Pacific Citizen* (Los Angeles) (Holiday Issue 1988).

John Tsuchida, ed., *Reflections: Memoirs of Japanese American Women in Minnesota* (Covina, Calif.: Pacific Asia Press, 1994).

Ray Yoshinaga, "George Aratani: The Nisei Behind Mikasa China," *Jade Magazine* 4, no. 3 (summer 1982).

Chapter 8: Gathering the Team

Interviews with George Aratani, Masuko Aratani, Mary Tamura, Kody Kodama, Ken Kitasako, Sakaye Aratani, Vickie Nakabayashi, Komano Ishikawa, Shig Kariya, Jean Kariya, Tad Yamada, and Tets Murata.

Key Sources

Toshitaro Ishikawa's original correspondence to George, written in Japanese, provided an essential source of facts and attitudes regarding the resurrection of All Star Trading.

Interviews in the book *The Salvage* (by Dorothy Swaine Thomas with the assistance of Charles Kikuchi and James Sakoda) were instrumental in painting a wide picture of attitudes concerning Santa Maria Valley. Although not identified by name, numerous subjects within *The Salvage* (see notes, Chapter 6) were formerly involved in farming in the valley before eventually relocating to Chicago.

The resettlement of Japanese Americans from camp is covered in *Nanka Nikkei Voices: Resettlement Years 1945–1955*, a 1998 publication of the Japanese American Historical Society of Southern California, edited by Brian Niiya. Also helpful was Kevin Allen Leonard's 'Is That What We Fought For?': Japanese Americans and Racism in California: The Impact of World War II," *Western Historical Quarterly* 21, no. 4 (November 1990). For more details on Santa Maria Valley resettlement experiences, see the War Relocation Authority Santa Barbara District's final report, written by district relocation officer Eric H. Thomsen on 31 January 1946.

Helpful was *Fortune* editor John Kenneth Galbraith's report on Japan's economy in the first year of the nation's defeat, "Japan's Road Back—The Hurdles: Starvation and Inflation, Reparations and Reform" (vol. 124, no. 31 [March 1946]).

Regarding the Sumitomo lawsuit, there are documents filed in both the Los Angeles County Law Library and Los Angeles Superior Court (*Maurice C. Sparling as Superintendent of Banks of the State of California and Liquidator of the Sumitomo Bank, Limited, Los Angeles Office* v. *Tetsuo Aratani, Superior Court of the State of California, in and for the County of Los Angeles, 1945–47*).

Chapter 9: The Voyage

Interviews with George Aratani, Sakaye Aratani, Shig Kariya, and Komano Ishikawa.

Key Sources

Shig Kariya, with the assistance of his wife Jean, provided a written summary of the history of Mikasa, Inc.

The following articles also painted a detailed picture of Occupied Japan, as seen by the American mass media: "Japan's Road Back" (*Fortune* 124, no. 31 [March 1946]); "Yet Another Land of Crisis" (*Newsweek* 30 [3 November 1947]); "A Lawyer's Report on Japan Attacks Plan to Run Occupation" (*Newsweek* 30 [1 December 1947]); "Two-Billion Dollar Failure in Japan" (*Fortune* 39, no. 4 [April 1949]); and "SCAPitalism Marches On: Japan's Economy Will Be Better Off When It Comes Marching Home" (*Fortune* 40, no. 10 [October 1949]).

Vividly describing life in Japan during the American Occupation, *My Bridge to America:*

Discovering the New World for Minolta (New York: E. P. Dutton, 1989) is the autobiography of Minolta leader Sam Kusumoto. Kusumoto is the husband of Kuniko Sumomogi, the daughter of George's half sister, Sadako.

Offering details on international trade regulations are "Documents Concerning the Allied Occupation and Control of Japan, Volume IV—Commercial and Industrial," compiled by Section of Special Records, Foreign Office, Japanese Government (24 December 1949).

Also notable is information provided by Cappy Harada, a native of Santa Maria, who served as Aide-de-Camp to Major General William F. Marquat during the Occupation. Harada went on to organize international goodwill baseball tours and eventually served as a scout for the San Francisco Giants.

Other Sources

Theodore Cohen, *Remaking Japan: The American Occupation as New Deal* (New York: The Free Press, 1987).

Robert A. Fearey, *The Occupation of Japan, Second Phase: 1948–50* (New York: MacMillan Company, 1950).

D. Clayton James, *The Years of MacArthur: Triumph and Disaster, 1945–1964* (Boston: Houghton Mifflin Company, 1985).

William Raymond Manchester, *American Caesar: Douglas MacArthur, 1880–1964* (Boston: Little, Brown and Company, 1978).

Chapter 10: Nisei in Manhattan

Interviews with George Aratani, Shig Kariya, Jean Kariya, Ken Kolker, Sakaye Aratani, Tad Yamada, and Ken Funabashi.

Key Sources

Invaluable were the essays of Roku Sugahara, "A Nisei in Manhattan," published in the *Pacific Citizen* in the early 1950s. Not only did Mr. Sugahara write of Japanese Americans and Japanese nationals in postwar New York, he also focused on international start-up trading companies. For an early history of Issei in New York, refer to Mitziko Sawada's *Tokyo Life, New York Dreams: Urban Japanese Visions of America, 1890–1924* (Berkeley and Los Angeles: University of California Press, 1996), and Scott T. Miyakawa's "Early New York Issei: Founders of Japanese American Trade," in *East Across the Pacific* (Santa Barbara: ABC-CLIO, 1972).

Both the *Pacific Citizen* and the *New York Times* also provided accounts of protests generated against the resettlement of Japanese Americans in New York City during the war. Refer to the *Pacific Citizen* regarding specific mention of the New York JACL activities (1 July 1944, 2 December 1944, and 23 June 1945).

Regarding the abalone trade, see *Abalone Book* by Peter C. Howorth (Happy Camp, Calif.: Naturegraph Publications, 1978).

Other Sources

Veronica P. Johns, *She Sells Seashells* (New York: Funk and Wagnalls, 1968).

A. Hyatt Verill, *Shell Collector's Handbook* (New York: G. P. Putnam's Sons, 1950).

George Zappler, *Grosset All-Color Guide Series* (New York: Grosset & Dunlap, Inc., 1973).

Chapter 11: Making It to Macy's

Interviews with George Aratani, Shig Kariya, Tad Yamada, Ken Funabashi, Joe Orshan, Vickie Nakabayashi, Maria Funabashi, Ken Kolker, Yae Aihara, Linda Kimura, and Donna Kwee.

Key Sources

Earl Lifshey's in-depth article, "The Mikasa Story," in *HFD: Retailing, Home, Furnishings* (1 December 1980: 19–21) outlines the roles of George Aratani, Al Funabashi, Joe Orshan, and Alf Blake. Joe Orshan was kind enough to send Mikasa's first color catalogue—a project he oversaw during his tenure with the company.

Three books about department stores were useful: Robert Hendrickson's *The Grand Emporiums: An Illustrated History of America's Great Department Stores* (New York: Stein and Day, 1979); John William Ferry's *A History of the Department Store* (New York: MacMillan Company, 1960); and Frank M. Mayfield's *The Department Store Story* (New York: Fairchild Publications, Inc., 1949).

Regarding the Japanese ceramics trade, there are a number of collector's groups for Nippon ware, as well as numerous collector's guides (see below). However, few individuals seem to be collecting Mikasa china from the late forties and early fifties. Numerous resources in the Japanese language are available about the Nagoya chinaware industry and Japan's ceramics industry in general. Of particular note are *Kindai Togyo-shi* by Kozo Mitsui (1979) and *Nagoya Togyo no Hyakunen*, published by the Nagoya Tojiki Kaikan (1987). Mr. Mitsui also authored a series of articles under the banner of "Showa Togyo-shi."

Articles in women's magazines discuss chinaware in general terms: "Facts to Know When Shopping for China" in *Good Housekeeping* (August 1962); "A Brief Dictionary of Dinnerware Terms" in *Good Housekeeping* (February 1957); "Why Don't They Make . . ." in *American Home* (May 1956); and "Start Here and Set Your Heart on the China, Glass, and Silver to Set Your Dream Table" in *Good Housekeeping* (March 1961).

AMCO Inc.'s company history was kindly provided by Tad Yamada. In addition, AMCO also sent over the firm's early brochures, which provide a sampling of the medical equipment it imported to Japan in the early 1950s and 1960s. A series of articles on Japan's atomic energy was instructive, as was *Sapio* magazine's 9 September 1989 article on the introduction of the nuclear reactor in Harumi Bay.

A videotape of a graveside ceremony commemorating the twentieth anniversary of Alfred Funabashi's death documents the great respect his colleagues had for the former Mikasa president.

Telegrams saved by Sakaye Aratani in her scrapbook provided accurate dates of George's travels to and from Japan.

Other Sources

Aimee Neff Alden and Marian Kinney Richardson, *Early Noritake China* (Lombard, Ill.: Wallace-Homestead Book Company, 1987).

Regina Lee Blaszczyk, "Reign of the Robots: The Homer Laughlin China Company and Flexible Mass Production," *Technology and Culture* 36, no. 4 (October 1995): 863–911.

Barbara Coddington, Sanford Sivitz Shaman, and Patricia Grieve Watkinson, eds., *Noritake Art Deco Porcelains: Collection of Howard Kottler* (Pullman, Wash.: Museum of Art, Washington State University, 1982).

Daniel Cohen, "Grand Emporiums Peddle Their Wares in a New Market," *Smithsonian* 23, no. 12 (March 1993): 122–29.

Money Hickman and Peter Fetchko, *Japan Day by Day: An Exhibition Honoring Edward Sylvester Morse* (Salem, Mass.: Peabody Museum of Salem, 1977).

Ken Itsuki, *The Dawns of Tradition* (Japan: Nissan Motors, 1983).

Kashu Mainichi, 19 November 1969.

Hugo Munsterberg, *The Ceramic Art of Japan: A Handbook for Collectors* (Tokyo: Charles E. Tuttle Company, 1964).

Leila Philip, *The Road Through Miyama* (New York: Random House, 1989).

Shin Nichibei, 30 November 1956.

Joan F. Van Patten, *Collector's Encyclopedia of Nippon Porcelain* (Paducah, Ky.: Collector Books, 1997).

Chapter 12: Going Solid State

Interviews with George Aratani, Tad Yamada, Frank Chuman, Bill Kasuga, Komano Ishikawa, Donna Kwee, Sakaye Aratani, Tets Murata, and Yoshie Nakase.

Key Sources

Journalists Peter Pringle and James Spigelman provide a good overview of the early nuclear age in *The Nuclear Barons* (New York: Holt, Rinehart and Winston, 1981). They include a section on the involvement of Matsutaro Shoriki, the founder of *Yomiuri Shimbun* and Japanese baseball supporter, in furthering the use of nuclear energy in Japan.

Regarding the electronics industry, articles in *Popular Electronics* (January 1961, July 1961, October 1961, January 1962, January 1963, August 1963, November 1965, September 1966, October 1966) were particularly helpful in revealing the state of audio technology in the mid-1960s. Japan's advancements in solid-state technology were documented in Charles Lincoln's article, "The Stereo Scene: Sayonara to the Stigma 'Made in Japan,'" in the July 1969 issue of *Popular Electronics*, and in "Japanese IC's" in the November 1966 issue of the same magazine. Also important were old issues of *High Fidelity* (January 1966, April 1966, June 1966, October 1966, December 1966, January 1968, October 1969).

Profiles on George Aratani and his activity with Kenwood are highlighted in "Kenwood's Aratani" in *Sight and Sound Marketing* (1978); a program for the Fourth Annual Audio Hall of Fame Awards dinner (1976); and *Kenwood Stereoletter* 1, no. 701 (January 1970).

Newsletters and articles in local vernaculars heralded the inaugural Japanese American Debutante Ball, including the *Japanese American Society of Southern California Journal* (1965), *Los Angeles Times*, *The Rafu Shimpo*, and *Kashu Mainichi*.

Other Sources on Atomic Energy

Atoms for Power: United States Policy in Atomic Energy Development (New York: The American Assembly, Columbia University, 1957).

Commercial Nuclear Power 1984 (Washington, D.C.: U.S. Energy Information Administration, 1984).

Gilbert M. Masters, *Introduction of Environmental Science and Technology* (New York: John Wiley and Sons, 1974).

Power Reactors (Washington, D.C.: United States Atomic Energy Commission Technical Information Service, 1958).

Robert Rienow and Leona Train Rienow, *Our New Life with the Atom* (New York: Thomas Y. Crowell Company, 1959).

United States Atomic Energy Commission, *Atomic Energy Facts* (Washington, D.C.: U.S. Government Printing Office, 1957).

Other Sources on the Audio Industry

Forest H. Belt, *Easi-Guide to Hi-Fi Stereo* (Indianapolis: Howard W. Sams and Co., 1973).

Melvin Berger, *The Stereo Hi-Fi* (New York: Lothrop, Lee and Shepard Books, 1979).

Electronics World (January 1966).

Hans Fantel, *ABC's of Hi-Fi and Stereo* (Indianapolis: Howard W. Sams and Co., 1975).

Joel Goldberg, *Fundamentals of Stereo Servicing* (Englewood Cliffs, N.J.: Prentice-Hall, 1983).

HiFi/Stereo Review (October 1963).

Donald Carl Hoefler, *Hi-Fi Guide* (New York: Arco Publishing Co., 1957).

Roy H. Hoopes Jr., *The High Fidelity Reader* (Garden City, N.Y.: Hanover House, 1955).

Delton T. Horn, *Basic Electronics Theory*, 4th ed. (New York: TAB Books, 1994).

Robert Oakes Jordan and James Cunningham, *The Sound of High Fidelity* (Chicago: Windsor Press, 1958).

Sumner N. Levine, *Principles of Solid-State Microelectronics* (New York: Holt, Rinehart and Winston, Inc., 1963).

Akio Morita, with Edwin M. Reingold and Mitsuko Shimomura, *Made in Japan: Akio Morita and Sony* (New York: E. P. Dutton, 1986).

David Rutland, *Behind the Front Panel: The Design and Development of 1920s Radios* (Philomath, Ore.: Wren Publishers, 1994).

Harvey Swearer, *Selecting and Improving Your Hi-Fi System* (Blue Ridge Summit, Penn.: G/L Tab Books, 1973).

U.S. News and World Report, 25 May 1970.

F. F. Y. Wang, *Introduction to Solid State Electronics*, 2nd ed. (Netherlands: North-Holland, 1989).

E. Patrick Wiesner, *Practical Transistor Theory* (Indianapolis: Howard W. Sams and Co., 1964).

Other Sources on Japan

Edwin O. Reischauer, *Japan: The Story of a Nation* (New York: Alfred A. Knopf, 1970).

Morton S. Schmorleitz, *Castles in Japan* (Rutland, Vt.: Charles E. Tuttle, 1974).

Edward Seidensticker, *Tokyo Rising: The City Since the Great Earthquake* (New York: Alfred A. Knopf, 1990).

Chapter 13: Rebuilding the Community

Interviews with George Aratani, Frank Chuman, Shig Kariya, Jean Kariya, Ken Funabashi, Tets Murata, Bill Kasuga, Linda Kimura, Donna Kwee, Mary Tamura, and Isamu Oku. Telephone conversations with Joe Orshan, Maria Funabashi, Alf Blake, and Ray Dingman.

Key Sources

George Aratani's application for redress under the Japanese American Evacuation Claims Act can be followed through correspondence between him and attorney David McKibbin of the law firm Chuman and McKibbin in Los Angeles. Also helpful were correspondence from the Committee on Japanese American Evacuation Claims, and correspondence with Mike Masaoka.

Regarding Mikasa's recent history, probably the most informative article is Damon Darlin's "Accessorizing the Dinner Table" (*Forbes* 154, no. 14 [19 December 1994]: 288–90). Touring Golden State Porcelain in Santa Maria, courtesy of Isamu Minami, was also instructive for getting a sense of chinaware decoration.

On the topic of Little Tokyo redevelopment in the 1970s, there are more critical analyses in publications like *The Rafu Shimpo* and *Gidra*.

Other Sources

John R. Dorfman, "Mikasa Shareholders Could Face Big Tax Bills as the Firm's Chairman Unloads Some Stock," *Wall Street Journal*, 23 August 1996.

Ernest B. Furgurson, *Hard Right: The Rise of Jesse Helms* (New York: W. W. Norton and Company, 1986).

Kashu Mainichi, 1 August 1980.

Kenwood Audio Product Catalog (1997).

Los Angeles Herald Examiner, 4 December 1983.

Los Angeles Times, 11 December 1983.

Karen E. Martin, "Mikasa Offers Upscale Look with Outlet Prices," *Chain Store Age Executive* 70, no. 8 (August 1994): 48–49.

Mikasa Annual Report (1995, 1996, 1997, 1998).

Moody's Industrial Manual (1993, 1994, 1995, 1996, 1997, 1998).

Douglas Neiss, "Tabletop Report 1997: Industry Tops 3% Growth," *HFN*, 15 September 1997.

Nisei Week Japanese Festival Booklet (1980).

The Rafu Shimpo, 11 November 1977; 20 May 1983.

Marilyn Sano, "George Aratani: A Profile in Multicultural Harmony," *The Japan Times Weekly International Edition*, 30 October–5 November 1995.

Ryo Takasugi, *Sokoku e Atsuki Kokoro o: Tokyo ni Orimpikku o Yonda Otoko* (Biography of Fred Wada) (Tokyo: Kodansha Bunko, 1992).

Chapter 14: A Second Look

Interviews with George Aratani, Shig Kariya, Alfred Blake, Min Endo, Tets Murata, Isamu Oku, Ray Dingman, Tad Yamada, Bill Kasuga, Donna Kwee, Linda Kimura, Isamu Minami, Mary Tamura, Kody Kodama, and Ken Kitasako. Telephone conversations with Alf Blake and Jean Ishii-Marshall.

Key Sources

Vince Tajiri assembled both a booklet and video script, "A Salute to George Aratani," for a Keiro Services dinner on 4 November 1987. The text and interviews proved helpful in assessing the dominant perceptions of George Aratani by community members. Reuters News Service reported the news of Verrerie Cristallerie d'Arques's purchase of Mikasa, Inc., on 12 September 2000.

Other Sources

Laurie Becklund, "Guadalupe: A Tiny Town with a Big Crime Problem," *Los Angeles Times*, 11 December 1983.

Jaime Ee, "Hi, Meet Melissa of Project Access," *The Business Times*, 4 December 1997.

Andy Furillo, "Little Town of Horrors: Raiders Evict Guadalupe's Prostitutes, Drug Dealers," *Los Angeles Herald Examiner*, 4 December 1983.

Goh Hwee Leng, "Kwee Access," *Singapore Tatler* (January 1998).

Visi R. Tilak, "George Aratani," in *Notable Asian Americans* (Detroit: Gale Research, 1994): 6–8.

Oral History Interviews

All of the following oral history interviews, conducted by the author and/or researcher, are part of the permanent collection of the Japanese American National Museum:

George Aratani (7 August 1997, Los Angeles), (21 August 1997, Los Angeles), (28 August 1997, Los Angeles), (10 September 1997, Los Angeles), (18 September 1997, Los Angeles), (26 September 1997, Los Angeles), (4 November 1997, Los Angeles), (26 November 1997, Los Angeles), (9 December 1997, Los Angeles), (13 December 1997, Los Angeles), (28 January 1998, Los Angeles), (10 April 1998, Los Angeles), (25 June 1998, Los Angeles), (8 July 1998, Los Angeles), (1 March 1999, Los Angeles), (8 March 1999, Los Angeles), (9 March 1999, Los Angeles), (11 March 1999, Los Angeles), (12 March 1999, Los Angeles), (17 March 1999, Los Angeles)

Masuko Aratani (12 November 1997, Los Angeles)

Sakaye Aratani (17 August 1997, Los Angeles), (14 October 1997, Los Angeles), (19 March 1999, Los Angeles), (22 March 1999, Los Angeles)

Minoru "Min" Endo (7 October 1997, Secaucus, N.J.)

Kensuke "Ken" Funabashi (20 November 1997, Carson, Calif.)

Tsuneo "Cappy" Harada (5 November 1997, Palm Desert, Calif.)

Masato Inouye (2 February 1998, San Pedro, Calif.)

Komano Ishikawa (4 March 1998, Los Angeles)

Jean Kariya (26 February 1998, Torrance, Calif.)

Seiichiro Shigeyoshi "Shig" Kariya (4 October 1997, North Bethesda, Md.), (26 September 1997, Los Angeles)

Hiroshi William "Bill" Kasuga (13 October 1997, Long Beach, Calif.)

Linda (Aratani) Kimura (18 November 1997, Rancho Palos Verdes, Calif.)

Kenji "Ken" Kitasako (17 September 1997, Arroyo Grande, Calif.)

Kody Kodama (6 March 1999, Palm Desert, Calif.)

Donna (Aratani) Kwee (12 November 1997, Los Angeles)

Tetsuo "Tets" Murata (20 August 1997, Carson, Calif.), (20 March 1998, Carson, Calif.)

Tatsuo Nakase (22 March 1999, Los Angeles)

Mary Tamura (6 March 1998, Pasadena, Calif.)

Tadao "Tad" Yamada (7 October 1997, Secaucus, N.J.)

Acknowledgments

I was literally in the middle of America—Wichita, Kansas—when the Japanese American National Museum called to see if I would be willing to take on a biography project on Nisei entrepreneur George Aratani. I was completing a nine-month creative writing fellowship at Newman University and would soon head back home to Los Angeles. Writing about the Japanese American experience in the land of wild sunflowers and wind-blown cornfields led to many epiphanies. One of them was that, yes, people—and not just those on the West Coast—want to hear the story of Japanese Americans. One very effective way to communicate this story is in a biography, and if the subject were connected to such well-known brand names as Mikasa and Kenwood, all the better.

To tackle a biography of this size, however, I needed a good research partner, and I found a great one in Teru Kanazawa Sheehan. Although we had never worked together prior to this project, Teru and I discovered that we had much in common: as former editors at Japanese American vernaculars, we had both been responsible for monitoring and reporting the pulse of our ethnic communities. While Teru had worked in Manhattan, I had spent my days in Los Angeles. Our different personal styles and backgrounds are reflected in the creation of this book: Teru could be depended on to be tenacious and aggressive in digging out information during interviews, while I opted to coax and ease out the details. By inadvertently playing "good cop, bad cop," we were a perfect research-and-interview team.

Such a collaboration was necessary to uncover the "real" George Aratani. Within the local Little Tokyo community in downtown Los Angeles, the generosity of George Aratani, the philanthropist, is legendary. His companies,

Mikasa and Kenwood, are well known by consumers who are shopping for either dinnerware or electronics. Yet who is this Nisei entrepreneur who seems so congenial and good-natured? Could we tear through the exterior and get to the heart of the man?

In search of background information, I first went to my former employer, *The Rafu Shimpo* newspaper. There I discovered only a thin manila folder that held a single dinner program. I found no press releases issued by large public-relations firms. It was obvious that this George Aratani was not into self-promotion.

Shortly thereafter, I met George at his home in the Hollywood Hills for the first time. At that time he spoke enthusiastically about the manufacture of chinaware, but he offered little in terms of the details of his personal life. Would he open up to me, a woman young enough to be his granddaughter? And would I be up to the task of accurately capturing his point of view and life experiences that spanned almost an entire century?

During the course of the next year and a half, through countless interviews and over meals around the Aratani kitchen table, at Burger King, and in high-tone Japanese restaurants, I began to break through and see the world according to George Aratani. His manner of recounting facts without emotion, even in the telling of devastating events, was not unfamiliar to me.

I thought back to the time my own grandmother, a Hiroshima atomic bomb survivor, took me, then a teenager, through the Peace Museum. Dry-eyed, she pointed to a diorama of ground zero and identified the area where her husband—my grandfather—had most likely died. She spoke evenly and calmly as schoolchildren in black uniforms wandered through the haunting exhibition halls. If she had allowed sorrow to consume her, she would not have been able to raise three children on her own.

In the same way, George does not dabble in sentimentality. He is a "man of action," a consummate businessman who doesn't dwell on problems but instead solves them. A realist, he looks toward the future, not the past. Also, as the only son of a successful entrepreneur and community leader raised in the fresh country air of Guadalupe, California, George has always seemed to live his life with a strong sense of confidence and self-assurance.

In this era of confessional memoirs, such a sunny approach to life seems false—or at the very least, undramatic. We want to hear the timbre of pain and anger, feel the depths of passion and sorrow, and taste bitterness, but here we read about a way of life that is steady and dependable. However, this steadiness belies the very real human drama that was eventually unearthed through our interviews and research efforts.

Most invaluable was the discovery of George's financial papers and personal correspondence written during the war years. Without those papers we would have not understood how George was temporarily stymied by physical illness and a relentless chase by the Superintendent of Banks while he was incarcerated in Gila River, Arizona. These struggles revealed to me—a daughter of a gardener who is more inclined towards stories of the unknown everyman and everywoman—the importance of the "Big Men" and "Big Bosses" in sustaining an ethnic community. The story of George Aratani shows how influential businessmen and leaders were targeted by the government during the racist frenzy of the World War II incarceration; perhaps the government sought to weaken the community by going after its most powerful figures. However, these individuals—as well as the effort and sweat of manual laborers—fueled the comeback of Japanese Americans during the resettlement period.

To reflect George's manner of communicating his affections and passions—through his actions—I wanted the actions to speak on their own. As a result, I've attempted to follow George's life by acting almost as a camera on his shoulder. Actions and interactions are documented and presented in their historic context but without much interpretation. Here, interviews with a number of George's relatives, friends, and associates were key for weaving a large and accurate picture of times and events.

There were, of course, editorial decisions on what scenes to include and exclude. I took the license of re-creating dialogue, but only when based closely on the recollection of interviewees. Whenever possible, personal correspondence, journals, and documents serve to support each chapter.

Archival research proved to be invaluable. The Japanese American National Museum was itself a wonderful source of moving images. Reels of Aratani family home movies have been preserved and archived at the institution, and they provide a rare look into one family's life from the 1930s to the 1970s.

Approximately 100 personal photo albums were examined by the research team, and now more than 200 photos are housed at the National Museum. These images will greatly contribute to the general scholarship of Japanese American researchers.

Other sources of material were the Santa Barbara County Hall of Records; Santa Maria Public Library; Los Angeles County Law Library; Los Angeles Superior Court; Mikasa headquarters (Long Beach, California, and Secaucus, New Jersey); Department of Special Collections, UCLA; Asian

American Studies Center's Reading Library, UCLA; Bancroft Library, UC Berkeley; Brand Library and Art Center, Glendale, California; *The Rafu Shimpo*; and *Pacific Citizen*.

We were also able to add to the wealth of the National Museum's oral history collection by conducting dozens of interviews. Unfortunately, over the course of the past four years, some subjects have passed away, notably Shig Kariya, instrumental in launching the New York office of Mikasa, as well as Komano Ishikawa, the widow of Toshitaro Ishikawa.

Others interviewed and those who donated photographs and other materials for the book include Yae Aihara, Min Endo, Ken Funabashi, Maria Funabashi, Cappy Harada, Jane Imamura, Masato Inouye, Jean Kariya, Bill Kasuga, Ken Kitasako, Kody Kodama, Sam Maenaga, Isamu Minami, Tets Murata, Vickie Nakabayashi, Masasuke Oishi, Isamu Oku, Joe Orshan, Mary Tamura, Masayoshi Tomooka, Richard P. Weldon, and Tad Yamada.

Also helpful were conversations with Kent Haldan, Jose Rubalcaba, Shirley Boylston, Donna Crippen, Yuji Ichioka, Masakazu Iwata, Sister Mercedes M. Martin, Haruyo Ogawa Kuroiwa, Dr. William Stead, Gordon Chang, Jean Ishii-Marshall, Frank Chuman, Ken Kolker, Alfred Blake, Ray Dingman, and members of the New York chapter of the Japanese American Citizens League.

After the research and interviews came the writing of the manuscript, and of course, the rewriting. Discerning readers include Jim Hirabayashi, Lloyd Inui, Karin Higa, Nancy Araki, Akemi Kikumura, Eileen Kurahashi, Eiichiro Azuma, Sojin Kim, Kristine Kim, James Gatewood, and Buddy Takata, all of the Japanese American National Museum. Author and editor Kathy Ishizuka provided feedback on the book's content and marketing. A longtime friend and colleague, Brian Niiya, was instructive concerning the shape of the book, as well as details concerning dates. Professor Arthur Hansen, another kindred spirit, astutely examined sections regarding the Santa Maria Valley, his old stomping ground, and the Gila River concentration camp. Grant Ujifusa, an experienced bookman, provided both constructive criticism and encouragement, while Professor Daniel I. Okimoto generously took time out of his busy schedule to pen the introduction. Many thanks also go to the Japan Minister of Foreign Affairs, His Excellency Yohei Kono, as well as Consul General Tsuneo Nishida and his Los Angeles staff, Toshihisa Ono and Nancy Hamai. On a more personal note, Teru and I would like to acknowledge our families: my husband, Wesley Fukuchi, and Teru's husband, James Sheehan, and their two sons,

Mikio and Terence. They spent their share of weekends and evenings on their own while we traveled north to Guadalupe.

The visionary behind this biography concept was scholar Gary Kawaguchi, now project director of Global Diasporas at California State University, Dominguez Hills. Overseeing the project was Darcie Iki, Japanese American National Museum's Life History curator, who moved this pioneering project forward. Alison Kochiyama, Laura Rubenstein, and Karen Otamura transcribed and indexed the interviews, while Shirley Ito had the yeoman's task of indexing the completed manuscript. Grace Murakami, Theresa Manalo, Toshiko McCallum, and Norman Sugimoto were key for access to and duplication of photographs. Sharon Yamato, the master organizer, supervised and implemented the book's actual publishing and production schedules. My mentor and teacher, Virginia Stem Owens, edited early drafts of the manuscript, while copy editor Sherri Schottlaender did a magnificent job in sharpening the narrative flow of this lengthy work. Kudos also go to graphic artist Koji Takei, who transformed the text and images into a beautiful visual product. David Gray Gardner of Gardner Lithograph in Buena Park, California, generously donated a portion of in-kind printing services. Carol Komatsuka, Chris Komai, Maria Kwong, and Cameron Trowbridge all aided in the book's marketing and promotion.

The leadership at the Japanese American National Museum, specifically executive director and president Irene Y. Hirano, must be acknowledged in this publishing endeavor, along with the support of Fred Hoshiyama, Manabi Hirasaki, and Dr. Takashi Makinodan.

Most of all, thanks go to the entire Aratani family. Sakaye generously welcomed us many times with hot tea, snacks, and sometimes a homemade meal. Masuko, always radiant with humor despite many physical ailments, was also extremely hospitable. Donna and Linda, the daughters of George and Sakaye, also shared their memories with us. Of course, a very special acknowledgment must go to George Aratani, who allowed Teru and me to probe into his past. It must have been quite a challenge for a "man of action" to be so reflective of such a long, illustrious life in countless interviews and conversations. This experience has resulted in a much clearer picture of how an American son and his community impacted the course of a nation during the past century. My hope is that this story will resonate not only in places like Guadalupe, Los Angeles, New York, and Nagoya, but also in cities and small towns across this vast land we call America.

Naomi Hirahara

Chronology
The Life and Times of George Aratani

1917   22 May. George Tetsuo Aratani born to Setsuo and Yoshiko Aratani in South Park, California, a community near the strawberry-growing center of Gardena.

1919   Aratani family moves from South Park to Pacoima in San Fernando Valley.

1920   Second Alien Land Law prevents Issei—all ruled ineligible for citizenship by legislation—to "acquire, possess, enjoy, use, cultivate, occupy and transfer real property."

1921   Setsuo Aratani family moves to Guadalupe, a town along California's Central Coast.

1923   May. Guadalupe Produce Company founded by Setsuo Aratani in partnership with Issei Naoichi Ikeda and Reiji "Ben" Kodama.

1928   1 August. The "Aratanis" baseball team, including 11-year-old George, travels to Japan.

1933   Setsuo Aratani temporarily moves family to Santa Maria.

1935   June. George Aratani graduates from the Santa Maria Union High School.

        16 July. The "four musketeers"—George Aratani, Jimmie Hamasaki, Masato Inouye, and Bob Ishii—set sail from San Francisco for Japan aboard the *Tatsuta Maru*.

        20 December. Yoshiko Aratani dies at age 46 of asthma and heart failure.

1936   April. The four musketeers enroll in Japanese colleges. George Aratani begins studies at Keio University.

1936	31 May. Setsuo Aratani marries Masuko Matsui in Japan.
	August. All Star Trading Company established to import sake and fish meal from Japan.
1939	January. Setsuo Aratani admitted to Maryknoll Sanatorium in Monrovia, California, after contracting tuberculosis.
1940	16 April. Setsuo Aratani dies of meningitis at the age of 54.
	Spring. George Aratani attends Stanford University. He leaves after two months to take over leadership of Setsuo Aratani's businesses, including Vegetable Farms and Guadalupe Produce Company.
1941	7 December. Bombing of Pearl Harbor and U.S. entry into World War II. Government begins arrests of prominent Issei.
	8 December. California Superintendent of Banks assumes control of Sumitomo Bank, where Setsuo Aratani had substantial yen deposits.
	14 December. George Aratani officially becomes general manager of the Guadalupe Produce Company.
1942	February. Approximately 250 Issei arrested by the FBI in Santa Maria Valley, including businessmen, ministers, and managers.
	19 February. Executive Order 9066 signed by President Franklin D. Roosevelt ordering all persons of Japanese ancestry in the Western region—citizens and aliens—into concentration camps.
	April. Vegetable Farms, Santa Maria Produce, and General Farms enter into a trust agreement with the Puritan Ice Company, which operates the three farms.
	George Aratani and stepmother Masuko Aratani are temporarily detained at the Tulare Assembly Center at the Tulare Fairgrounds in Tulare, California.
	August. George and Masuko Aratani incarcerated at the Gila River concentration camp in Rivers, Arizona.
	12 September. Meeting with attorney Leo McMahon results in a lease arrangement with purchase option of Vegetable Farms by the trustee, California Lettuce Growers.
1943	February. George Aratani suffers from valley fever, which recurs in 1944.
	30 June. George Aratani, Naoichi Ikeda, and Ben Kodama officially liquidate Guadalupe Produce.

December. George summoned to appear before the Superior Court of Los Angeles regarding the repayment of business loans that his father had secured before the war.

1944 George Aratani engaged to Sakaye Inouye during her visit to Gila River from the Poston concentration camp.

1 May. George Aratani leaves Gila River for the Military Intelligence Service Language School (MISLS) at Camp Savage, Minnesota (later moved to Fort Snelling, Minnesota).

23 November. George Aratani weds Sakaye Inouye in Minneapolis, Minnesota.

1945 10 March. Largest U.S. firebombing of Japan (Tokyo/Yokohama); an estimated 83,000 to 100,000 people die.

6 August. Atomic bomb dropped on Hiroshima; three days later, a second atomic bomb dropped on Nagasaki.

15 August. Japan officially surrenders.

1946 22 January. First child, Donna Naomi Aratani, born to George and Sakaye Aratani in Minnesota.

June. U.S. War Department moves MISLS to the Presidio in Monterey, California.

After a few months in Monterey, George Aratani leaves the language school to start his own business. The Aratanis move in with Sakaye's family in Lakewood, California, near Long Beach.

All Star Trading company revived by George Aratani, who rents his first office in Little Tokyo section of Los Angeles.

Trio, forerunner of Kenwood Electronics, established in Japan by the Kasuga brothers.

1947 Winter. Shig Kariya joins All Star Trading company.

5 November. Second child, Linda Yoshiko Aratani, born at the Japanese Hospital in Los Angeles.

1948 March. George Aratani departs Los Angeles for first business trip to Japan. After he returns, he decides to change the name of All Star Trading to American Commercial, Inc. (ACI).

2 July. The Japanese American Evacuation Claims Act issued by the U.S. government to compensate for the loss of property during the incarceration of Japanese Americans during World War II.

1949	George Aratani decides to open an East Coast office in New York City. Shig Kariya becomes head of New York office. ACI begins to import shell buttons and chinaware.
1950	Winter. ACI sets up first exhibit in a hotel room at the annual china-and-glass trade show in Pittsburgh, Pennsylvania.
1951	January. ACI establishes AMCO, a Tokyo-based company to import and market medical equipment.
	The Aratanis purchase a house in Montebello, California.
	ACI moves to a larger office and showroom at 212 Fifth Avenue in New York. In Los Angeles, ACI expands to a larger office at Maple and 11th streets.
	George Aratani hospitalized with hepatitis.
1952	ACI makes its official debut at the annual china-and-glass show in Pittsburgh.
	Sakaye Aratani and other Nisei women form the Montebello Japanese Women's Club.
	ACI makes first department store sale to Jerry Stone, china-and-glass buyer for Macy's department store.
1956	The 1948 Japanese American Evacuation Claims Act amended to provide for appeal to the U.S. Court of Claims.
1957	December. The brand name Mikasa introduced to the American public.
1958	Aratani family moves from Montebello to a custom-built house in the Hollywood Hills.
	November. *Aratani* v. *Robert F. Kennedy* formally filed with the U.S. Court of Appeals, District of Columbia circuit, a class-action suit to recover yen deposits confiscated by the Alien Property Custodian.
	AMCO moves to a three-story building in Tokyo. ACI and AMCO open offices in Nagoya.
1959	12 May. AMCO, along with American Technology Laboratory, holds the first postwar demonstration of a nuclear reactor in Japan at the International Science Exhibition in Tokyo.
1961	George Aratani travels to Japan to visit Trio Corporation and concludes a deal involving exclusive distribution of the Japanese company's stereo equipment. Kenwood registered as the new name of the stereo company. Bill Kasuga becomes head of the New York office.

1963	The Department of Justice settles the class-action suit filed by George Aratani against the U.S. government for unfair compensation of yen deposits confiscated by the Alien Property Custodian.
1965	Kenwood introduces a wide range of solid-state high-fidelity products, which eventually outsell vacuum-tube units.
1967	George Aratani and philanthropist Fred Wada travel to Japan to raise money for Keiro Services, a nonprofit organization dedicated to serving the elderly in the Japanese American community. He later becomes involved in other philanthropic efforts for numerous organizations.
1969	Mikasa and Kenwood move West Coast headquarters to Gardena, California.
1976	Al Funabashi dies of a heart attack; Alfred Blake, originally from Austria, appointed new president of Mikasa.
1977	George Aratani inducted into the Audio Hall of Fame.
1983	Sakaye Aratani receives *kunshō* (Order of the Sacred Treasure, Fourth Order) from the Japanese government for her service on behalf of U.S.–Japan relations.
1986	Trio Corporation in Japan acquires Kenwood's U.S. operation and changes its name to Kenwood.
1988	April. George Aratani receives *kunshō* (Order of the Sacred Treasure, Gold Rays with Rosette) from the Japanese government.
1994	Mikasa, Inc., traded publicly on the New York Stock Exchange.
	George and Sakaye Aratani establish the Aratani Foundation, an endowment that funds various nonprofit organizations serving the Japanese American and larger Asian American community.
2000	September. Mikasa acquired by France-based J. G. Durand Industries, the parent company of the world's largest glass and crystal maker. Mikasa principals, including George Aratani, remain major shareholders.

Index

Nisei. *See* generational issues between Issei and Nisei

Nisei Week (Japanese festival), 267–68; beauty pageant, 244; grand marshals, *254*

Nishi Hongwanji Temple, 11, 15, *27, 50,* 66, *66,* 169, 225, 259

Nokai. *See* Japanese Agricultural Association

Noritake Company, 161, 185–202, 213, 260

nuclear technology industry, xii, 234–37

"Nylons for Japan," 226

O

Obata, Chiura, 5

Office of Strategic Services (OSS), 169

Ohio Chemical Company, 215

Okada, Peter K., xii, 179

Olivers Club, 32

Olympic Games (Los Angeles, 1932), 38

Olympic Hotel (Little Tokyo, Los Angeles), 38, 61, 114

100th Infantry Battalion, 117, 129, 145, 203. *See also* 442nd Regimental Combat Team

Order of the Sacred Treasure, Gold Rays with Rosette. *See* Aratani, George, *kunshō* (national award)

Orshan, Joe, 220

OSS. *See* Office of Strategic Services

Otoi, Chester Masunosuke, 74, 93, 97, 98, 131, 138–39, 157–58; settlement, 162. *See also* Santa Maria Chili Dehydrating Company

Otoy. *See* Otoi, Chester Masunosuke

P

Pacific Citizen (newspaper), 113, 116, 193, 194, 198, 207, 208

Pearl Harbor, after the attack on, 85–100, 114–115, 154; bombing of, xi, 82–83

philanthropy. *See under* Aratani, George, charities and philanthropy; Aratani, Sakaye; Aratani, Setsuo, philanthropy and community service

Phillips, Leon R., 97

"picture brides," 8

Pismo Beach, Calif., 26, *39*

Pismo-Oceano Vegetable Exchange, 234, 281

Planted in Good Soil (book), 13

Popular Electronics (magazine), 233, 248, 249, 250

porcelain and pottery, history in Japan, 177, 184–87. *See also* ceramics, dinnerware industry, and specific Japanese manufacturers

Poston concentration camp (Chandler, Ariz.), 108, 114–16, 123–24, 130, *123,* 135, 140–41, 160

Preisker, C. L., 37

Produce Dealers Exchange, 30

Project Access, 279

property ownership and losses, xi, 78–79, 89, 98–99, 109–10, 121, 127, 140, 223; redress, 256

Puritan Ice Company, 15–16, 97

PWP Japan, Inc., 179

R

racial discrimination against Japanese. *See* anti-Japanese sentiment; discrimination

RadioShack Corporation, 238

The Rafu Shimpo (newspaper), 20, 22, 169, 175

Rancho de Guadalupe Historical Society, 2, 281

Rasmussen, Capt. Kai E., 133–36, *145,* 147

redress. *See under* property ownership and losses

Republican National Committee, 277

resettlement of Japanese, xii, 124–25, 137, 155–56, 160–63, 167, 171, 204, 233

Richter, Joe, 274

Roosevelt, President Franklin D., 30, 79, 96, 194, 277

Rose China (porcelain), 188–89

Royal Japanese Agricultural Society, 66

Rubalcaba, Jose, 2

Rusch, Paul, 56–57, 59, 129, 214, 260

Russo-Japanese War, 5, 231

S

"Safe at Home" (packing label), 73

Saji-Kariya Company, 161

Sakata, Tetsuo, 215

sake (rice wine), importing of, 2, 52, 72, 75, 126, 146, 169, 234; homemade, 17

San Francisco, 5, 20, 46, 52; earthquake, 6

San Francisco Chronicle (newspaper), 5

San Francisco Examiner (newspaper), 80

Santa Barbara County Fair, 31, 75, 76, 81

Santa Fe Justice Department camp (N.M.), 109, 126–27

Santa Maria Chili Dehydrating Company, 2, 73–74, 93, 98, 105, 131, 138–39, 162

Santa Maria Country Club, 2, 40, 77, 120

Santa Maria Daily Times (newspaper), 34, 37, 65, 66, 67, 75, 76, 77, 80, 81, 85, 88, 89, 90, 91

Santa Maria Farms, 233. *See also* Tomooka Farms

Santa Maria Produce, 25, 32, *86,* 95, 97, 98, 156

Santa Maria Rotary Club, 31

Santa Maria Union High School, 33–36, 42, 45–46

Santa Maria Valley (Calif.), 3, 13, 14–16, 30, 33–36, 38, 41, 45, 52, 61, 65, 66, 70, 72–80, 85, 89, 93, 99–100, 120, 131, 138, 153–54, 155, 233; after World War II, 53–54

Santa Maria Valley Chamber of Commerce, 31

Sato, Arthur "Ace," 40

Sawada, Madame Miki, 257

SCAP. *See* Supreme Commander of Allied Powers

scarlet fever. *See under* Aratani, George, health of

Security-First National Bank, 81, 92

Seto (porcelain), 185

Shimizu, Harold, 82

Shimizu, Mitsuhiko, *267*

Shoichiro, 4

Sino-Japanese War, 58, 61, 68

Skinner, A. E., 127

solid-state components, 247–48

sometsuke (chinaware), 185

Sony Corporation, 238

St. Mary's Episcopal Church, 259

Stanford University, xiii, 18, 25, 42, 61, 68, 73, 120, 279

Stoklos, Rudy, 242

Stone, Jerry, 208, 228–30

Strawberry Growers Association, 7

subversive activity investigations, 75, 76

Suenaga, Howard, 82

Sugahara, Kay, xii, 169, 179

Sugahara, Roku, 193, 194, 195, 198, 205, 207, 208, 221